School Secretary's Encyclopedic Dictionary

Cherie Fehrman

PRENTICE-HALL, INC.
ENGLEWOOD CLIFFS, NEW JERSEY

Prentice-Hall International, Inc., *London*
Prentice-Hall of Australia, Pty. Ltd., *Sydney*
Prentice-Hall Canada Inc., *Toronto*
Prentice-Hall of India Private Ltd., *New Delhi*
Prentice-Hall of Japan, Inc., *Tokyo*
Prentice-Hall of Southeast Asia Pte. Ltd., *Singapore*
Whitehall Books, Ltd., Wellington, *New Zealand*
Editora Prentice-Hall do Brasil, Ltda., *Rio de Janeiro*

10 9 8 7 6 5 4 3

Library of Congress Cataloging in Publication Data

Fehrman, Cherie
  School secretary's encyclopedic dictionary.

  1. Education—Dictionaries. 2. School management
and organization—Dictionaries. 3. School secretaries—
Handbooks, manuals, etc. 4. Secretaries—Handbooks,
manuals, etc. I. Title
LB15.F34   1984   371.2′003′21   84-3185

ISBN 0-13-794446-2

Printed in the United States of America

A Preview of This Useful Working Tool

When you are in a hurry and you need fast and accurate information about school operations, *School Secretary's Encyclopedic Dictionary* will provide you with the answers. Within these pages is a complete alphabetical listing of operational methods necessary for the efficient running of a school, from elementary through college, whether a private or public institution.

Do you need to know the correct form for addressing a letter? Look under **ADDRESS, FORMS OF** and you will find the answer. Are you having problems with drug abuse or student behavior? Is your punctuation or grammar less than perfect? If so, you can rest assured that the pertinent alphabetical sections will give you the answers you need.

Following is a partial listing of the topics that are covered in this book:

- **SCHOOL RECORDS**
  Medical, counseling and guidance, teacher files, test scores, accident reports, tuition refunds, address records, federal and state reports, accreditation reports, teacher certification records, statistical reports.

- **SOLUTIONS TO TYPING PROBLEMS**
  How to cope with stencils, typing layouts; what to do about poor mimeograph copies; how to set up and type an outline; when to use footnotes; abbreviations used in footnotes; typing tricks.

- **TELEPHONE TECHNIQUES**
  Effective telephone methods and manners; how to use a PBX switchboard; dealing with crank calls and irate calls; telephone tapping; placing difficult calls; how to get the most from your telephone service.

- **SCHOOL EQUIPMENT EXPLAINED**
  Audio-visual equipment including film projectors, opaque projectors, overhead projectors, and sound equipment; sources for obtaining supplies

and equipment; charts and diagrams explaining equipment; the latest information about typewriters and copy equipment; reproduction systems explained; tips and tricks for coping with less than perfect equipment.

- **SCHOOL FINANCES**
  Payroll methods; verifying time records; forms used when enrolling an employee and terminating employment; how to prepare paychecks and maintain employee attendance records; coping with school budgets, including student, PTA, and fund-raising events.

- **PUNCTUATION AND GRAMMAR**
  A review of the basic rules of spelling, punctuation, capitalization, syllabication and usage.

- **PRINTING MADE EASY**
  Printing processes explained; tips on designing the copy; artwork preparation tips; choosing the best typeface for the job; dealing with revisions, galley proofs, page proofs, a chart of proofreader's symbols; a glossary of graphics and printing terms.

- **SCHOOL COMPUTERS**
  Computer systems explained including software and hardware packages; glossary of computer language; applications of small computers in the school: sources and manufacturers.

- **SCHOOL FILING SIMPLIFIED**
  Listings of basic school filing categories; how to tailor a filing system to your school's needs; correct cross-referencing; development and maintenance of a records retention schedule.

School Secretary's Encyclopedic Dictionary will supply you with valuable information for efficient ways to deal with faculty meetings, board meetings, and committee meetings; from preparing the agenda, to recording motions and resolutions, to outlining, writing, and typing the minutes. Requisitions, purchasing, and supplies are also covered, including such topics as placing textbook orders, setting up and maintaining a film log, how to order, receive, and verify deliveries, and the best ways to deal with invoices, lost orders, and delays.

There are also invaluable reference lists for you, such as abbreviations of test titles, lists of textbook publishers, a glossary of testing terms, a list of testing services, metric conversion charts, tables of weights and measures, as well as lists of educational suppliers, educational organizations, and scholastic publications—even a guide to copyright laws in the school.

In case you need quick first aid advice, you will find it under **FIRST AID,** where emergency procedures are clearly outlined for such problems as bleeding, burns, choking, convulsions, fainting, heart attack, poisoning, shock, and childhood illness.

School Secretary's Encyclopedic Dictionary is as easy to use as ABC. All listings are alphabetically arranged so that you will waste no time in hunting through sections for the answer you need.

Cherie Fehrman

Contents

ABBREVIATIONS COMMONLY USED IN SCHOOLS

A.A.	Associate in Arts
A.B.	Bachelor of Arts (see also B.A.)
abbr.	abbreviation
AC	alternating current
acad.	academic, academy
acct.	account
ack.	acknowledge
A.D.	anno Domini (in the year of our Lord)
add.	addition, address
adj.	adjective, adjacent
ad loc.	to or at the place (Latin: ad locum)
admin.	administration
adv.	adverb, advertise
AEC	Atomic Energy Commission
AFL-CIO	American Federation of Labor & Congress of Industrial Organizations
agr.	agriculture
agt.	agent, agreement
alg.	algebra
A.M. or a.m.	before noon (Latin: ante meridiem)
Amer.	America
amt.	amount
anal.	analogy, analysis
ans.	answer
APO	Army Post Office
appt.	appoint, appointment

approx.	approximate
Apr.	April
AR	account receivable
ASAP	as soon as possible
assoc.	associate
assn.	association
asst.	assistant
attn.	attention
atty.	attorney
Aug.	August
ave.	avenue
avg.	average
AWOL	absent without official leave
B.A.	Bachelor of Arts (see also A.B.)
bal.	balance
B.B.A.	Bachelor of Business Administration
B.C.	before Christ
bd.	board, bond, bound
B.D.	bank draft, bills discounted
bdl.	bundle
B/E	bill of entry, bill of exchange
bet.	between
bf	boldface, brought forward
Bib., bib.	Bible, biblical
bibliog.	bibliography, bibliographer
biog.	biography, biographer
biol.	biology, biologist
bkg.	banking
bkpg.	bookkeeping
bkpt.	bankrupt
B/L	bill of lading
bldg.	building
blvd.	boulevard
B/P	bills payable
br.	branch
B.S.	Bachelor of Science (see also S.B.)
BTU	British thermal unit
bu.	bushel
bur.	bureau
bull.	bulletin
bus.	business
c.	carat, cubic

C.	Celsius, centigrade
CAB	Civil Aeronautics Board
cal.	calendar
canc.	cancel
CARE	Cooperative for American Remittances to Europe
C.B.D.	cash before delivery
cc	cubic centimeter
cc.	chapters
c.c.	carbon copy
C.D.	civil defense
Cdr.	commander
cert.	certificate, certified
C.F.I.	cost, freight, and insurance
char.	charter
chg.	charge
CIA	Central Intelligence Agency
cit.	citizen, citation
cm.	centimeter
cml.	commercial
C/N	credit note
co.	company, country
c/o	in care of
COD	cash on delivery
co.	collect
Co.	company
com.	commission
comm.	communication, commerce
cont.	continued
cp.	compare
C.P.A.	certified public accountant
cpd.	compound
cr.	credit
ct.	cent, court
ctn.	carton
ctr.	center
cu.	cubic
cur.	currency
c.w.o.	cash with order
cwt.	hundredweight
D.	doctor (in academic degree)
D.A.	district attorney
DAR	Daughters of the American Revolution

d.b.a.	doing business as
dbl.	double
DC	direct current
D.D.S.	Doctor of Dental Science
dec.	deceased
Dec.	December
def.	definite, definition
deg.	degree
del.	delegate, delete
Dem.	Democrat
dep.	deposit, deputy
dept.	department
dia.	diameter
dim.	dimension
dir.	director
disc.	discount
div.	division
dlvy.	delivery
dol.	dollar
doz.	dozen
dup.	duplicate
D.V.M.	Doctor of Veterinary Medicine
ea.	each
econ.	economics
ed.	edition, editor
educ.	education
e.g.	for example (Latin: exempli gratia)
elec.	electric
elem.	elementary
enc.	enclosed, enclosure
eng.	engineer
Eng.	English
E.R.B.	Educational Records Bureau
esp.	especially
Esq.	Esquire
est.	established, estimate
et al.	and others (Latin: et alii)
etc.	and so forth (Latin: et cetera)
Eur.	Europe
ex.	example
exec.	executive, executor
exp.	expenses, express

F.	female, Fahrenheit
F.B.I.	Federal Bureau of Investigation
F.C.C.	Federal Communications Commission
F.D.I.C.	Federal Deposit Insurance Corporation
Feb.	February
fed.	federal, federation
fl. oz.	fluid ounce
F.O.B.	free on board (cost plus freight)
fpm	feet per minute
Fri.	Friday
frt.	freight
ft.	foot
fut.	future
fwd.	forward
g.	gram
gal.	gallon
GAW	guaranteed annual wage
gds.	goods
gen.	general
geog.	geography
geom.	geometry
G.I.	government issue
gm	gram
GNP	gross national product
GOP	Grand Old Party (Republican party)
gov.	governor
govt.	government
G.P.	general practitioner
gr.	grade, group
grad.	graduate
G.R.E.	Graduate Records Examination
guar., gtd.	guaranteed
h., ht.	height
hdqrs.	headquarters
HEW	Department of Health, Education, and Welfare
hon.	honorable, honorary
hor.	horizontal
hosp.	hospital
hp	horsepower
hr.	hour
H.S.	high school
hyp.	hypothesis

is.	island
ib., ibid.	in the same place (Latin: ibidem)
I.D.	identification
i.e.	that is (Latin: id est)
in.	inch
inc.	incorporated, increase, income
inst.	institute
int.	interest, interior, international
inv.	invention, invoice, inventory
IQ	intelligence quotient
IRS	Internal Revenue Service
ital.	italic
Jan.	January
J.D.	Doctor of Laws (Jurisprudence)
jour.	journal
J.P.	Justice of the Peace
jr., Jr.	junior
k.	karat
kc	kilocycle
kg.	kilogram
km	kilometer
kw	kilowatt
l	liter
lab.	laboratory
lat.	latitude
Lat.	Latin
lb.	pound
l.c. or lc	lower case
L/C	letter of credit
l.c.d.	lowest common denominator
leg.	legislation
lf	lightface
lg.	large
lib.	liberal, library
lit.	literature, literary
LL.B.	Bachelor of Laws
LL.D.	Doctor of Laws
loc. cit.	in the place cited (Latin: loco citato)
log.	logarithm
long.	longitude
ltd., Ltd.	limited
M	meter, male

M.A.	Master of Arts
Mar.	March
masc.	masculine
math.	mathematics, mathematical
max.	maximum
M.B.A.	Master of Business Administration
Mc	megacycle
m.c.	master of ceremonies
M.D.	Doctor of Medicine
mdse.	merchandise
M.E.	mechanical engineering, Middle English
meas.	measure
mech.	mechanical
med.	medical, medieval
M. Ed.	Master of Education
mem.	member
memo	memorandum
Messrs.	plural of Mr.
mfg., mfr.	manufacture
mi.	mile
min.	minute, minimum
misc.	miscellaneous
mkt.	market
ml.	milliliter
mm	millimeter
MMPI	Minnesota Multiphasic Personality Inventory
mo.	month
m.o., M.O.	money order, mail order, medical officer
mol.	molecule
mon.	monetary
Mon.	Monday
M.P.	member of parliament, military police
mpg	miles per gallon
mph	miles per hour
Mr.	Mister
Mrs.	Mistress (married woman)
Ms.	title for woman instead of Miss or Mrs.
ms.	manuscript
mtg.	meeting, mortgage
mtn.	mountain
mun.	municipal
mus.	music, museum

N.A.	North America
nat.	natural, national, native
NATO	North Atlantic Treaty Organization
nav.	naval
n.b.	note carefully (Latin: nota bene)
neg.	negative
no.	number, north
nos.	numbers
Nov.	November
N.P.	Notary Public
obj.	object, objective
Oct.	October
O.D.	Doctor of Optometry
OD	drug overdose, overdraft, overdrawn
OLMAT	Otis-Lennon Mental Ability Test
org.	organization, organic
o/s	out of stock
oz.	ounce
p	page
P/A	power of attorney, public address
Pac	Pacific
par	paragraph, parallel, parenthesis
pat.	patent
payt., pt.	payment
pct.	percent
pd.	paid
pf	preferred
Ph.B.	Bachelor of Philosophy
Ph.C.	Pharmaceutical Chemist
Ph.D.	Doctor of Philosophy
phar.	pharmacy, pharmaceutical
philos.	philosophy
pk.	pack, peck
P.M., p.m.	after noon (Latin: post meridiem)
P.O.	postal order, post office
POE	port of entry
pol.	political
poss.	possession
POW	prisoner of war
pp.	pages
ppd.	postpaid
pr.	pair

PR	public relations
pre.	preparatory
pres.	present, president
prim.	primary
prin.	principal
prof.	professor
pro tem	temporarily (Latin: pro tempore)
PS	post script, public school
P.T.	physical therapy
PTA	Parent-Teacher Association
pub.	public, publisher
pvt.	private
quad.	quadrant, quadrangle
quot.	quotation
qt.	quantity, quart
rd.	road
R.D.	rural delivery
R.E.	real estate
re	concerning, in reference to
recd.	received
ref.	reference
reg.	register, region, regularly
rep.	representative, repair, report
Rep.	Republican
req.	require
RFD	rural free delivery
rpm	revolutions per minute
R.R.	rural route, railroad
r.s.v.p.	please reply (French: répondez s'il vous plait)
S.B.	Bachelor of Science (see also B.S.)
Sat.	Saturday
S.A.T.	Stanford Achievement Test; Scholastic Aptitude Test
sc.	scene
s.c.	small capitals
sch.	school
sci.	science
S.D.	special delivery
S.E.C.	Securities and Exchange Commission
sec.	secretary, second
Sen.	senator
Sept.	September
sgd.	signed

sgt.	sergeant
shpt.	shipment
shtg.	shortage
sic	thus, so
sign.	signal, signature
sing.	singular
sm.	small
soc.	society, social
SOP	standard operating procedure
soph.	sophomore
SOS	distress signal
sp.	special, spelling
sq. ft.	square foot, square feet
sq. yd.	square yard
Sr.	senior, sister (religious)
SRO	standing room only
SSAT	Secondary Schools Admission Test
st., St.	street, state, saint
std.	standard
stk.	stock
sub.	substitute, subscription
subj.	subject, subjunctive
Sun.	Sunday
sup.	above (Latin: supra)
supt.	superintendent
surg.	surgeon, surgery
sym.	symbol, symphony
syn.	synonym
TB	tuberculosis
tbs., tbsp.	tablespoon
tech.	technical
tel.	telegram, telegraph, telephone
temp.	temporary
Thurs.	Thursday
tkt.	ticket
tpk.	turnpike
treas.	treasurer
Tues.	Tuesday
TV	television
U., univ.	university, universal
UN	United Nations
U.S.A.	United States of America, United States Army

v	volt
VA	Veterans' Administration
var.	variable, various
VIP	very important person
vol.	volume, volunteer
VP	vice president
vv	vice versa
w	watt
Wed.	Wednesday
whse.	warehouse
whsle.	wholesale
wkly.	weekly
w.o.c.	without compensation
wt.	weight
x	unknown factor
XL	extra large
Xmas	informal for Christmas
YMCA	Young Men's Christian Association
yr.	year
YWCA	Young Women's Christian Association
zool.	zoology

ABILITY GROUPING   A system of placing students in a learning situation according to their tested abilities, usually in fast, average, or slow sections. The grouping may be based on such factors as I.Q., learning disabilities, or physical handicaps.

ABSENCE, STUDENTS'   Most schools dealing with minors require that parents call in if a student will be absent from school on that day. Some schools require a written excuse in addition to the phone call when a student returns to school. When accepting incoming calls relating to attendance, do the following:

1. Make sure that it is actually the parent or legal guardian who is calling. (Sometimes students will have their friends telephone.)
2. Find out why the student will be absent, whether due to medical appointments, illness, or personal reasons.
3. Ask how long the student may be absent from school.
4. Keep a daily record of the absentees by grade.

A daily absentee report is made up showing the absentees by grade. This report can be as simple as a stencilled form or as elaborate as a computer printout.

When dealing with students in regard to absences, maintain a skeptical attitude, but do not appear to mistrust them. If you keep a businesslike attitude balanced with a sense of humor, the students will not feel that you are "checking up on them" or "out to get them." If a student is absent but the parent does not call in, you may have to track down the parent at home or at the office. If the parent is unaware of the student's absence, assume that the student has cut school and is truant. Inform the appropriate administrator. If a student is absent for over five days, most schools require a physician's letter for reentry.

ABUSE, CHILD   Child abuse can take many forms—physical abuse, mental abuse, or sexual abuse. The abused child often has a very poor self-image and feels that he must be at fault or must have done something bad, or in fact that he must BE bad and therefore deserving of such treatment. The abused child will seldom volunteer information about the abuse and will often try to hide it and protect the abuser because of confusion, misplaced loyalty, guilt, or shame. Repeated or unaccounted for marks, scars, and bruises should be considered suspect. Bring any such concerns to the attention of your administrator. Sometimes a child will really want you to guess what the problem is and will throw out hints in conversation. Try to be sensitive in picking up these hints, but remember also that children love to dramatize a situation. There may not be an abuse situation at all, but they may relish the attention they get from making one up. This is a difficult area to cope with. Rely on the training and wisdom of your administrator or a professional counselor. Also, most cities have child abuse centers or hot lines that can help and will investigate suspected child abuse situations.

ACCIDENT REPORT   It is usually necessary to file an accident report whenever a student or staff member is injured seriously enough to require medical treatment. An accident report form is provided by the school's insurance carrier, and should include the following information pertaining to the accident:

Name of school
Name of injured person
Addresses of school and of injured party
Date and time of injury
Site where injury occurred (gymnasium, stairs, etc.)
Brief description of the accident
Extent of injury

Names and addresses of witnesses

Description of action taken (e.g., gave first aid and called parents)

Date of report

Name of person making the report

The facts from the accident report could be used if a lawsuit were to be brought against the school. Be sure that all facts are accurate before they are written into the report and become a part of the permanent file.

ACCIDENTS   See FIRST AID.

ACCREDITATION   It is usually required that independent (private) schools be accredited by the state in order to operate. This entails the filling out of numerous forms explaining the school's particular purpose and method of operation, and also entails personal interviews and visits from the accrediting body.

Accreditation Body

The group that evaluates a school in order to grant accreditation privileges is known as the accrediting body or accreditation group. The state usually requires evaluation of schools in order for them to operate, but private organizations such as WASC (Western Association of Schools and Colleges) also follow set accreditation procedures before a school may join the organization. In the case of independent schools, it is desirable to join such prestigious organizations to maintain credibility.

Accreditation Report

The completed evaluation of a school made by the accreditation body is known as an accreditation report. Such reports are usually quite extensive and may contain well over one hundred pages. Evaluation teams visit accredited schools (or schools applying for accreditation) at regular intervals, usually every two to five years, to verify that goals and methods are being adhered to. The evaluation team visits for several days and thoroughly investigates all aspects of the school before preparing the accreditation report. The completed report may include commendations for outstanding features of a school, or recommendations for improving problem areas.

ADDRESS, FORMS OF   See FIGURE 1.

FORMS OF ADDRESS

PERSON	ENVELOPE AND INSIDE ADDRESS	SALUTATION		ORALLY
		INFORMAL	FORMAL	
Ambassador of the U.S.	The Honorable (full name) American Ambassador Address	My dear Mr. (or Madam) Ambassador:	Sir (or Madam):	Your Excellency OR Mr. (or Madam) Ambassador
Ambassador (foreign)	His Excellency (full name) Ambassador of (country) Washington, DC	My dear Mr. (or Madam) Ambassador:	Sir (or Madam): OR Your Excellency:	Your Excellency OR Mr. (or Madam) Ambassador
Archbishop (Catholic)	The Most Reverend (full name) Archbishop of (city) Address	Most Reverend and dear Sir:	Your Excellency: OR Most Reverend Sir:	Your Excellency
Baron	The Right Honorable Lord (name) Address		My Lord: OR Dear Sir:	Lord (name)
Baroness	The Right Honorable Baroness (name) Address		My Lady: OR Dear Madam:	Lady (name)
Baronet	Sir (full name), Bart Address		Sir: OR Dear Sir:	Sir (given, name)
Baronet's Wife	Lady (full name) Address		Madam: OR My Lady:	Lady (given name)
Bishop (Methodist)	Bishop (full name) Address		Dear Bishop (surname):	Bishop (surname)
Bishop (Episcopal)	The Right Reverend (full name) Address	Dear Bishop (surname):	Right Reverend and dear Sir:	Bishop (surname)
Bishop (Catholic)	The Most Reverend (full name) Bishop of (diocese) Address	Dear Bishop (surname):	Your Excellency: OR Most Reverend Sir:	Bishop (surname)
Cabinet Office (U.S.)	The Honorable (full name) Secretary of (the cabinet) Washington, DC	My dear Mr. (or Madam) Secretary:	Sir (or Madam):	Mr. (or Madam) Secretary
Cardinal (Catholic)	His Eminence (given name) Cardinal (surname) Archbishop of (city) Address		Your Eminence:	Your Eminence
Chancellor of a University	Dr. (full name) Chancellor of (name of university) Address	Dear Sir (or Madam): OR Dear Chancellor (surname):	Sir (or Madam):	Dr. (surname)

14

Common Form		Dear Mr. (surname):	My dear Mr. (surname): OR My dear Sir: OR Gentlemen: (pl.)	Mr. (surname)
Male	Mr. (full name) Address	Dear Mr. (surname):	My dear Mr. (surname): OR My dear Sir: OR Gentlemen: (pl.)	Mr. (surname)
Female	Mrs. (husband's full name) OR Miss (own full name) OR Ms. (own full name) Address	Dear Mrs. (or Miss, or Ms.) (surname):	My dear Mrs. (or Miss, or Ms.) (surname) OR Mesdames: (pl.)	Mrs., Miss, or Ms. (surname)

NOTE: A fictional couple is traced from childhood through adulthood to clarify forms of address relating to marriage and divorce:

	MALE	FEMALE
	MALE (John Jones)	FEMALE (Mary Smith)
Children	Master John Jones	Miss Mary Smith
Young Adults (Unmarried)	Mr. John Jones	Miss or Ms. Mary Smith
Married Adults	Mr. John Jones	Mrs. John Jones OR Mrs. John Smith-Jones OR Ms. Mary Smith
Divorced	Mr. John Smith	Ms. Mary Smith OR Mrs. Mary Jones (The dropping of the husband's first name indicates that the couple is divorced. This prevents confusion should the male remarry.)
Professional Title	Dr. John Jones, etc. Professor Jones	Dr. Mary Smith OR Dr. Mary Jones OR Professor Smith OR Professor Jones (Depending on whether the female wishes to use her married or maiden name with her title.)

In the past, a woman holding a doctor's degree was not usually acknowledged in correspondence and was referred to as simply Miss Mary Smith rather than Dr. Mary Smith. This has now changed and women are referred to by their earned title, so Dr. Mary Smith is now the accepted form. If both husband and wife hold doctor's degrees they may be addressed as:

INFORMAL   Mr. and Mrs. John Jones

FORMAL   The Drs. John Jones

If the wife holds a doctor's degree and the husband does not, it can be a bit tricky as past etiquette demanded that the wife not use her title socially in deference to her husband (Mr. and Mrs. John Jones); however, many women today are demanding to be accorded the respect of their earned titles and request to be addressed as:

Mr. and Dr. John Jones OR

Mr. John Jones and Dr. Mary Smith

FIGURE 1
Forms of Address

15

SALUTATION

PERSON	ENVELOPE AND INSIDE ADDRESS	INFORMAL	FORMAL	ORALLY
Congressman	The Honorable (full name) House of Representatives Washington, DC	My dear Mr. (or Mrs., Miss, Ms.) (surname):	Sir (or Madam):	Mr., Mrs., Miss, or Ms. (surname)
Consul	(full name), Esq. American (or other) Consul Address	My dear Mr. (or Madam) Consul:	Sir (or Madam): OR My dear Sir (or Madam):	Mr., Mrs., Miss, or Ms. (surname)
Dean of a College or University	Dr. (full name) Dean of (university name) Address OR Dean (full name) (if no doctor's degree) Address	Dear Sir (or Madam): OR Dear Dean (surname): OR Dear Dr. (surname):	My dear Sir (or Madam): OR My dear Dean (surname):	Dr. (surname) Dean (surname)
Doctor (of philosophy, medicine, etc.)	(full name), PhD (or M.D. etc.) Address OR Dr. (full name) Address	Dear Dr. (surname):	My dear Dr. (surname):	Dr. (surname)
Duchess	To Her Grace, the Duchess of (name) Address	Dear Duchess:	Madam:	Duchess
Duke	To His Grace, the Duke of (name) Address	Dear Duke:	Sir:	Duke
Earl	The Right Honorable The Earl of (name) Address		My Lord:	Lord (name)
Earl's Wife	The Right Honorable The Countess of (name) Address		My Lady:	Lady (name)
Governor of a State	The Honorable (full name) Governor of (state) Address	My dear Governor (surname):	Sir (or Madam):	Governor (surname)
Instructor at a College or University	(full name), PhD (if a doctor) OR Dr. (name) OR Mr., Mrs., Miss, Ms. (full name) Title/Department Name of University or College Address	Dear Sir (or Madam): OR Dear Dr. (surname): OR Dear Mr., Mrs., Miss or Ms. (surname):	My dear Sir (or Madam):	Dr. (surname) Mr., Mrs., Miss or Ms. (surname)

Judge	The Honorable (full name) (Name of Court) Address	My dear Judge (surname):	Sir (or Madam):	Judge (surname)
Supreme Court Associate Justice	The Honorable (full name) Associate Justice of the U.S. Supreme Court Washington, DC	My dear Mr. (or Madam) Justice:	Sir (or Madam):	Mr. (or Madam) Justice
Supreme Court Chief Justice	The Honorable (full name) Chief Justice of the United States Washington, DC	My dear Mr. (or Madam) Chief Justice:	Sir (or Madam):	Mr. (or Madam) Chief Justice
King	His Most Gracious Majesty, King (name) Address		May it please Your Majesty:	Your Majesty OR Sir
Knight	Sir (full name) (initials of order if any) Address		Sir:	Sir (given name)
Mayor	The Honorable (full name) Mayor of (city) Address	My dear Mr. (or Madam) Mayor; OR My dear Mayor (surname):	Sir (or Madam):	Mr. (or Madam) Mayor
Member of a Religious Order Male	Brother (name) (initials if any) Address	Dear Brother (name):	My dear Brother:	Brother (name)
Female	Sister (name) (initials if any) Address	Dear Sister (name):	My dear Sister:	Sister (name)
Minister (Protestant)	The Reverend (full name) Address		My dear Mr. (or Dr.) (surname):	Mr. or Dr. (surname)
Monsignor (Catholic)	The Right Reverend Monsignor (full name) Address		Right Reverend Monsignor (surname):	Monsignor
President of the U.S. (current)	The President The White House Washington, DC	My dear Mr. (or Madam) President:	Sir (or Madam):	Mr. (or Madam) President
President of the U.S. (former)	The Honorable (full name) Address	My dear Mr. (surname):	Sir:	Mr. or Sir

FIGURE 1, *continued*

SALUTATION

PERSON	ENVELOPE AND INSIDE ADDRESS	INFORMAL	FORMAL	ORALLY
President of a University	Dr. (full name) OR (full name) PhD (or other appropriate degree initials) OR President (full name) Address	Dear Sir (or Madam): OR Dear President (surname):	Sir (or Madam):	Dr., Mrs., Mr., Miss, or Ms. (surname)
Priest (Catholic)	The Reverend (full name) Address	My dear Father (surname):	Reverend and dear Sir:	Father (surname)
Prince or Princess	His (Her) Royal Highness Prince(ss) (given name) Address	Sir (or Madam):	Your Royal Highness:	Your Royal Highness
Professor	(full name) PhD, (or other degree initials) OR Professor (full name) OR Dr. (full name) (if doctor's degree) Department (name) Address	Dear Dr. (surname): OR Dear Professor (surname):	Dear Sir (or Madam): OR My dear Sir (or Madam):	Dr. (surname) OR Professor (surname)
Queen	Her Most Gracious Majesty, Queen (name) Address		May it please Your Majesty:	Your Majesty OR Ma'am
Rabbi	Rabbi (full name) Address		My dear Rabbi (or Dr. if a doctor's degree) (surname):	Rabbi (or Dr.) (surname)
Representative of a State	The Honorable (full name) Member of Assembly (OR) State Assemblyman Address	My dear Mr. (or Mrs., Miss, Ms.) (surname):	Sir (or Madam):	Mr., Mrs., Miss or Ms. (surname)
School Officials (other than previously listed)	Mr., Dr., Mrs., Miss or Ms. (full name) Title School Name Street Address City, State, ZIP Code	Dear Dr., Mr., Mrs., Miss, or Ms. (surname):	My dear Dr., Mr., Mrs., Miss, or Ms. (surname): OR Sir (or Madam):	Dr., Mr., Mrs., Miss, or Ms. (surname)

Senator (U.S.)	The Honorable (full name) United States Senate Washington, DC	My dear Senator (surname):	Sir (or Madam):	Senator (surname) OR Mr. (or Madam) Senator
Senator (state)	The Honorable (full name) (name of state) Senate Address	My dear Senator (surname):	Sir (or Madam):	Senator (surname)
Speaker of the House of Representatives	The Honorable (full name) The Speaker of the House of Representatives Washington, DC	My dear Mr. (or Madam) Speaker:	Sir (or Madam):	Mr. (or Madam) Speaker
Vice President of the U.S.	The Vice President Washington, DC	My dear Mr. (or Madam) Vice President:	Sir (or Madam):	Mr. (or Madam) Vice President

FIGURE 1, *continued*

ADDRESS RECORDS   Current and accurate address records are vital to the efficient operation of any school. It is often difficult to maintain accuracy in address records since people often forget to notify the school of changes. Keep a sharp eye for returned mail and check with the post office for forwarding addresses. An effective method of maintaining current address records is to keep the pertinent information on separate 3×5 cards for each student and staff member. Special file jackets designed to hold these cards in sequential order are available. When a change occurs it is then easy to remove and replace the address card. Rotary files may also be used for this purpose, but the advantage of the jacket system is that emergency information cards can be filed behind each address card making them easily accessible in critical moments. While this method is useful in smaller schools, large institutions handle this function by computer. It is usually required that all student address changes be filed with the central office of the school district. This applies to both public and private schools.

ADDRESSING MAIL   Following are some basic rules to follow when addressing mail:

DO NOT use a # sign before a street number.

41 Maple Drive	NOT	#41 Maple Drive
		No. 41 Maple Drive

Spell out the street names of numbered streets under 20.

85 Fifth Avenue	NOT	85 5 Avenue
1600 Nineteenth Avenue		1600 19 Avenue

Use the numerical form *without* th, rd, or st following the number, for numbered streets larger than 20.

83 21 Street		83 21st Street
586 89 Avenue	NOT	586 89th Avenue
51 43 Avenue		51 43rd Avenue

Use the numerical forms for all residence or building numbers except "one," which should be written:

One Century Plaza	NOT	1 Century Plaza

DO NOT abbreviate anything in the address except the state (if desired).

433 Maple Drive		433 Maple Dr.
San Francisco, CA	NOT	S.F., CA 94103
94103		

For Packages

Mark all packages in waterproof ink or cover the address lines with scotch tape.

```
Form 52-C        EMERGENCY INFORMATION CARD      Grade..............................
Please Print                                     Home Room....................

Student's Name ............................................................................................Bus. No...........................
                        Last                    First
Address ....................................................................................... Home Tel.............................
      Where can parents be reached if not at home?      Birth date..........................

Mother: .........................................................................................  Tel.................................
               First Name              Address
Father: .........................................................................................  Tel.................................
               First Name              Address
      List two neighbors or nearby relatives who will assume temporary care of your child if you
      cannot be reached.

1.  Name ..........................................................................................................................

    Address ............................................................................... Tel.................................

2.  Name ..........................................................................................................................

    Address ............................................................................... Tel.................................
School Service Co., Inc., 157 W. Ontario St., Chicago, Ill. 60610                      (over)
```

```
Date ...................................................................

      In case of accident or serious illness, I request the school to contact me. If the school is
unable to reach me, I hereby authorize the school to call the physician indicated below and to
follow his instructions. If it is impossible to contact this physician, the school may make whatever
arrangements seem necessary.

Signature of parent or guardian ..............................................................................................

Remarks:

Allergies:


Other Conditions:


Local Physician's Name..............................................................................................................

Address...........................................................................................................................

Office Telephone No........................................... Other Telephone No...................................
                        (over)
```

Courtesy, School Service Co., Chicago, Illinois

FIGURE 2

**This is a sample of the front and back of a typical emergency in-
formation card used in schools. If you use the flat file jacket system mentioned in the text, you can easily file the emergency
card behind the student's address information, where it will be
readily available.**

Always place a card with sender and receiver's name and address INSIDE the package in case the wrapping is damaged or unreadable.

Mark packages with appropriate warnings to postal employees, "DO NOT BEND," "FRAGILE," "PLEASE HANDLE WITH CARE," "PERISHABLE."

ADMINISTRATOR, WORKING WITH   Being the administrator or head of a school is comparable to running any large corporation—plus much more. The school administrator performs such executive functions as hiring and firing teachers and staff, personnel supervision, overseeing the budget and school finances, meeting with the Board, participating in fund-raising or funding allocations, and participating in community programs or affairs. In addition to these tasks, the administrator also has to deal with the disciplining of unruly students including suspension and expulsion from school; irate or concerned parents; faculty and staff problems; and press relations. On top of this he or she must maintain a public image that is beyond reproach.

A good school administrator is worthy of all the respect and help that you are able to muster. It is a difficult job at best, but you as the secretary can make things run more smoothly for your administrator, and this in turn will make your life and your job easier. It helps to remember that the administrator is a person with the same feelings and human frailties present in all of us. He or she has a personal life and personal problems to deal with as well as all the requirements of the job.

In addition to performing your regular duties efficiently, here are some additional suggestions for helping your administrator:

1. BE PUNCTUAL. Your administrator may rely on you to handle early morning telephone calls, to set up or cancel appointments, or to perform duties on schedule. If your administrator knows that you are reliable, it will ease his burden. If you run into difficulties on a project and know that you will be unable to be punctual, let your administrator know as soon as possible. That way an alternative may be arranged that is mutually advantageous.

2. BE RELIABLE. If you are given a task, do it or delegate it, but be sure it is accomplished. Your administrator has enough on his mind without having to worry about whether or not everyday projects are being completed.

3. BE THOUGHTFUL. When you have worked with someone for a time, you learn when he is having a bad day, or is not feeling particularly

well. Try to ease up on those days. Instead of overloading the administrator with appointments, decisions that need to be made, and problems that need to be solved, attempt to postpone such items until another day.

4. COMMUNICATE. Early communication can forestall many problems. Make a habit of telling your administrator about problems and pleasant happenings relating to work. Try not to dwell on the negative, but to achieve a balance between negative and positive occurrences. This can really help to overcome the feeling that things never go right.

5. BE COOPERATIVE. In an ideal situation, you and your administrator work together as a well-matched team, each performing his own duties efficiently, yet each ready to fill in and compensate as necessary.

6. BE NEAT. Your personal appearance, your work, and your work space should be neat and organized. If you have public contact, the image you present will influence visitors and students alike.

ADMISSIONS Admissions refers to the set of operational procedures involved with application and acceptance to the school. Schools with admission requirements usually ask that the student (or parent) fill out an application, submit transcripts of previous grades pertinent to the application (usually the previous two or three years), and pass any necessary admission tests. After the admission requirements have been met, an individual or group forming an admissions committee may meet to review the applicant's qualifications and decide whether to accept or reject the applicant. (See ENROLLMENT PROCEDURES for further information on this topic.)

AGENDA An agenda is simply a list of what will take place at a meeting. Your administrator may gather items for the agenda and present them to you for typing, or you may be responsible for collecting pertinent data and preparing the agenda. Items may be brought to your attention by teachers, parents, or students, that will require discussion at a meeting. Keep a record of these items by maintaining a 3×5 file card system on which you can jot down topics as they are suggested. It is helpful to reread the minutes of previous meetings and make a note of any business unresolved or carried over that will need further discussion. Prior to typing the agenda, take a few minutes to go over the file cards with your administrator. He or she will then decide which items to include. Try to have the agenda distributed to those who will be attending the meeting far enough in advance to give time to mull over the topics. Some administrators prefer not to set time limits for each topic on the agenda. However, this can lead to exceedingly long meetings. Others will allow five, ten, or fifteen minutes per speaker or per topic area. The drawback to this system is that free and

```
        THE JOHN DOE SCHOOL

  Faculty Meeting, April 14, 19__


            AGENDA


3:00 P.M.        Meeting will come to order

3:05 P.M.        Administrator's Report

3:15 P.M.        English Department Report

3:25 P.M.        History Department Report

3:35 P.M.        Math Department Report

3:45 P.M.        Science Department Report

3:55 P.M.        Routine Business

                 -Faculty salary increases

                 -Student behavior

                 -Volunteer program

                 -Awards and contests

4:15 P.M.        New Business

4:30 P.M.        Adjournment
```

FIGURE 3

Sample agenda of a faculty meeting employing the time-limit method.

open discussion is limited and frustration and poor decision making may occur. Some administrators prefer to set the time that a meeting will adjourn, leaving the interim period for free discussion and then carrying over unfinished items to the next meeting. If time limits are given, they may be indicated as on the sample agenda.

The items on **an** agenda include ACTION ITEMS, which require a formal motion and must be seconded and voted upon; INFORMATION ITEMS, which consist of reports, statistics, data and proposals (while such information items may be presented orally, there is usually written backup information); and REFERENCE DATA, which are supporting documents further explaining an oral presentation.

It is helpful to bring additional copies of the agenda to the meeting, as those in attendance may have misplaced or forgotten their copies.

ALCOHOLISM, STUDENT Seventy-five percent of high school students say they have used alcohol before the age of eighteen and one-third say they drink regularly. A large number of young people start drinking as early as age twelve or thirteen. Adolescence is a difficult time at best: there are so many physical changes to integrate, so many new sensations to understand, so many important decisions to make, and so much pressure from parents and society to succeed, and from peers to fit in.

According to the National Institute on Alcohol Abuse and Alcoholism, there are at least 450,000 alcoholics in the nine to eighteen age range. Having a parent who is an alcoholic can also be detrimental to the student. The child may never take a drink but may still have to live with the problems of alcoholism without understanding the situation. The student may feel somehow responsible and guilty because the parent is an alcoholic.

Alcoholism is treatable if the alcoholic is willing to be treated. Realistically, the school secretary cannot expect to solve such a massive problem as adolescent or adult alcohol abuse, but here are some suggestions that you can implement:

- Be aware that alcohol abuse is on the increase among students, often as young as eight or nine years old.
- Be alert to the students. If you suspect that a student has an alcohol or other drug problem, do not hesitate to discuss it with the administrator.
- Never glorify alcohol to a young person, even in a joke, and be honest and factual when discussing drinking or alcoholism. Explain that alcohol

is a drug that may be used socially, but that it is illegal for minors to use. Morality and values aside, any minor who uses alcohol is breaking the law and is subject to its penalties.

If the parents of a minor who has a drinking problem are contacted by the administration, be prepared to deal with their disbelief or hostility. It may take some time for the parents to come to terms with the problem—or they may choose to ignore it entirely refusing to believe that it exists. (For further information, see DRUG ABUSE.)

APPOINTMENTS, HANDLING   See TIME MANAGEMENT.

ATTENDANCE   A record of time spent in school by students (which is often kept for faculty also). Attendance records are kept in roll books (for an entire grade) or on attendance cards (for individuals). It is essential that attendance records be kept accurately since they are a part of the student's permanent file. It is necessary to keep track of minor students' movements during a school day, and medical appointments, tardiness, and absenteeism must all be accounted for by an excuse note from the parent or verification by telephone if that is the school's policy.

Attendance Records Maintenance

Very large institutions often use a computer to keep track of attendance. The following information is provided for schools in which the secretary is directly responsible for keeping attendance records.

How to Set Up an Attendance Roll Book

1. Find out the actual number of school days, including vacations, from the school calendar.
2. Write the dates in the boxes provided in the roll book.
3. Draw a line through vacation periods. Here you could also choose to save space by leaving vacation periods out of the book altogether; simply end a section with the last day before vacation, then begin the next section with the first day following vacation.
4. Count the number of students per grade and determine the amount of space you will need to record each grade.
5. Set up your book in sections, indicating the grade level at the top of each page. Six-week sections are the norm for most attendance record books, but if your school uses different grading periods, simply add or delete pages as necessary.

6. List students in alphabetical order, last name first.

7. Double-check the number of students when you have finished listing them to avoid accidentally dropping someone from the roll.

8. Type your attendance symbol code and tape it to the inside front cover of your attendance book. (See ATTENDANCE SYMBOLS.)

9. You are now ready to record the daily attendance.

10. Each day, record in pencil. There are often many changes during the day because of medical appointments, tardiness, and so on. At the end of the day, take a few minutes to verify all changes; then record in pen over the pencil. Your roll book will always be neat, accurate, and easy to read.

11. If a student enrolls or drops out at midterm, list the date of enrollment or dropping next to the name. This saves time when doing transcripts.

Attendance Symbols

Attendance symbols, which are used to record attendance on cards or roll books, may vary from school to school. If your school does not have an existing system, here is one you can adopt or modify according to your needs:

X	Absent all day due to illness
/	Absent morning only due to illness
#	Absent afternoon only due to illness
T or L	Tardy or late
TE or LE	Excused tardiness for medical reasons
E	Excused absence other than illness—all day
E/	Excused morning only
E#	Excused afternoon only
*	Absent for over one hour but less than one-half-day (four *s count as one half-day)
C	Cut school
S	Suspended
EXP	Expelled

AUDIO-VISUAL EQUIPMENT   Equipment such as tape recorders, record players, microphones, amplifiers, film projectors, overhead projectors, opaque projectors, slide projectors, and videocassette recorders are used in schools and are referred to as audio-visual or AV equipment. Large schools often have AV centers that handle equipment checkout and maintenance, but in the smaller school the secretary and/or librarian will usually handle AV systems.

The AV equipment used in schools may be broken down as follows:

AUDIO	tape recorders
	record players
	stereo component systems
	microphones
	amplifiers
VISUAL	16 mm film projectors
	8 mm film projectors (or super 8mm)
	overhead projectors
	opaque projectors
	slide projectors
	videotape or videocassette recorders
TYPICAL AV SUPPLIES	film reels
	tape reels or cassettes
	transparency film for overhead projectors
	transparency pencils
	tape head cleaner
	demagnetizer tape
	projector lamps
	slides and/or films
	film rental/sales catalogs
	necessary replacement parts

Audio-Visual Equipment Explained

Projectors – 8mm and 16mm film projectors

These are used for educational and other films. Most projectors now have an automatic loading feature. Once you switch on the automatic lever all you need do is place the film reel on the arm, place the film into the appropriate slot, and the projector does the rest. Most 16mm projectors used in education have very clear instructions right on the machine. One thing to remember though: NEVER RUN THE FILM BACKWARDS or you will tear the sprocket holes and ruin the film. There is a separate procedure for rewinding the film after it has been shown.

If you are responsible for checking out AV equipment to the faculty, be sure that you thoroughly understand how to use the equipment yourself. If this area is new to you, ask a knowledgeable staff member, or ask the supplier for product information pamphlets. They are extremely informative and will tell you practically anything you could want to know about the equipment.

Projectors – opaque

An opaque projector has the capability of projecting opaque images onto a screen. It has many uses in the school, especially in science classes. For example, a teacher may want to show the class a shell or a leaf and the opaque projector allows the enlarged image to be viewed by the whole class at one time—preferable to trying to pass around a small object.

Projectors – overhead

Overhead projectors are used by teachers for various subjects from elementary school through college. The instructor may use commercially prepared transparencies (transparent film on which information is drawn or printed), or may choose to prepare his own. Special felt or grease pencils can be used to write on the film which comes in sheets or continuous rolls, or the transparency may be made by the photocopy process. The projector then shows the enlarged image to the class.

Projectors – slide

Slide projectors are available in carousel or straight tray models, both with and without rear-screen projection capabilities.

Projectors – filmstrip

Filmstrip projectors are available in sound and silent models, and are frequently used in the classroom for various educational applications.

Videotape Recorders (VTR) or Videocassette Recorders (VCR)

Reel-to-reel or cassette, these are similar to the videocassette devices manufactured for home use. In education, the VTRs or VCRs may be used in the classroom to show films or specially prepared educational material. They are also used in faculty seminars and are a wonderful teaching aid for the creative faculty member.

Projection Screens

Screens are used with various types of projection equipment. They are available in portable models with a tripod base, in pull-down versions that operate like roller window shades, and stationary models that may be operated automatically from either ceiling-mount or wall-mount positions.

Audio-Visual Equipment, Tips for Handling

Slides and Films

The prime factors that can ruin the quality of slides and film are light, moisture, and heat. Therefore, films and slides should be stored in a dark, dry, cool place. Dealing specifically with slides, the life of such color transparencies depends on the amount of light and heat from the projection lamp, and upon the total projection time. Protect slides from excessive light and heat by:

- Never using a higher wattage projection lamp than that recommended by the manufacturer for use with the projector.
- Never removing glass lens covers or shields.
- Never restricting the air flow to the projector, and not blocking ventilator openings.

Protect film and slides from physical damage by:

- Keeping them as clean and dust-free as possible.
- Never touching them with your fingers except at the edges.
- If spots or fingerprints are already on them, you can clean them in a special solution such as Kodak Photo-Flo Solution, used according to package directions.
- Sometimes the storage rooms in old buildings may be visited by insects who can feast on stored slides or film. Such damaged items should be discarded, but you may be able to save some slides by remounting the transparencies in new mounts. Slides and films are best stored in metal or hard plastic containers.
- Transparencies should not be stored in basements or attics that may be too hot or too damp. Storage in high-humidity areas can result in the growth of fungus. Too low humidity results in possible brittleness and breakage.
- You can remove lint from transparencies by lightly dusting with a dry camel's hair brush available in art supply or camera supply shops.

Maintaining the Projection Room

Whether your school uses portable AV equipment that is moved from classroom to classroom, or whether you have a permanent projection room, there are basic requirements that apply to both situations: room size; seating capacity; lighting; and sound reproduction quality. Here are some tips to help you efficiently utilize the projection facilities:

1. The projection screen should be large enough for everyone present to view it easily. The screen should be at least on the same level (or higher) as the projector.

   A rule of thumb for showing slides is that the last row of seats should be no farther from the screen than eight times the height of the projected

Selecting the Correct Screen Size

HOW TO FIND EXACT SCREEN SIZE:
Aperture Width x Projection Throw in inches ÷ Lens Focal Length = width of screen needed. For example: Aperture .380" (16mm movie projector) x 320" (projection throw...desired distance from screen) ÷ 2" (lens focal length) = a 60" screen.

Tables prepared according to ANSI PH7.6.
1. Overhead and Opaque projection distances are measured from lens to screen.
2. All other projection distances are measured from film to lens.
3. Because of lens manufacturing tolerances, projection distances shown may vary 6 inches either way.

16 MM MOTION PICTURES—APERTURE WIDTH—.380"

LENS FOCAL LENGTH	40"	50"	60"	70"	84"	96"	9'	10'	12'	14'	16'	18'	20'	22'	24'	26'	28'	30'
12.7 mm — ½"	4.5	5.7	6.7	7.8	9.3	10.6	11.9	13.2	15.9	18.5	21.1	23.8	26.4	29.0	31.7	34.3	36.9	39.6
15.875 mm — ⅝"	5.6	7.0	8.3	9.7	11.6	13.3	14.9	16.6	19.8	23.1	26.4	29.7	33.0	36.3	39.6	42.9	46.2	49.4
19 mm — ¾"	6.7	8.3	10.0	11.6	13.9	15.9	17.9	19.9	23.8	27.8	31.7	35.7	39.6	43.5	47.5	51.4	55.4	59.3
25.4 mm — 1"	8.9	11.1	13.3	15.5	18.6	21.2	23.9	26.5	31.7	37.0	42.3	47.5	52.8	58.1	63.3	68.6	73.9	79.1
38.1 mm — 1½"	13.4	16.7	20.0	23.3	27.9	31.8	35.8	39.7	47.6	55.5	63.4	71.3	79.2	87.1	95.0	102.9	110.8	118.7
50.8 mm — 2"	17.9	22.3	26.7	31.0	37.2	42.4	47.7	53.0	63.5	74.0	84.5	95.1	105.6	116.1	126.6	137.2	147.7	158.2
63.5 mm — 2½"	22.3	27.8	33.3	38.8	46.5	53.0	59.6	66.2	79.4	92.5	105.7	118.8	132.0	145.2	158.3	171.5	184.6	197.8
69.85 mm — 2¾"	24.6	30.6	36.6	42.7	51.1	58.4	65.6	72.8	87.3	101.8	116.2	130.7	145.2	159.7	174.1	188.6	203.1	217.6
76.2 mm — 3"	26.8	33.4	40.0	46.6	55.8	63.7	71.6	79.4	95.2	111.0	126.8	142.6	158.4	174.2	190.0	205.8	221.6	237.3
88.9 mm — 3½"	31.3	39.0	46.6	54.3	65.1	74.3	83.5	92.7	111.1	129.5	148.0	166.4	184.8	203.2	221.6	240.1	258.5	276.9
101.6 mm — 4"	35.8	44.5	53.3	62.1	74.4	84.9	95.4	105.9	127.0	148.0	169.1	190.1	211.2	232.2	253.3	274.4	295.4	316.5

SUPER 8MM MOTION PICTURES—APERTURE WIDTH—.209"

LENS FOCAL LENGTH	40"	50"	60"	70"	84"	96"	9'	10'	12'
12.7 mm — ½"	8.1	10.1	12.0	14.0	16.8	19.2	21.6	24.0	28.7
14.88 mm — 9⁄16"	9.0	11.3	13.5	15.7	18.9	21.5	24.2	26.9	32.3
17 mm — 21⁄32"	10.8	13.5	16.1	18.8	22.6	25.8	29.0	32.2	38.6
18.5 mm — 23⁄32"	11.8	14.7	17.6	20.5	24.6	28.1	31.6	35.1	42.0
19 mm — ¾"	12.1	15.1	18.1	21.1	25.2	28.8	32.4	36.0	43.2
22 mm — ⅞"	14.0	17.5	21.0	24.4	29.3	33.5	37.6	41.8	50.1
25.4 mm — 1"	16.1	20.1	24.1	28.1	33.7	38.5	43.2	48.0	57.6
27 mm — 1 1⁄16"	17.1	21.3	25.5	29.8	35.7	40.8	45.8	50.9	61.0
28 mm — 1 3⁄32"	17.7	22.1	26.5	30.9	37.0	42.3	47.6	52.8	63.3
32 mm — 1¼"	20.3	25.3	30.4	35.4	42.4	48.4	54.5	60.5	72.6

2"x2" 126 INSTAMATIC SLIDES—APERTURE WIDTH—1.04" (SQUARE SCREEN SIZE)

LENS FOCAL LENGTH	40"	50"	60"	70"	84"	96"	9'	10'	12'
1.4"	4.7	5.8	7.0	8.1	9.7	11.0	12.4	13.7	16.4
2"	6.7	8.4	10.0	11.6	13.8	15.7	17.6	19.6	23.4
3"	10.1	12.5	14.9	17.3	20.7	23.6	26.5	29.3	35.1
4"	13.5	16.7	19.9	23.1	27.6	31.4	35.3	39.1	46.8
5"	16.9	20.9	24.9	28.9	34.5	39.3	44.1	48.9	58.5
6.5"	21.9	27.1	32.3	37.5	44.8	51.1	57.3	63.6	76.1
7"	23.6	29.2	35.0	40.4	48.3	55.0	61.7	68.5	81.9
8.5"	28.7	35.5	42.3	49.1	58.6	66.8	75.0	83.2	99.5
9"	30.4	37.6	44.8	52.0	62.1	70.7	79.4	88.0	105.4
10"	33.7	41.8	49.8	57.8	69.0	78.6	88.2	97.8	117.1
11"	37.1	45.9	54.7	63.5	75.9	86.5	97.0	107.6	128.9
12.5"	42.2	52.2	62.2	72.2	86.2	98.3	110.3	122.3	146.3
15.5"	52.3	64.7	77.1	89.5	106.9	121.8	136.7	151.6	181.4
20"	67.5	83.5	99.5	115.5	138.0	157.2	176.4	195.7	234.1

2"x2" DOUBLE FRAME—35MM SLIDES—APERTURE WIDTH—1.35"

LENS FOCAL LENGTH	40"	50"	60"	70"	84"	96"	9'	10'	12'	14'	16'	18'	20'
1"	2.6	3.3	3.9	4.5	5.4	6.1	6.8	7.6	9.1	10.5	12.0	13.5	15.0
1.4"	3.7	4.6	5.4	6.3	7.5	8.5	9.6	10.6	12.7	14.8	16.8	18.9	21.0
2"	5.3	6.5	7.7	9.0	10.7	12.2	13.7	15.2	18.1	21.1	24.0	27.0	30.0
3"	7.9	9.8	11.6	13.5	16.1	18.3	20.5	22.7	27.2	31.6	36.1	40.5	44.9
4"	10.6	13.0	15.5	18.0	21.4	24.4	27.3	30.3	36.2	42.2	48.1	54.0	59.9
5"	13.1	16.3	19.4	22.4	26.8	30.5	34.2	37.9	45.3	52.7	60.1	67.5	74.9
5.5"	14.5	17.9	21.3	24.7	29.4	33.5	37.6	41.9	50.1	58.6	66.1	74.3	82.4
6"	15.8	19.5	23.2	26.9	32.1	36.6	41.0	45.5	54.3	63.2	72.1	81.0	89.9
6.5"	17.1	21.2	25.2	29.2	34.8	39.6	44.4	49.2	58.9	68.5	78.1	87.8	97.4
7"	18.5	22.8	27.1	31.4	37.5	42.7	47.8	53.0	63.4	73.8	84.1	94.5	104.9
7.5"	19.8	24.4	29.0	33.7	40.2	45.7	51.2	56.8	67.9	79.0	90.1	101.3	112.4
8"	21.1	26.0	31.0	35.9	42.8	48.7	54.7	60.6	72.5	84.3	96.2	108.0	120.0
8.5"	22.4	27.7	32.9	38.2	45.5	51.8	58.1	64.4	77.0	89.6	102.2	114.8	127.4
9"	23.7	29.3	34.8	40.4	48.2	54.8	61.5	68.2	81.5	94.8	108.2	121.5	134.8
9.5"	25.1	30.9	36.8	42.6	50.9	57.9	64.9	72.0	86.0	100.1	114.2	128.3	142.3
10"	26.4	32.6	38.7	44.9	53.5	60.9	68.3	75.6	90.6	105.4	120.2	135.0	149.8
12.5"	33.0	40.7	48.4	56.1	66.9	76.2	85.4	94.7	113.2	131.7	150.2	168.8	187.3
15.5"	40.5	50.0	59.5	68.9	83.0	94.4	105.9	117.4	140.4	163.3	186.3	209.3	232.2
20"	52.8	65.1	77.4	89.8	107.1	121.9	136.7	151.5	181.1	210.8	240.4	270.0	299.7

2"x2" SUPER SLIDES—APERTURE WIDTH—1.5" (SQUARE SCREEN SIZE)

LENS FOCAL LENGTH	40"	50"	60"	70"	84"	96"	9'	10'	12'	14'	16'	18'	20'
1"	2.4	2.9	3.5	4.1	4.8	5.5	6.2	6.8	8.2	9.5	10.8	12.2	13.5
1.4"	3.3	4.1	4.9	5.7	6.8	7.7	8.6	9.6	11.4	13.3	15.2	17.0	18.9
2"	4.8	5.9	7.0	8.1	9.7	11.0	12.3	13.7	16.3	19.0	21.8	24.7	27.0
3"	7.2	8.8	10.5	12.2	14.5	16.5	18.5	20.5	24.5	28.5	32.5	36.5	40.5
4"	9.6	11.8	14.0	16.2	19.3	22.0	24.7	27.3	32.7	38.0	43.3	48.7	54.0
5"	12.0	14.7	17.5	20.3	24.2	27.5	30.8	34.2	40.8	47.5	54.2	60.8	67.5
5.5"	13.2	16.2	19.3	22.3	26.6	30.3	33.9	37.6	44.9	52.3	59.6	66.9	74.3
6"	14.4	17.7	21.0	24.3	29.0	33.0	37.0	41.0	49.0	57.0	65.0	73.0	81.0
6.5"	15.6	19.2	22.8	26.4	31.4	35.8	40.1	44.4	53.1	61.8	70.4	79.1	87.8
7"	16.7	20.6	24.5	28.4	33.8	38.5	43.2	47.8	57.2	66.5	75.8	85.2	94.5
7.5"	17.9	22.1	26.3	30.4	36.3	41.3	46.3	51.3	61.3	71.3	81.3	91.3	101.3
8"	19.1	23.6	28.0	32.5	38.7	44.0	49.3	54.7	65.3	76.0	86.7	97.3	108.0
8.5"	20.3	25.0	29.8	34.5	41.1	46.8	52.4	58.0	69.3	80.8	92.1	103.4	114.8
9"	21.5	26.5	31.5	36.5	43.5	49.5	55.5	61.5	73.5	85.5	97.5	109.5	121.5
9.5"	22.7	28.0	33.3	38.5	45.9	52.3	58.6	65.0	77.6	90.3	102.9	115.6	128.3
10"	23.9	29.5	35.0	40.6	48.4	55.0	61.7	68.3	81.7	95.0	108.3	121.7	135.0
12.5"	29.9	36.8	43.8	50.7	60.4	68.7	77.1	85.4	102.1	118.8	135.4	152.1	168.8
15.5"	37.1	45.7	54.3	62.9	74.9	85.3	95.6	105.9	126.6	147.3	167.9	188.6	209.3
20"	47.9	58.9	70.1	81.2	96.7	110.0	123.4	136.7	163.4	190.0	216.7	243.4	270.0

2¼"x2¼" SLIDES—APERTURE WIDTH—2.1875" (SQUARE SCREEN SIZE)

LENS FOCAL LENGTH	40"	50"	60"	70"	84"	96"	9'	10'	12'	14'	16'	18'	20'
5"	8.5	10.4	12.3	14.2	16.8	19.1	21.4	23.7	28.3	32.8	37.4	42.0	46.6
6.5"	11.0	13.5	16.0	18.4	21.9	24.9	27.8	30.8	36.8	42.7	48.6	54.6	60.5
7"	11.9	14.5	17.2	19.9	23.6	26.8	30.0	33.2	39.6	46.0	52.4	58.8	65.2
8.5"	14.4	17.6	20.9	24.1	28.6	32.5	36.4	40.3	48.1	55.8	63.6	71.4	79.1
10"	17.0	20.8	24.8	28.4	33.7	38.3	42.8	47.4	56.5	65.7	74.8	84.0	93.1
12.5"	21.2	25.9	30.7	35.4	42.1	47.8	53.5	59.3	70.7	82.1	93.5	100.8	116.4
15.5"	26.3	32.2	38.1	44.0	52.2	59.3	66.4	73.5	87.6	101.8	116.0	130.1	144.3
20"	33.9	41.5	49.1	56.7	67.4	76.5	85.7	94.8	113.1	131.4	149.6	167.9	186.2
24"	40.7	49.8	58.9	68.1	80.9	91.8	102.8	113.8	135.7	157.6	179.6	201.5	223.4

35MM SINGLE FRAME FILM STRIPS—APERTURE WIDTH—.885"

LENS FOCAL LENGTH	40"	50"	60"	70"	84"	96"	9'	10'	12'	14'	16'	18'	20'
3"	11.8	14.6	17.5	20.3	24.4	27.8	31.0	34.4	41.2	48.0	54.7	61.5	68.3
4"	15.7	19.5	23.3	27.0	32.3	36.8	41.3	45.9	54.9	63.9	73.0	82.0	91.1
5"	19.7	24.4	29.1	33.8	40.4	46.0	51.7	57.3	68.8	80.0	91.2	102.5	113.8
6"	23.6	29.3	34.9	40.6	48.5	55.2	62.0	68.8	82.4	95.9	109.5	123.0	136.6
7"	27.5	34.1	40.7	47.3	56.5	64.4	72.4	80.3	96.1	111.9	127.7	143.5	159.4
8"	31.5	39.0	46.5	54.1	64.6	73.7	82.7	91.7	109.8	127.9	146.0	164.0	182.1

3¼"x4" SLIDES (LANTERN)—APERTURE WIDTH—3.0"

LENS FOCAL LENGTH	50"	60"	70"	84"	96"	9'	10'	12'	14'	16'	18'	20'
6"	9.4	11.0	12.7	15.0	17.0	19.0	21.0	25.0	29.0	33.0	37.0	41.0
6.5"	10.1	11.9	13.7	16.3	18.4	20.8	22.8	27.1	31.4	35.8	40.1	44.4
8"	12.5	14.7	16.9	20.0	22.7	25.4	28.0	33.3	38.7	44.0	49.3	54.7
8.5"	13.3	15.6	18.0	21.3	24.1	26.9	29.8	35.4	41.1	46.8	52.4	58.1
10"	15.6	18.4	21.1	25.0	28.3	31.7	35.0	41.7	48.4	55.0	61.7	68.3
12"	18.7	22.1	25.4	30.0	34.0	38.0	42.0	50.0	58.0	66.0	74.0	82.0
12.5"	19.5	23.0	26.4	31.3	35.4	39.6	43.8	52.1	60.4	68.8	77.1	85.4
14"	21.9	25.7	29.7	35.0	39.7	44.4	49.0	58.4	67.7	77.0	86.3	95.7
15"	23.4	27.6	31.7	37.6	42.5	47.5	52.5	62.5	72.5	82.5	92.5	102.5
15.5"	24.2	28.5	32.8	38.8	44.0	49.1	54.3	64.6	74.9	85.3	95.6	105.9
16"	25.0	29.4	33.8	40.1	45.4	50.7	56.0	66.7	77.4	88.0	98.7	109.3
18"	28.1	33.1	38.1	45.1	51.0	57.0	63.0	75.0	87.0	99.0	111.0	123.0
20"	31.2	36.8	42.3	50.1	56.7	63.4	70.1	83.4	96.7	110.0	123.4	136.7
22"	34.3	40.4	46.5	55.1	62.4	69.7	77.1	91.7	106.4	121.0	135.7	150.4
24"	37.5	44.1	50.7	60.1	68.1	76.1	84.1	100.0	116.0	132.0	148.0	164.0
26"	40.6	47.8	55.0	65.1	73.7	82.4	91.1	108.4	125.7	143.0	160.4	177.7

OVERHEAD PROJECTION—MOUNT APERTURE WIDTH—9.5"

LENS FOCAL LENGTH	50"	60"	70"	84"	96"	9'	10'	12'	14'	16'	18'	20'
10.5"	5.5	6.4	7.3	8.6	9.7	10.8	11.9	14.3	16.5	18.8	20.8	23.0
12.0"	6.3	7.3	8.4	9.8	11.1	12.4	13.6	16.2	18.7	21.2	23.7	26.3
12.5"	6.5	7.6	8.7	10.3	11.6	12.9	14.2	16.9	19.5	22.1	24.7	27.4
12.75"	6.7	7.8	8.9	10.5	11.8	13.1	14.5	17.2	19.8	22.5	25.2	27.9
13.5"	7.0	8.2	9.4	11.1	12.5	13.9	15.3	18.2	21.0	23.9	26.7	29.6
14.0"	6.9	8.1	9.8	11.5	13.0	14.4	15.9	18.9	21.8	24.7	27.7	30.6
15.5"	8.1	9.5	10.8	12.7	14.3	16.0	17.6	20.9	24.1	27.3	30.5	33.9
16.0"	8.3	9.8	11.2	13.1	14.8	16.5	18.2	21.5	24.9	28.3	31.7	35.0
22.0"	11.5	13.4	15.3	18.0	20.4	22.7	25.0	29.6	34.2	38.9	43.5	48.1
40.0"	20.9	24.4	27.9	32.8	37.0	41.2	45.4	53.9	62.3	70.7	79.1	87.5
50.0"	26.1	30.5	34.9	41.0	46.3	51.5	56.8	67.3	77.8	88.4	98.9	109.4

OPAQUE PROJECTION—APERTURE WIDTH—10" (SQUARE SCREEN SIZE)

LENS FOCAL LENGTH	50"	60"	70"	84"	96"	9'	10'	12'
18"	9.0	10.5	12.0	14.1	15.9	17.7	19.5	23.1
22"	11.0	12.8	14.7	17.2	19.4	21.6	23.8	28.2
26"	13.0	15.2	17.3	20.4	23.0	25.6	28.2	33.4

© Copyright Da-Lite Screen Company, Inc.

Courtesy, Da-Lite Screen Company, Inc.

FIGURE 4

This chart will help you to select the correct screen size and projection distance for a variety of projection needs.

image. (If the image on the screen is four feet high, then the last row of seats should be no farther than thirty-two feet away.)

2. Position the projector the correct distance from the screen. When the projector is in the best location for the space, place a piece of masking tape on the projector table under each projector foot, and trace the location. If the projector is accidentally moved, it can be relocated quickly and easily.

3. Check to see that the electrical outlets are adequate for the equipment required.

4. Carpeting or soundproofing material placed on the wall directly opposite speakers will greatly improve sound quality.

5. A flat-finish neutral hue such as gray is a good choice for projection room walls.

6. Make sure that any extension cords used are capable of carrying the necessary electrical load.

Audio-Visual Equipment and Supplies, Sources

Carts, Projection Tables, Stands

Accessories Manufacturers, Ltd.
P.O. Box 70
595 St. Remi Street
Montreal, Quebec, Canada H4C 3G6

Advance Products Company, Inc.
P.O. Box 2178
1101 East Central
Wichita, Kansas 67214

Bretford Manufacturing, Inc.
9715 Soreng Avenue
Schiller Park, Illinois 60176

Gruber Products Company
P.O. Box 5556
5254 Jackman Road
Toledo, Ohio 43613

Kimchuck, Inc.
Audio-Visual Division
34 Del Mar Drive
Brookfield, Connecticut 06804

Luxor Corporation
P.O. Box 830
104 Lake View Avenue
Waukegan, Illinois 60085

H. Wilson Corporation
555 West Taft Drive
South Holland, Illinois 60473

Front-Projection Screens

Da-Lite Screen Company, Inc.
P.O. Box 629
Warsaw, Indiana 46580

Knox Manufacturing Co.
111 Spruce Street
Wood Dale, Illinois 60191

Wilcox-Lange, Inc.
3925 North Pulaski Road
Chicago, Illinois 60641

Rear-Projection Screens

Da-Lite Screen Company, Inc.
P.O. Box 629
Warsaw, Indiana 46580

Draper Shade and Screen Company
411 South Pearl Street
Spiceland, Indiana 47385

Spectrovue, Inc.
7853 El Cajon Boulevard
La Mesa, California 72104

3M Company
Visual Products Division
Bldg. 220-10W
3M Center
St. Paul, Minnesota 55101

Trans-Lux News-Sign Corporation
625 Madison Avenue
New York, New York 10022

Miscellaneous Equipment and Supplies

A-V Services, Inc.
263 Hillside Avenue
Nutley, New Jersey 07110

Arion Corporation
825 Boone Avenue, North
Minneapolis, Minnesota 55427

AudioVisual Laboratories
420 Highway 36
Belford, New Jersey 07718

Avtek
28 Woodard Road
Walpole, Massachusetts 02081

Bergen Expo Systems, Inc.
1088 Main Avenue
Clifton, New Jersey 07011

Buhl Optical Company
1009 Beech Avenue
Pittsburgh, Pennsylvania 15233

Clear Light Productions, Inc.
P.O. Box 391
57B Chapel Street
Newton, Massachussetts 02158

Columbia Scientific Industries, Inc.
AVC Division
P.O. Box 9908
11950 Jollyville Road
Austin, Texas 78766

EEG Enterprises, Inc.
82 Rome Street
Farmingdale, New York 11735

Electrosonic Systems, Inc.
4575 West 77th Street
Minneapolis, Minnesota 55435

Impact Communications, Inc.
P.O. Box 28639
Dallas, Texas 75228

E. Leitz, Inc.
Link Drive
Rockleigh, New Jersey 07647

Mackenzie Laboratories, Inc.
P.O. Box 3085
5507 North Peck Road
Arcadia, California 91006

Montage Productions, Inc.
9 Industrial Drive
Rutherford, New Jersey 07070

Optisonics HEC Corporation
1802 West Grant Road
Tucson, Arizona 85705

RMF Products, Inc.
P.O. Box 413
Batavia, Illinois 60510

Sight and Sound Systems
5619 St. John Avenue
Kansas City, Missouri 64123

Skirpan Lighting Control Corporation
61-03 32 Avenue
Woodside, New York 11377

George R. Snell Associates, Inc.
Genarco Division
155 U.S. Route 22 E.
Springfield, New Jersey 07081

Spindler and Sauppe, Inc.
13034 Saticoy Street
North Hollywood, California 91605

Technamics Company
2232 Gardner Station
St. Louis, Missouri 63109

Technicraft
P.O. Box 9098
405 Greenlawn Drive
Columbia, South Carolina 29290

Tempo Audivision, Inc.
290 Larkin Street
Buffalo, New York 14210

3M Company
Visual Products Division
Bldg. 220-10W
3M Center
St. Paul, Minnesota 55101

United Audio Visual Corporation
1730 Mojave Road
Las Vegas, Nevada 89104

Wollensak/3M Company
Bldg. 223-5E
3M Center
St. Paul, Minnesota 55101

B

BANK

Deposits

It is not prudent to keep sums of money at the school. In fact, many school districts require any cash collected to be deposited every day. School funds are usually paid in small cash sums, so all coin should be rolled in bank wrappers and currency should be bundled according to denomination and held with rubber bands. Fill out the deposit slip before you get to the bank, and be sure the contents are counted by the teller in your presence; then get a receipt. Always make up duplicate deposit slips so that you can have one stamped as the receipt. When writing a deposit slip, list the coin and currency separately in the appropriate sections, and write the identifying ABA (American Bankers Association) number (e.g., $\frac{1\text{-}113}{1210}$) that appears in the upper right hand corner of the check in the correct space on the deposit slip. As you list each check, verify that the dollar amount and written amounts coincide and that each check is signed and endorsed.

Endorsement of Checks

A rubber stamp is usually used for check endorsement. Such a stamp may be worded "Pay to the order of ＿＿＿＿＿ Bank. For deposit only." If you do not have a stamp, type or write this on each check.

Withdrawals

Withdrawals from school savings or checking accounts usually require two signatures. The principal is most often one of these authorized to sign. The second party authorized to sign may be a financial officer of the PTA or student body, the school business manager, board chairman, or vice principal. NEVER keep a supply of pre-signed checks on hand.

Writing Checks

Most schools have their own printed checks showing the school name, address, ZIP code and telephone number. They are usually "business style" checks, bound into a large book, three checks to a page, with all checks prenumbered. A stub is attached to each check, on which is recorded the reason for which payment is being made, the name of the payee, and the date. Sometimes a separate ledger page is provided for this rather than individual stubs. No errors are permitted on checks. Do not alter or erase. If you have made a mistake, write "VOID" across the check and its stub and write a new check. Keep all voided checks on file in numerical order for statement reconciliation.

Reconciling Bank Statements

Do this each month or whenever the statement is sent by the bank. (Some are sent every three months.) Reconciling is a matter of balancing the figures in your checkbook against the bank figures. The reverse side of the statement generally provides a printed form for reconciling and gives detailed bank instructions. If you have trouble following them, call your bank for help. If checks are returned marked "NSF" (not sufficient funds) tell the appropriate administrator immediately. Any errors or discrepancies in the bank statement should be reported to the bank right away.

BEHAVIOR PROBLEMS, SUPERVISION OF   Children are often sent to the office when the teacher has reached wit's end in dealing with them. It is the administrator's responsibility to determine disciplinary actions for such students, but it is wise to discuss this with the administrator in advance in case you have to deal with such an issue in the administrator's absence. Usually, the student is expected to sit quietly out of the way for a period of time—often the remainder of the period during which the behavior problem occurred. If you are faced with this issue while the administrator is gone and there is no one else in charge:

- Write down the student's name and grade and the name of the teacher who has sent him to the office. Present this information to your administrator when he returns. Also, make a note of the reason why the student was sent to the office.
- In the case of a young child, you could have him sit quietly for a short period or give him some "busy work" if he is to be kept in the office for a longer period. Counting forms or papers into bundles, sharpening pencils, or performing some other such task will usually keep him occupied.

– In cases where an older student has caused severe difficulties, get help from the administration—a teacher, or security personnel. Do not attempt to deal with this alone.

BELLS, WORKING WITH   Bells ring automatically, according to times set inside the master clock. The school electrician sets the times according to the needs of the school program. If there is a sudden temporary change of program, you will need to ring the bells manually. Breakdown of the master clock, a shortened schedule, or power failure may cause the need for manual ringing. It is wise to keep a portable cooking timer on hand to help you remember to ring bells at the proper times.

BIBLIOGRAPHIES, GUIDELINES FOR TYPING   The bibliography, or list of books consulted in the preparation of a written work, should conclude a report. It is not necessary to include the titles of standard dictionaries in a bibliography. Here are samples of the correct forms to use when typing bibliographies:

Books and Pamphlets

List in alphabetical order:

– Full name of author, last name first
– Complete title and subtitle of work, underlined
– Name of the editor, or the number of the edition, or the name of the translator, or the number of volumes in the work
– The place of publication, name of the publisher, and date of publication

Each part of each reference should be separated by commas, with a period at the end.

Sample:

Noma, Seiroko, Japanese Costume and Textile Arts, The Heibonsha Survey of Japanese Art, Vol. 16, New York, Weatherhill/Heibonsha, 1974.

Encyclopedia Items

– Author's name
– Title of article in quotation marks
– Edition if available
– Place of publication, name of publisher, date of publication
– Volume and page numbers

Sample:

Kandel, I.L., "History of Education," Collier's Encyclopedia, 1974, Vol. 8, 564–576.

Magazine Articles

- Author's name. If unknown, type "anonymous."
- Title in quotation marks
- Name of magazine, underlined
- Volume of magazine in Roman numerals
- Date in parentheses
- Page numbers for entire article

Sample:

Bone, Dorothea, "Making Calculators Count," Independent School (May, 1981), 45–47.

BILLING   Some private schools operate on a "cash only" basis, while others allow students to charge items to their accounts which are then billed on a monthly basis. Such items as lunches, supplies, textbooks, and field trip costs may be included on the monthly statement. Tuition payments may often be paid on a monthly billing basis and sent along with the monthly statement, or they may be due on dates as specified in the enrollment agreement. If the tuition is outstanding, the student may be suspended from school until payment is received. Of course, this policy will vary from school to school, and there is usually considerable leeway for extenuating circumstances.

BINDING   Pamphlet or booklet binding is usually done in five steps: scoring, folding, gathering the materials or collating, stitching or stapling, and trimming. Scoring is the creasing of the paper prior to folding. Pamphlets can be obtained in four, six, eight, twelve, or sixteen-page folders. Anything over sixteen pages is usually bound as a book form.

If stitching is used, it might be saddle-stitch or side-stitch. The method used depends on the thickness of the booklet. Saddle-stitching is used for smaller, slimmer volumes where the staples are forced through the center backbone of the booklet. This method allows the booklet to lie flat for easy reading. When the bulk is too great for saddle-stitching, side-stitching is used. In this case, the stapling or stitching is done on the side of a stack of sheets rather than through the center backbone. In bookbinding, the most common methods are:

Edition Binding

This method is used in most school textbooks. The pages are collated and sewn together, the pages are trimmed, and the sewn sections are coated with glue. The backbones or spines are then sent through a special machine that rounds them and will allow the book to open and close properly. The books are then covered, dried in a hydraulic press and packed for shipment

Perfect Binding

This is a cheaper method than edition binding as it eliminates the expense of sewing and case-binding. The pages are held in place by an adhesive rather than stitching, and the cover is glued into place. The telephone book is an example of perfect binding.

Mechanical Binding

This method is often used for school notebooks and other books that must lie flat. The sheets are punched with holes, and coils or rings are inserted. Loose-leaf or spiral-bound notebooks are examples of this process. This method is not very durable, however, as the pages easily pull loose.

BLUEPRINTS, FILING OF   Schools are usually being redone on a more or less constant basis to keep up with growing needs. This requires the frequent use of a building's blueprints. Storage of these blueprints presents a problem. They are large and bulky and difficult to file unless your school has blueprint file drawers available. Ideally, they should lie flat in a drawer, but if this is not possible, they can be rolled. Do not fold blueprints as this causes rapid deterioration along the fold lines, and they are costly to replace. Blueprints should be retained for as long as the building is standing.

BOARD OF EDUCATION, FUNCTION OF   All schools in the United States are governed by a Board of Education or Board of Trustees. Board members are usually elected, or in the case of private institutions, sometimes appointed. It is their job to work with the superintendent of schools. Boards of Education must take into consideration the needs of the students as well as the wishes of taxpayers, parents, teachers, and school staff. There are also limits set by state laws. The major responsibilities of the school board are to establish policies for running schools, to establish a curriculum and course of study, to approve the budget to cover salaries and operating costs, and to consider these factors in relation to the taxpayers' wishes and the educational needs of the students. Board meetings are held at regular intervals and detailed minutes are kept by a secretary.

BUDGETS

Student Body Budgets

The treasurer of the student body is responsible for keeping track of student body funds. In reality, however, the school secretary is often asked to lend a hand, perhaps in holding monies collected, or in helping to count and sort money. Whether or not you get involved in this area is up to you and your administrator. If you do handle student funds, however, it is best to verify totals and issue receipts in the presence of at least one other person so that there can be no question of your honesty should the totals be out of balance.

The PTA Budget

The Parent-Teacher Association sometimes stages fund-raisers in order to provide the school with extra money for special events or enrichment programs. Such events are usually sponsored by the PTA, but you may be asked to collect funds or to hold money until it can be picked up by a PTA representative. Here again, keep accurate records of collections and only count and verify funds with someone else present. While probably no one will accuse you if funds are short, there may always be seeds of doubt in someone's mind. It is far better to avoid unpleasant situations whenever possible by simply protecting yourself to begin with.

Departmental Budgets

These are usually controlled by department heads or other administrators, but you may be asked to help in verifying or balancing them. Just follow the procedures outlined in PETTY CASH, BALANCING. The figures may be much larger, but the procedure remains the same, and is no more difficult than balancing your checkbook.

BULLETIN BOARDS   Often the art department, a branch of student government, or a special committee will take care of the school bulletin boards, but here are some suggestions just in case this task falls to you:

- Keep one area for important messages and mark it with a sign or an arrow cut from construction paper.
- Space each item so it is set apart from the rest and is easily visible.

- Do not overlap or pile things on top of one another.
- Avoid clutter by removing outdated material.
- Use topic headings or subject labels and group announcements in the appropriate area. You can purchase commercially made letters from art supply and stationery stores at a reasonable cost. These give the bulletin board a professional appearance.
- Use your creativity to produce an effective, attractive information center.

BULLETINS, PREPARING   Bulletins have a twofold use: (1) within the school, (2) between the school and the home. Preparing school bulletins is usually your responsibility. You will need to collect data, type it, copy it, and distribute it. Some typical items in a bulletin are:

- Announcements such as social, athletic, or special events, rehearsals, assemblies, or programs.
- Fund-raising drives such as Red Cross, March of Dimes, or other charities.
- Praise of students or faculty for outstanding accomplishments.
- Notifications of PTA meetings, faculty meetings, etc.
- Reminders
- Calendar listings

Copy for the bulletin can come from the administration, from the officers of school clubs, from the PTA, the central office, from teachers, department heads, etc. Your job is to coordinate all these fragments into an easily readable cohesive whole. Give yourself time. Set deadlines for insertions at least two days prior to the publication of the bulletin. Don't break your own rule once you have established it, or you leave the door wide open for people to take advantage.

Suggestions for setting up the bulletin:

- The bulletin should be easy to read, concise, and accurate.
- Breaking down the data into sections marked "Faculty," "Students," "Parents," etc., can make it easy to find information fast.
- You may wish to make two separate bulletins, one for in-school use and one to go home with announcements that relate only to the parent community. In the smaller school, one can usually suffice.
- Block style is the easiest to read.
- Leave plenty of space between topics to set off headings.

- Do not crowd or you will lose impact.
- Date each bulletin.
- Any important messages should be boxed.
- Keep daily bulletins to one page if possible, otherwise they may not be read.
- Be sure to proofread before copying and distributing.
- Always keep a few extra copies for the file.

BYLAWS The PTA, student organizations, or the board of trustees may sometimes wish to correct or amend their bylaws (constitution). Any such changes are made by the executive body of the group and are approved by its membership. If you are given a set of bylaws changes to be typed:

- Mark through areas to be deleted with a series of hyphens. For example: The committee will not meet at regular intervals.
- Words proposed for addition are underlined. For example: In that this event . . .
- Words that are to remain unchanged are retyped as is.

CALENDAR, SCHOOL The school calendar provides the basis for scheduling all major meetings, special events, vacation periods, and field trips. Major vacation periods and legal holidays are scheduled first. In a smaller school, a main calendar usually suffices to cover all events, and every event is written on the calendar to avoid conflicts. In large institutions, while the major vacation periods and holidays are scheduled on a main calendar, departmental calendars are usually kept, which are then coordinated with the main calendar. In addition to the main school calendar and departmental calendars, you may be required to keep the administrator's personal calendar. Usually, both you and the administrator will have desk calendars that must be coordinated; your administrator may also carry a personal calendar or appointment book which will also have to be considered.

Tips for Maintaining the Calendar

1. When making entries, make sure that all calendars are taken into consideration.

2. Each Friday, scan the appointments or events for the coming week and double-check for conflicts or cancellations. Remind the administrator of any particularly important events.

3. Check with your administrator *each day* to see if he has forgotten to tell you of any new appointments.

4. Encourage your administrator to let you know when he has made appointments. If you develop the habit of coordinating your calendars on a daily basis, it can prevent chaos.

5. Inform your administrator of any new appointments and write them on all the calendars.

6. If there are personal appointments, days when you know he will be absent, or other necessary information, also write these on the administrator's calendar.

7. Be sure the calendar shows major vacation periods, holidays, and recurring events.

8. Each day, turn the calendar to the appropriate date. On your desk calendar it is also helpful to list dates and times when reports or projects are due, telephone calls or appointments you must make, or any other information that you need to spot at a glance.

CALLS

Administrator's Calls

Some administrators prefer to take all calls, while others prefer the secretary to screen their calls. Some administrators now feel that screening calls is not recommended for good public relations and they wish to be available at all times. Others, however, feel that if they take all their incoming calls they will have little time to do anything else. When you answer the administrator's telephone:

– Be alert, friendly, and helpful.
– Identify yourself. "This is Ellen Reeves, Mrs. Fletcher's secretary."
– Try to give a reason why the administrator cannot come to the telephone without going into details:
 "She's on another line. Would you like to wait?"
 "He's in a meeting. May I take a message?"
 "He's out of the office until this afternoon. May I ask him to return your call?"

Calls During a Crisis

If there is any kind of emergency, whether real or rumored, the school will be deluged with telephone calls. Parents will call to find out the details of the emergency, or to give instructions for disposition of their children. Much confusion can be avoided if the school has a stated emergency policy whereby the school community is aware of proper procedures to follow in case of natural disasters or other emergency situations. This will cut down on some of the crisis calls, but there is always an element of the population that either does not get the message or ignores it and calls anyway. How you should respond to calls during times of crisis depends on the nature of the emergency. During a fire, for example, the building would be evacuated immediately, so answering the telephones would not be a problem for you. During natural disasters, the telephone lines should be kept clear. The emergency may be of a personal nature where the caller has to relate news of death or injury to a member of a student's family. Since you will be the one receiving these calls, it is up to you to know how to deal with them effectively. However, since emergencies or crises are unexpected, it is impossible to establish a pat formula for dealing with them. You will need to think on your feet and respond in the best way you can. Here are some guidelines that can help you to deal with crisis calls:

- Know in advance whom to call upon for help in emergency situations that you cannot handle.
- Keep an accurate referral list of emergency names and numbers near your telephone. Note any pertinent information next to each name. For example:

  Bob Walsh Ext. 448   water and gas shutoff
  Mary Alexander 427-8041   health department disease control

- When the administrator is away from the office, arrange in advance for him to telephone you at specific times so that you can relay emergency or important information to him.
- During a serious emergency when the administrator is away, rely on the assistant administrator for help, or make arrangements with your administrator ahead of time to designate a person who will help out in emergency situations.
- If the emergency is of a nature that can wait for its solution until the administrator's return, you could simply tell the caller: "The principal is not in at the moment, but he should be calling in soon and I will refer your problem to him." Make sure you then record the message accurately.

Faculty Calls

Keep close at hand a copy of teachers' schedules so that you can see when they are free. Teachers should not be called from the classroom except in extreme emergencies. Tell the caller that the teacher is not available and offer to take a message. "Miss Smith is in class now. May I ask her to return your call later?" Write down the message accurately and clearly and leave it for the teacher. Usually, the telephone messages are left in the teachers' mailboxes. In rare cases of extreme emergency, when a teacher must be called to the telephone immediately, the class should not be left unattended (unless they are adults), so you may be asked to fill in for a few moments, or to quickly find another faculty member to do so.

General Calls

When a call comes in requesting general information, find out the nature of the call and either respond yourself, transfer the caller to someone who can help, or take a message. When recording messages, be as precise as possible. State:

- the name of the caller (ask for the spelling if necessary)
- the number of the caller (if long distance, get the area code)
- the date and time of the call
- a brief but accurate message
- your initials in case the recipient of the message has any questions

You will save time and energy if you write each message on a separate piece of paper which can be given directly to the appropriate person. It wastes time to list calls on one sheet which then have to be rewritten. Telephone message pads are ideal time-saving tools.

The telephone is often your only link to people outside the school. When you contact the administration and staff of other schools, repair personnel, order departments, or some parents, your ability to communicate effectively by telephone may be your only available tool. The use of your voice is vital in communicating emotions, in being courteous, and in transmitting the intent of your message. The person at the other end cannot see you and is therefore unable to draw conclusions from your physical manner and body gestures. The caller is unable to see your smile, or the concern in your eyes, so your telephone voice is the sole method of effective communication.

Irate Calls

The irate caller has one thing in mind—he is angry and he wants satisfaction. He does not want to hear reasons or explanations. He wants a solution to his problem—immediately. It is helpful to keep this in mind when dealing with an irate caller. The tone of voice will give him away instantly even if he does not state his purpose right away. Be on your guard because you will need to handle the irate caller very tactfully in order to avoid further unpleasantness. As the school secretary, you will probably not have the authority necessary to meet the caller's demands, and the call will most likely need to be transferred to someone at the administrative level. If the appropriate administrator is not available right away this may cause the caller to become even angrier—remember, he wants immediate satisfaction. Here are some suggestions to help you cope with an irate caller:

- Remain calm. This is easier said than done when someone is being abusive and angry, but if you too become angry, you will only make matters worse.

— Let the caller speak freely without interruption. Sometimes just being able to say what is making him angry vents the emotion and causes him to simmer down.

— Listen carefully. While very angry people sometimes make little sense and tend to seem irrational, listen carefully and try to ascertain the crux of the problem.

— Write down the details of the call. As soon as you know the caller is irate, begin jotting down notes about the conversation. Your notes could be very important to the administrator or whoever is left to deal with the problem. Be accurate. Here are some points that you will need to note:

  — The complete name of the caller.

  — The caller's telephone number and area code if long distance.

  — The nature of the call.

  — Who else is involved with the problem—a teacher, a student, the administration.

  — Has the caller contacted anyone else about the problem?

  — What solution, if any, would the caller like to see put into action?

  — The date, time, and duration of the call.

— Be a listener, not a talker. Listen to the person's complaints, but do not agree with him (even if you really do). It is not your place to make judgments, just to take down the information and give it to the appropriate party. Do not make any commitments. Do not give out confidential information. Simply say that you do not know the answer, if confidential questions are asked.

— Be concerned but businesslike. Let the caller know that you are sorry he has a problem, and that you will see that the information is referred to the appropriate person, but say no more and do no more. With this type of call it is always best to confer with the administration unless you have made other arrangements previously.

— Close the call on a pleasant note, if possible, with the caller knowing that his call will receive attention.

Long Distance Calls

Direct Distance Dialing (DDD) is the fastest way to make long distance calls. You usually begin the procedure with an area code or access number (1) followed by the regular number. If you reach a wrong number, ask the person who answers for the name of the city. Then dial the operator (0) immediately, give this information, and you will not be charged for the call. If you need directory assistance in placing your call, dial the area code of the city you wish to reach, followed by 555-1212. When the operator answers, give the name of the city, then the name of the person whose number you want. When you wish to make a person-to-person call, a collect call, a credit card call, a call charged to another number, or a time and charges call: dial the operator (0) + area code + telephone number. The operator will come on the line to assist you.

International Direct Distance Dialing (IDDD) is now available in many areas of the country. Information will be provided by your local telephone company when the service becomes available in your area. In the meantime, dial the operator to place an international call.

Obscene Calls

If you receive an obscene call, say nothing to the caller, as this will only aggravate the problem, and hang up immediately. Note the date and time of the call and tell your administrator. Sometimes the police will ask to tap the school telephone in the case of repeated obscene or threatening calls. If this is the case, act as naturally as possible when answering the tapped phone, even though you know the call is being monitored. Follow to the letter any instructions given by the administration or the police, and remain alert and ready to deal with any new developments. Give out no information to parents, students, or the press without the express permission of the administrator and/or authorities. Usually, if you hang up immediately, an obscene caller will not call back.

Operator-Assisted Calls

These include collect, credit card, time and charges calls, or coin telephone calls requiring an operator intercept. This type of phone call will cost you as much as one and one-half times more than direct dial calls.

Parent Calls

Most parents want to feel that the school their child attends is a friendly, caring place that is capable of providing an education and of effectively coping with any emergency that may arise during the course of a school day. You, as the school secretary, are the one who presents the image of the school over the telephone. If you seem harried and unable to cope, that message will be transmitted to parents, who may in turn assume that the whole school is ineffective. Parent calls are the most difficult to deal with since they often involve some crisis, complaint, or problem. At times you may be assaulted by a barrage of daily calls, especially if there is a special event or new program. Requests for information about dates, times, and places are endless. Remember to answer each call as if it were the only call of the day. Keep abreast of current school events by reading all bulletins and correspondence that cross your desk and by keeping alert to information passed on by faculty, parent groups, the administration, and custodians. It is helpful to keep a personnel list and write down any special duties or events so that you can refer calls accurately and give correct information about times and dates. Do not give out information unless you are absolutely sure of its accuracy. It is better to tell the caller that you are not sure and return the call with the proper information. Part of your job is to protect the administration by not giving away confidential information or by implying anything negative by the way you make statements. If you are unsure about whether to make a statement, DO NOT MAKE IT. Simply say that you do not know the answer and ask if the caller would like to speak with an administrator. Then try to arrange for the two parties to confer.

Parents will call daily for a thousand little things: "What time is the school play?"; "When does Easter Vacation begin?"; "Johnny forgot his lunch. May he borrow money to eat at the cafeteria?" You can handle some of these calls by transferring the caller to the appropriate person, and you can handle some of them directly. Try to remain courteous and factual at all times.

Person-to-Person Calls

This type of operator-assisted call is the most costly and may run twice as much as a direct dial call. Compare your local telephone company's rate charts before deciding to place this type of call.

Receiving Calls

When you receive a telephone call, answer promptly, and identify yourself. If the call is coming in over the general school line, say: "Good Morning (or Afternoon), Ridgeway School, Mary Smith speaking" or "Ridgeway School, Principal's office, Mary Smith speaking" or "Mr. Farley's office, Mary Smith speaking. May I help you?"

When receiving calls, all you need to do is identify the particular line on which you are speaking. If it is a school line, answer with the school name. If it is a department line, answer with the department name. If it is a personal office line, answer with the person's name—but always identify yourself also.

Be friendly. Make the caller feel good about calling. Be a good listener so that the caller will not have to repeat anything. Show interest in the caller. Use the caller's name whenever possible. If you are sincere, this will be transmitted to the caller. Never have a side discussion or make comments to others while someone is waiting on the line. If it should become necessary to confer with someone else during a call, either ask the caller to wait and place the line on hold, or offer to return the call.

If you have to leave the line to get information, always give the caller the option of waiting or being called back. Let the caller know approximately how long it will take to get the information. When you leave the line, use the hold button if you have one, or place the handset face down on the desk using a book or paper as a cushion. (If you place the handset down on a hard surface, it sounds unpleasant to the caller.) When you return to the line, let the caller know you are back. "Mr. Jones, I have that information for you now" or "Mr. Jones, I will need to search further for that information. May I call you back?" If you will be away from the line for several minutes, return to the line periodically to let the caller know you have not forgotten him. "Mr. Jones, I'm still checking for you." Be sure to thank the caller for waiting.

Transferring calls

If you are unable to provide information to a caller and it becomes necessary to transfer the call:

- Explain why you want to make the transfer. "Mr. Smith is the Dean of Boys and he handles that. May I transfer you?"
- Be sure the caller wants to be transferred rather than called back.
- Be sure you know how to transfer calls correctly according to your school's system. It is extremely aggravating to be disconnected while waiting to be transferred. Ask the caller for his number, just in case the transfer is not completed correctly. If you are disconnected, call the person back immediately.
- Never ask "Who is calling?" before transferring a call to another party. Instead say, "May I tell Mr. Smith who is calling?" Many people take offense at being questioned although a courteous caller should identify himself without having to be asked.

Completing the call

Always try to close a call on a friendly note. Let the caller end the conversation. Say "Goodbye" courteously and place the receiver down gently.

Screening Calls

If you are asked to screen calls, be tactful. Remember never to ask "Who's calling?'' as this gives a negative impression to some callers. If the administrator is in but wants to receive only selected calls, try this:

> "He's not available at the moment. May I tell him you called?" After the person identifies himself, you have the option of putting the call through by saying, "If you'll hold a moment I'll see if he's free now," if it is someone the administrator wishes to speak to.

Always give the reason for the administrator's unavailability before asking the name of the caller. Otherwise, it will seem that you are making excuses not to put the call through. If the administrator is available simply ask, "May I tell him who's calling?" If the administrator is out, say "He's out at the moment. May I take a message?" Listen carefully and give your full attention to the caller.

Special Area Code Calls

Some organizations use Wide Area Telephone Service (WATS) which allows the caller to dial toll-free. If you need to locate a WATS number, dial 800 + 555-1212 and ask the operator. You may find that many of your suppliers have this type of service, which can make ordering much easier and faster for you.

Student Calls

Usually, students will not be receiving calls at school, except in emergency situations. Such calls are usually referred to the administration unless you have been instructed otherwise. If you are authorized to handle calls for students, they are handled in a manner similar to faculty calls. Students should not be called from class except in real emergencies. You may offer to take a message, but feel free to interrogate the caller, find out exactly who is placing the call, and the reason for the call. In the case of minor students, the school is responsible for their safety and well-being, so be sure to refer any suspicious calls directly to the administrator. Many schools have a bulletin board for student messages, but this is at the discretion of the administration.

Threatening Calls

If a caller gives a bomb threat or other threatening message, it may just be a prank, but assume that the call is serious. Try to write down as much information as you can about the call and the caller. Note the location of the threatened incident. Where is the action to take place? What time is the event to take place? On what date? Jot down anything that will help authorities identify the caller. Take note of the caller's voice. Is it male or female? Can you guess the age of the caller? Does the voice seem natural or disguised? Does the caller have an accent or speak in a dialect? Notify the administrator immediately. You will then probably need to contact the police to make a full report. Depending on the nature of the threat, the school may need to be searched or evacuated.

Tips for Improving Calls

- Keep a list of frequently called numbers near your phone.
- Keep a telephone directory near your phone.
- If you have a call-director or button telephone, be sure that the line is not in use before picking up the receiver. Check to see that the button is not lighted.
- Listen for the dial tone before placing a call. (If you don't have a clear dial tone, you could reach a wrong number or no number at all.)
- If you are using a rotary dial telephone and your finger slips, hang up and dial again.
- If you have a Touch-Tone telephone, depress each button firmly, but do not play with the buttons after the call is completed or you may disconnect.
- If you reach a wrong number, always apologize. Do not just hang up.
- The trend today is for administrators and executives to place their own calls, but if you are asked to place a call for someone, say ''Mr. Smith of Menlo School is calling Miss Jones,'' or ''Mr. Smith of Parkview College is calling you, Miss Jones.''
- Plan your conversation for long distance calls. Before placing the call, take a moment to jot down the important points you will need to cover.
- Schedule your calls wisely. If you call someone frequently, try to arrange a specific time for the calls so that neither of you will waste time.
- If you reach a wrong number, report it to the operator and you will not be charged for long distance or toll calls.
- If you reach a bad connection or are disconnected, both parties should hang up. Whoever placed the call should dial again or report the bad connection to the operator so that the billing can be adjusted if necessary.

Toll-Free Calls

In addition to WATS lines, some organizations have telephone numbers preceded by ENTERPRISE or ZENITH prefixes. These are also toll-free. Check your local telephone directory to see if the company you wish to call offers such a service.

CAPITALIZATION, RULES OF

DO	DON'T
Capitalize conjunctions of more than four letters in titles: Coming *Through* the Rye	Do not capitalize conjunctions or articles of four letters or fewer in titles unless they begin the title: a, an, the, when, with, if, so, to, or, nor, for, and, but, at, of, by, oh, in, up, etc. The Miracle Worker Wind in the Willows
Capitalize compass points when they indicate a *specific* geographical region: Why do people assume that schools in the *East* are better?	Do not capitalize the points of a compass if only indicating direction: We live on the north side of town.
Capitalize all words referring to God or Jesus except who, whom, whose: God, Christ, Jesus, the Messiah	Do not capitalize words such as "god" or "goddess" in mythology: Was Ra the Egyptian sun god?
Capitalize references to satan only if they specifically denote personage: Go to the Devil! You are devilish.	
	Do not capitalize the seasons: summer, spring, autumn or fall, winter
Capitalize the names of specific days, months, and holidays: Father's Day, Christmas Day, Easter	
	Do not capitalize the first word following a colon unless it is a proper noun, "I," or begins a complete sentence. (If in doubt, ask yourself if the colon were not there, would the next word normally be capitalized.)

<u>DO</u>	<u>DON'T</u>
	Please list the following: shoes, socks, umbrellas in alphabetical order.
	I have lived in many cities: Paris, Athens, London, and Rome included.
Capitalize the first word of each line of poetry, whether or not it is a complete sentence.	
Capitalize the first word of each item of an outline.	
Capitalize college degrees: Master of Arts or M.A. Doctor of Philosophy or Ph.D.	
	Do not capitalize the names of school subjects unless they are the names of languages, religions, or specific courses: Bob is enjoying his philosophy class. If you take Algebra I, you will really have to work hard.
Capitalize names of historical periods and movements: Middle Ages, Roaring Twenties	
	Do not capitalize classes: freshman, sophomore, junior, senior
Capitalize proper names and derivatives of proper names: Greece, Freud, Elizabethan NOTE: As proper nouns become assimilated into our language with the passage of time, some proper nouns become common nouns. Here is a partial list:	

DO	DON'T
brazil nut, derby hat, epsom salts, french fries, saddle oxfords, panama hat, venetian blind, moroccan leather, pasteurized milk, cuban heel, scotch tape	
	Do not capitalize names of centuries: I am glad to be living in the twentieth century.
Capitalize the names of ethnic groups, races, religions, and languages: English language, French people, Jewish religion, Caucasian race	
	Do not capitalize the first word enclosed in parentheses if it is within another sentence, unless it is a proper name or "I": The fire (she later learned that it was caused by arson) resulted in serious damage.
Capitalize the first word of every sentence, whether enclosed within quotation marks, parentheses, or standing alone: The fire caused serious damage. The fire caused serious damage. (I later learned that it was caused by arson.) I said, "The fire caused serious damage."	
Capitalize the pronoun "I" always.	
Capitalize titles when they go in front of a proper name: Aunt Mame; Principal Rogers	

DO	DON'T
	Do not capitalize titles when they follow a name:
	Edith Cavelle, nurse, was a remarkable woman.
	Mame is her aunt.
Capitalize titles when they are part of an address: Professor Edward Smith 1234 Maple Drive	
	Do not capitalize titles unless they are before a person's name or are used *in place* of a name: Let's hear it for the senator. Let's hear it for the Secretary of the Interior. If in doubt substitute a name for the title in the sentence. If it makes sense, it is probably correct. (Let's hear it for the Bob would not make sense, so "senator" is not capitalized. However, Secretary of the Interior is capitalized because it is in the line of presidential succession.)
Capitalize titles in presidential succession: President, Vice President, Secretary of State, etc.	
Capitalize the main political position in any country: the Premier, the President	
Capitalize the names of companies, organizations, schools, churches, etc.: Fraternal Order of Elks St. John's Church	

<u>DO</u>	<u>DON'T</u>
	Do not capitalize "the late," "ex-," "elect," or "the former":
	ex-Vice President Smith
	the former President of the United States
	the late King of England
	President-elect Bradshaw
Capitalize nouns used as part of a proper name:	
He lives in Marin County.	
Capitalize the names of continents, states, cities, towns, mountains, rivers, lakes, valleys, parks, and buildings:	
England, San Francisco, the Rocky Mountains, Beacon Hill Park, Market Street, Hall of Justice, Nile River, Marin County, the Continent of Asia	
	Do not capitalize common nouns:
	We will meet at the <u>b</u>ank.
	I have an appointment at his <u>o</u>ffice.
	The <u>c</u>ompany is filing bankruptcy.
	This <u>c</u>ourse is so boring.
Capitalize product trade names but NOT the nouns that follow the trade name:	
Pyrex dish, Bates stapler	
Capitalize the words "sun," "moon," "earth," only when used in association with other celestial bodies which are proper names and are therefore capitalized:	
We like to watch the setting sun.	

<u>DO</u>	<u>DON'T</u>
Venus, Mercury, and Earth are three of the planets.	
Capitalize personification:	
. . . the sands of Time.	

CHAPERONING Chaperoning falls into two basic categories: short-term (dances, games, parties), and long-term (camping trips, etc.). The guidelines for being a successful chaperone are the same for both categories. While the school secretary is not usually asked to chaperone events, there may be occasions when it is a regular part of your duties. Usually, chaperoning an event is a happy occasion. Whether a dance, an outing, a field trip, or a camping trip, the prospects can be as exciting for the chaperone as for the student. You will have an opportunity to relate to the students on a more relaxed level, and they in turn will get a chance to view you in a new situation, away from your desk and daily duties. This can be a wonderful time to establish new relationships that will benefit both you and the student when you return to the daily routine. (Incidentally, it is best to have chaperones of both sexes available so that restrooms can be easily inspected if problems arise.)

The students will undoubtedly be excited and enthusiastic. One of the tasks of a chaperone is to direct this energy in a positive way, to keep the energy generated for the event, but at the same time to maintain discipline and order without being a "wet blanket." All in all, not an easy job.

However, there are some techniques that can help to make chaperoning an enjoyable learning experience for both the student and the chaperone. In order to exude an air of confident authority, you must first feel it yourself. If your role is clearly defined, it will be much easier to transmit instructions to your group and to have the group respond in a positive manner. If you follow the steps outlined below, you will have a good base for knowing what is expected of you. This will then enable you to assume your role as chaperone with confidence and authority.

1. Find out what the rules are. Never chaperone a group unless you are provided with a set of expectations from the administration (preferably in writing).
2. Learn the rules thoroughly. Know what is expected of you. Know what is expected of the student.

3. Find out who is ultimately responsible for the student in a given situation. Is it the school, the parent, or you? Find out if you are covered by liability insurance while you are chaperoning.

4. Uphold the set rules. Infractions could result in dismissal or a jail sentence as in the case of allowing minors to use alcohol.

5. Make sure the students know the rules. If the guidelines for conduct are thoroughly discussed before an event, there is no excuse for misbehavior.

6. What if a rule is broken? Determine in advance what is to be done with rule-breakers and behavior problems. Who is responsible for punishment?

7. Make sure any necessary parental permission forms are collected before the event. (The school may already have a blanket permission form on file to cover minors for all events. If not, it is wise to have the parents sign permission forms before taking on the responsibility of chaperone duty.)

8. An efficient permission form should include the following information: DATE, TIME, PLACE of the event, PURPOSE of the event, and METHOD OF TRANSPORTATION. (Some parents do not want their children to ride in carpools. If an accident occurs while a child is in a carpool and there is no written permission, you or the school could be held liable.)

If the rules of behavior for an event have already been set by administrative policy, make sure that the students are aware of the rules. Inform the students of the consequences of rule breaking. If rules are broken, see that the appropriate disciplinary action is taken.

If no rules of behavior have been set, it may be up to you and other chaperones to decide on such policy. If so:

- Arrange a meeting to discuss this well in advance of the event.
- Consider what behavior would be appropriate to the event. For example, behavior that would be acceptable on a camping trip or at a football game might be totally inappropriate at a theater or a museum.
- Make sure that the rules are reasonable for the time, place, and age of the students.
- Decide on a course of disciplinary action, should rules be broken.
- Write a list of the rules that you have decided upon and provide each chaperone with a copy. (This step can save much bickering and bad feelings later.)

- Clearly explain to the students the rules and the consequences of breaking the rules.
- Implement the rules.

How and When to Assume Responsibility

Unfortunately, some educators find chaperoning not to their liking, and sometimes mysteriously disappear at the beginning of an event. This of course, is unfair, and places double the responsibility on those who remain on chaperone duty. If it is at all possible, try to organize it so that each chaperone is responsible for a specific area, a specific group of students, specific duties, or a specific period of time. This is a good way to make sure that responsibilities are equally shared. If you agree to be a chaperone, you agree to be a responsible adult. As such, try to keep the following things in mind:

- You are present to maintain order.
- If you have a positive, trusting attitude tempered with common sense, the students will usually behave better.
- If you treat students as responsible people whom you expect to perform well, they will usually come up to your expectations. (There are always exceptions, but don't let a few malcontents ruin your attitude.)
- Enjoy yourself. Your interest and enthusiasm will rub off on others.
- Maintain a watchful eye without being overbearing and intrusive. (I've found that one of the best ways to chaperone a dance is by dancing right along with the students. You can see everything without being obtrusive.)
- If there is a problem that you cannot handle, get help right away.

COMMUNICATION WITH STUDENTS   Students are people. They respond as do any other humans in a given situation. Usually, if you treat them with respect and trust they will respond accordingly. Honesty spawns honesty. Be honest about your feelings, whether negative or positive. Students need to learn that school employees are not robots who materialize magically behind the desk each morning and have no other lives. If, for example, you have a bad headache, and a group of students is being particularly boisterous and loud, don't rush over and demand that they keep quiet. Instead, tell them that you have a bad headache and that you would appreciate their cooperation in quieting down. In most cases you will get cooperation and you will find that the students will be surprised and pleased that you have confided in them as equals. There are exceptions of course, but the old saying ''You can catch more flies with honey than with vinegar'' has never been better applied than when dealing with young people.

COMMUNICATIONS MEDIA   Most press contact will be handled by the administration. If you should be questioned by newspaper, television, or radio reporters, be careful that you do not let confidential information slip. Part of a reporter's technique is to ask leading questions. He will lead you to believe that he knows more facts than he actually does in order to get information from you. While the reporter is only doing his job, don't be fooled by this technique. Your job is to be discreet and refer any questions to the administration.

COMPUTER APPLICATIONS IN THE SCHOOL   As an educational tool, computers may be used in the following areas:

- to teach basic music reading
- as a mathematics tutor
- to aid in building vocabulary and spelling skills
- to create graphic/geometric designs
- to teach historical/chronological events

The school office can also benefit from the small computer in such areas as:

- inventory of textbooks
- inventory of supplies
- inventory of equipment
- tuition billings/payments
- maintaining tax records
- maintaining address records
- student records/medical and counseling files
- payroll
- personnel management; job descriptions; employee records; employee benefit files

COMPUTER GLOSSARY OF TERMINOLOGY

abend	a shortened form of "abnormal ending"; the computer has terminated the program, perhaps because of a problem in the system.
account	a label for a time-sharing computer system that identifies you or your group (like a bank account number).
A/D converter	a device which converts analog information into digital information.
ADP	automatic data processing.
ALGOL	a computer language best used to solve mathematical problems.
analog	an electronic method that can handle complex signals through fairly simple circuitry. In an analog computer, numbers are represented by varying electronic voltages.

APL	a programming language used between interactive terminals.
architecture	the way a computer is built; how the elements of a computer are organized.
artificial intelligence	programming that simulates thought in which computers can play chess, learn, and reason.
BASIC	a programming language used frequently for beginners. It is very commonly used in schools with small computers.
binary	the number system used by computers, using only two digits, 1 and 0. When used together, the 1 and 0 can represent an infinite number of combinations.
bit	(binary digit) the smallest unit of information used in computers; a simple dual-value piece of information, it stands for on/off and is written as 1 or 0.
bomb	a failed program.
bug	an error in a program that prevents proper functioning of the program.
byte	a grouping of eight bits of information. Bytes are used to express computer memory.
cache memory	a high-speed memory unit.
CAI	Computer Aided Instruction. Using the computer as teacher, it takes the student step-by-step through a programmed subject and lets the student know whether the answer is correct or not. Many computer games and teaching machines use this method. The student is able to progress at his/her own rate.
chip	a silicon flake that forms the basis of an integrated circuit (see microprocessor).
COBOL	a programming language designed for business applications.
COM	Computer Output Microfilm. A camera which is capable of photographing a video screen, resulting in microfilmed data.
core	the main memory device of a computer.
console	the control panel of a computer.
Cps	characters per second, referring to data transmission.

CPU	Central Processing Unit. The computer unit that contains all the elements necessary to do the actual computing.
crash	a sudden malfunction of the computer.
CRT	Cathode Ray Tube. The main tube in the viewing screen (same as your TV set).
cursor	a mark made on the video screen showing where the next digit will appear, as an aid to prevent you from losing your place.
data	the information dealt with by a computer.
data base	the basic information that must be fed into the computer for it to complete the program. For example, if a computer is to schedule classes, it must be informed of the courses being offered, the times, locations, dates, etc.
data link	a method of transferring data between locations via telephone lines, cable, microwave, radio waves, etc.
debugging	correcting errors or bugs in a program.
digital	a method of computing using a yes/no on/off approach with no levels in between.
DIP	Dual Inline Package. The form of most integrated circuits.
disk	a thin magnetic device that looks like a record and is capable of storing large amounts of data.
down	when a computer is not working, it is down.
EDP	Electronic Data Processing. The act of dealing with information by the computer.
first generation	refers to early computers using vacuum tubes.
floppy disk	a storage device that gives small computers an inexpensive means of data storage. It is similar to a disk, but smaller and less expensive. Floppy disks, while flexible, are not actually floppy.
FORTRAN	a computer language designed mainly for technical applications.
GIGO	garbage in, garbage out. In other words, faulty data give faulty results.
hard copy	information that can be carried away from the computer, such as a printout sheet

hardware	the physical equipment of a computer.
housekeeping	the time that a computer spends in "cleaning up after itself," such as rewinding tapes, etc.
IC	integrated circuit.
input	information that is fed into the computer.
interactive	a system that asks questions of the user.
I/O device	allows input of material in a form understood by humans which is transmitted to the computer in a form understood by the machine.
K	1,024 bytes of memory.
log-in	the process of identifying yourself to the computer so you can use the system.
magnetic tape	a storage system for large amounts of information (wider, but similar to the tape used in tape recorders).
memory	the part of a computer where results and information are stored.
microcomputer	a term used to describe a computer based on microprocessors.
microprocessor	in essence, a CPU on a silicon chip.
nybble	a piece of information half the length of a byte (four bits long).
OCR	Optical Character Recognition. A process by which texts using special typefaces can be read by a machine; this process is more accurate than manual keyboard entry.
off-line	not connected directly to the main computer system.
on-line	a system by which data are transmitted directly to the computer for immediate processing (rather than being stored and processed later).
output	the outcome of a computer's calculations.
PILOT	a computer programming language used in education.
program	a series of instructions fed into a computer.
RAM	Random Access Memory. Information is available in any sequence from the computer.
real-time	a system in which the computer can process data immediately and keep current with ongoing events at the same time.

real-time clock	a regulating device that keeps the computer informed of real-time events.
reset	returning the code to "O" so that processing can begin again. After an interruption in transmission it may be necessary to reset and refeed data input into the computer terminal.
ROM	Read Only Memory. A storage system that cannot be erased.
second generation	refers to early computers using transistors.
SNOBOL	a programming language developed in linguistics research.
software	computer programs.
software maintenance	keeping programs up to date.
terminal	a device used for communicating with the computer. It may be a keyboard, a video screen, or a teletypewriter.
time-sharing	enables many people to use the computer simultaneously from individual terminals. The computer shifts from one user to the next so rapidly that it is not noticeable to the user.
turnaround time	the time it takes for completion of a program.
up and running	a computer system that is on and operating properly.
video graphic display	computers can do graphic presentations including drawing in perspective, color, and 3-D presentations on a video screen.
video terminal	consists of a typewriter keyboard and a video screen like a TV set for transmitting and receiving information. The main problem with this system is that no permanent printout is available.

COMPUTER HARDWARE The term "computer hardware" refers to the actual physical components that make up the computer—the skin and bones. Computer hardware can be broken down as follows:

Keyboards

A keyboard is the most commonly used method of input into the small computer system. The calculator-type keyboard uses the same system found in pocket calculators. The switch-type keyboard is more expensive, more durable, and resembles electric typewriter keys. Some keyboards have a rollover feature (how the keyboard interprets two or more keys being pressed at the same time). For example, a two-key rollover feature means that the keyboard is able to store the identity of both keys that are pushed at the same time; is able to know which key was released first (or struck first); and is thus able to prevent some errors as information is being fed in. Some keyboards offer special features such as a repeat feature, which insures that a key will repeat the character as long as the key is held down; special characters that can be used for artwork, or graphics presentations, etc.; and programmability which incorporates a microprocessor in the keyboard and allows the user to code a given key.

CRT Displays

Most computers use a video display screen similar to your TV set, known as a CRT (cathode ray tube). Some design schools are now using the computer as a regular part of the curriculum. Students are able to "draw" both architectural and interior plans and specifications with the CRT, and can save many tedious hours of drafting and redrafting a project. By using the computer it is simple to move walls, change dimensions, and add levels to buildings. When the completed design is decided upon, the computer can then provide a printout of the plan.

Cassette Storage Devices

Audiocassette storage devices are commonly used in inexpensive microcomputer systems. Information is stored in the cassettes via differing sound frequencies.

Printers

Printers are used to obtain a hard-copy printout. There are two basic types of computer printers: impact, which makes an image on paper by means of an inked character; and non-impact, which forms an image by adhering a contrast material to paper, usually by electrostatic means.

COMPUTER LANGUAGES   For very simple operations, once the appropriate software has been obtained and loaded into the computer, the computer will then ask you a series of questions, so it is not necessary to know a computer language. However, in order to apply the computer to more sophisticated problems, or to reprogram, it is necessary to know a computer language, such as BASIC (Beginners All-Purpose Symbolic Instruction Code). BASIC is the easiest language to learn and is well suited to many microcomputer applications. Most microcomputer manufacturers have a few versions of the BASIC language available for their equipment, which can be geared to the needs of the user. The most elementary form of BASIC is the integer basic, which can only cope with simple arithmetic; it cannot handle "floating point" numbers (decimals). The most advanced forms of BASIC are available on floppy disks (diskettes).

Other computer languages include ALGOL, used to solve mathematical problems; APL, a programming language used between interactive terminals; COBOL, a programming language designed for business applications: FORTRAN, used mainly for technical applications; and PILOT, used frequently in education.

COMPUTER MICROSYSTEMS MANUFACTURERS

Alpha Microsystems
17875 Sky Park North
Irvine, CA 92714

APF Electronics, Inc.
444 Madison Avenue
New York, NY 10022

Apple Computer Inc.
10260 Bandley Drive
Cupertino, CA 95014

Bally Manufacturing Corporation
2640 West Belmont Avenue
Chicago, IL 60618

Bedford Computer Systems
3 Preston Court
Bedford, MA 07130

Commodore Business Machines, Inc.
901 California Avenue
Palo Alto, CA 94304

Compucolor Corporation
Subsidiary of Intelligent Systems,
Corp.
5965 Peachtree Corners East
Norcross, GA 30071

Control Logic, Inc.
Nine Tech Circle
Natick, MA 07160

Digital Equipment Corp.
One Iron Way
Marlborough, MA 07152

The Digital Group
P.O. Box 6528
Denver, CO 80206

Exidy, Inc.
969 West Maude Avenue
Sunnyvale, CA 94086

Heath Company
Benton Harbor, MI 49022

North Star Computers
2547 Ninth Street
Berkeley, CA 94710

Ohio Scientific Instruments
1333 S. Chillicothe Road
Aurora, OH 44202

Pertec Computer Corporation
12910 Culver Boulevard
Los Angeles, CA 90066

Polymorphic Systems, Inc.
460 Ward Drive
Santa Barbara, CA 93111

Processor Technology
7100 Johnson Drive
Pleasanton, CA 94566

Radio Shack
2617 West 7th Street
Fort Worth, TX 76107

Southwest Technical Products Corp.
219 W. Rhapsody
San Antonio, TX 78216

Texas Instruments Inc.
P.O. Box 2909
Austin, TX 78767

Vector Graphic, Inc.
31364 Via Colinas
Westlake Village, GA 91361

Zilog
10460 Bubb Road
Cupertino, CA 95014

COMPUTER SOFTWARE   Software is the program or instruction package that is given to the computer. It is packaged in various ways. It may use paper tape, magnetic tape or disks, or solid state memory devices. Software packages are sold much in the same way as stereo system components. As you can choose from a variety of packages such as cassette, 8-track, reel-to-reel tapes, or record albums, so you have your choice of the software package that is compatible with your school's computer. At the moment, one of the big problems with using microcomputers in the classroom is the lack of sufficient relevant software. Most of the micro software packages are being designed for business and home use.

Computer Software Manufacturers

Administrative Systems Inc.
1642 S. Parker Road
Denver, CO 80231

The Boston Systems Office Inc.
400 Totten Pond Road
Waltham, MA 02154

Digital Research Inc.
P.O. Box 579
Pacific Grove, CA 93950

MicroPro International Corp.
1299 Fourth Street
San Rafael, CA 94901

Microsoft
10800 NE Eighth
Bellevue, WA 98004

MicroSource
1425 W. Twelfth Place
Tempe, AZ 85281

Microware Systems Corp.
2035 East Ovid Avenue
Des Moines, IA 50317

Rothenberg Information Systems
260 Sheridan Avenue
Palo Alto, CA 94306

Michael Shrayer Software Inc.
1253 Vista Superba Drive
Glendale, CA 91205

Technical Systems Consultants Inc.
Box 2547
W. Lafayette, IN 47906

COMPUTER SYSTEMS You may not have much direct contact with computers in your secretarial position, but it is certain that computers will have at least an indirect link with your job. Hardly any phase of the business world is not guided by computers—and they are beginning to play a large role in the field of education. Computers are used in the classroom as teaching aids; they may be used to schedule classes; record grades; provide transcripts; keep supply inventories; prepare invoices and salary warrants—the list is endless. Computers are only as good as the humans who make, program, and operate them.

They are often classified by size. The maxis are capable of coping with many complex calculations. Such computers may be used by large universities for processing the administrative functions of the institution as well as for complex scientific applications. Minicomputers are scaled down in both size and capabilities, but can perform many necessary duties for the smaller school. The microcomputers are on the bottom of the size scale. Their function is based on an integrated circuit microprocessor. In layman's language, this is an electronic component that contains all the basic elements of computer functions on a tiny silicon chip. When the microprocessor is combined with other elements such as memory, a keyboard, and a display screen, a microcomputer results. Microcomputers are also known as personal or home computers.

CONFERENCES Conferences may be called for a variety of reasons, both positive and negative. Behavior problems, poor grades, scholarship requests, fund-raising activities, planning social events, plus innumerable other reasons may all require conferences. Conferences may be held between the parent/student/teacher/administrator in any combination. Unless the student is specifically invited to attend a conference, it is best to arrange parent/teacher meetings at a quiet time and place without students present. Sometimes teachers request that parent/teacher discussions be held in the presence of a third party such as the administrator or department chairman. This is a good idea in cases of conflict, as it can prevent comments from being misconstrued and later repeated incorrectly. In some instances, you might be asked to be present at such a conference to record the key points of the meeting. The main things to remember when setting up conference times are:

- Arrange the meetings so that time and place are suitable for all persons involved if possible.
- If you receive a "third party" request, refer this to the administrator.
- When an irate person arrives for a conference, try to be especially patient and understanding. To act otherwise will only make matters worse.

– Try to arrange for the privacy of all involved during the conference period.

– Some parents request an immediate appointment with the administrator the moment there is a misunderstanding, when the matter might be cleared up quicker and easier by speaking with the teacher or person in question. It is not your responsibility, however, to make such a decision. Just take the name and refer the matter to the administrator, or set up an appointment for a conference.

CONTRACTIONS   A contraction is a word shortened by the insertion of an apostrophe in place of one or more letters. Some of the most common are:

are not	aren't	would not	wouldn't
can not	can't	is not	isn't
will not	won't	they are	they're
have not	haven't	we are	we're

COPIERS   See REPRODUCTION SYSTEMS.

COPYRIGHT LAW APPLIED TO SCHOOLS   The school secretary will often be asked to make copies of various printed materials for use in the classroom. *The Chronicle of Higher Education* helps to clarify the law as related to schools:

What You May Do

You may make a *single copy* of:
- a chapter from a book
- an article from a periodical or newspaper
- a short story, short essay or short poem
- a chart, graph, diagram, drawing or cartoon

if the copy will be used for research, or in preparation for teaching a class.

You may make *multiple copies* of
- a complete poem if less than 250 words and printed on less than two pages
- an excerpt from a long poem if less than 250 words

- a complete article if less than 2,500 words.
- an excerpt from a prose work if less than 1,000 words or 10 percent of the work
- one chart, graph, diagram, drawing, or cartoon

if the copies are for classroom use only and are distributed one copy per student.

What You May Not Do

You may *not* make multiple copies of:

- a work for classroom use that has already been copied for another class.
- a short poem, article, story or essay from the same author more than once in a term
- the same work more than three times per term
- works more than nine times per term
- workbooks

CORRECTIONS, TYPING   Correction fluid makes it quick and easy to cover up mistakes IF its use is not obvious to the reader. Liquid Paper Corporation, among others, makes different correction fluids for many different needs, including typing, ink, and photocopies. Here are some suggestions for using correction fluid effectively:

- Shake the bottle well to thoroughly mix the contents.
- Wipe off excess fluid from the brush back into the bottle.
- For corrections on originals, lightly trace over the outline of the error with the fluid. Use as little fluid as possible to cover the error, as the correction will be less noticeable. If you are going to photocopy the original, you may be more liberal in your application, as the blotch will not photograph.
- Recap the bottle after each use to prevent the fluid from drying out.
- Allow the fluid to dry thoroughly before typing the correction. You can speed up the drying time by blowing on or fanning the spot.

- If a blotch is visible on the page, you have used too much fluid.
- Correction fluid comes in several colors and can even be custom ordered to match any color of paper exactly. Never use a different color correction fluid on an original.
- Remember to dot on correction fluids. If you paint them on, the fluid can mix with the ink and make a gray mess.

Correction paper or film is easy to use, but the correction is not permanent. Folding or handling the paper can cause the chalky material to flake off. It is very useful, however, for temporary papers, memos, etc. To use correction paper or film:

- Backspace to the error.
- Insert the correction paper or film over the error with the chalky side facing the mistake.
- Type the error again, and the chalky material is impressed over the error to cover it.
- Remove the correction paper or film, backspace again, and retype the correction.

Erasures are the most difficult of all typing corrections to execute neatly, and if not done correctly, the eraser crumbs can damage your typewriter.

- Always move the carriage to the far right or left before erasing so that the crumbs will not fall into the typewriter. If you are using a machine with a typing element, do not erase into the typewriter; remove the page before you erase.
- Take your typewriter eraser and rub lightly in one direction. Excessive pressure or rotary motion will damage the paper and make the correction visible.
- Blow or brush eraser crumbs from the page.
- A light application of chalk gently smoothed into the spot can fill in any indentations in the paper.
- Return the paper to the original position and type in the correction. If you have removed the paper from the machine, and are having trouble locating the exact spot, take a small piece of tissue paper, place it over the area you are trying to locate and test on it until you find the exact spot.

Self-correcting typewriters offer the fastest and easiest method of correcting errors. However, they cannot correct carbons or photocopies, so you will have to rely on erasures, correction fluids, or correction papers for all except the original. Here are some suggestions for getting the most from your self-correcting typewriter:

TYPEWRITER RIBBON CONVERSION CHART

IF YOUR MACHINE IS:	CHOOSE COLOR CODE:	
IBM Model D Standard IBM Model D Executive IBM Model C Standard IBM Model C Executive	YELLOW	#2004 correctable film typewriter ribbon (spool) #2005 correctable film typewriter ribbon (cartridge)
	PINK	#2104 single-use film typewriter ribbon (spool) #2105 single-use film typewriter ribbon (cartridge)
Correction Aids:	YELLOW	#2500 lift-off correction tabs
IBM Selectric II IBM Executive Mag Card Remington Basic SR-101	YELLOW	#2001 correctable film typewriter ribbon
	PINK	#2101 single-use film typewriter ribbon
	BLUE	#2201 multi-use film typewriter ribbon
Correction Aids:	YELLOW	#2500 lift-off correction tabs
IBM Correcting Selectric IBM Memory Typewriter IBM Mag Card "A" IBM Mag Card II Remington Correcting SR-101	YELLOW	#2000/ #2001 correctable film typewriter ribbon
	PINK	#2101 single-use film typewriter ribbon
	BLUE	#2201 multi-use film typewriter ribbon
Correction Aids:	YELLOW	#2501/ #2502 lift-off correction tape
	BLUE	#2503 cover-up correction tape
IBM Selectric 72 IBM M.T.S.T. 72	YELLOW	#2003 correctable film typewriter ribbon
	PINK	#2103 single-use film typewriter ribbon
	BLUE	#2203 multi-use film typewriter ribbon
	GRAY	#2403 nylon fabric typewriter ribbon
Correction Aids:	YELLOW	#2500 lift-off correction tabs
IBM Selectric 71 IBM M.T.S.T. 71 IBM Mag Card I	YELLOW	#2002 correctable film typewriter ribbon
	PINK	#2102 single-use film typewriter ribbon
Correction Aids:	YELLOW	#2500 lift-off correction tabs

NOTE:

In order to obtain optimum "lift-off" of the ink when correcting errors typed by a LIQUID PAPER correctable ribbon, it may be necessary to adjust the multiple Copy Control Lever and Impression Control. These adjustments may be needed when installing a LIQUID PAPER correctable ribbon on any of the following typewriters: IBM Model D Standard, IBM Model C Standard, IBM Model D Executive, IBM Model C Executive, Selectric II, Correcting Selectric II, Selectric 71, and Selectric 72.

FIGURE 5

This chart will help you to convert your noncorrecting typewriter into one that is self-correcting, by using Liquid Paper correctable ribbon. Just locate your typewriter in the left column, then find the suitable Liquid Paper product in the right column.

- Handle correctable ribbons very carefully. They are delicate. Be sure you do not touch the coated portion of the ribbon, as it damages easily.
- Use high-quality rag content paper. Correctable ribbons do not work well on erasable paper, coated paper, or shiny paper such as labels.
- Make sure your impression control lever and multiple control lever are properly adjusted. If not, the paper may appear embossed and corrections will be visible.

Many typewriters that are not self-correcting can be converted by using a self-correcting ribbon system especially designed for the particular make and model of typewriter.

CORRESPONDENCE

Letter Styles

Many schools today use the block style in correspondence, and most administrators will accept any form that is neat and uniform throughout the school. In a large school where there are several secretaries, you may have to comply with set standards, whereas in a single-secretary school, you may be able to set the policy for correspondence—with the approval of the administrator, of course. It is best if all secretaries within the same school use the same format; the overall presentation will be cohesive and professional. The block style is fast to type and easy to read. Please see Figures 6 and 7 for samples of school correspondence in common use today.

Parts of a Letter

The School Logo or Letterhead

Practically all institutions today use printed letterheads on stationery. There are wide variations in size: some schools use small sheets such as $6'' \times 9\frac{1}{2}''$ or $7\frac{1}{4}'' \times 10\frac{1}{2}''$ for informal notes, while the norm remains the standard $8\frac{1}{2}'' \times 11''$ sheet. If the margins can be set to align with the perimeters of the printed letterhead, it will make a cleaner, more professional looking presentation.

The Date Line

Always strive for accuracy here. If a letter will not be mailed for a day or so, postdate it to coincide with the actual mailing date. If working from dictation, however, it should usually be dated as of the dictation day. The date line should be complete and not abbreviated:

July 15, 1990

San Francisco State University

1600 HOLLOWAY AVENUE ● SAN FRANCISCO, CALIFORNIA 94132

DEPARTMENT OF HOME ECONOMICS

September 14, 19

Miss Emily Levine, Secretary
St. Mark's School
Pittsburgh, PA 15224

Dear Miss Levine:

This is a sample of a full-block style letter. This style is
distinguished by the fact that the inside address, all paragraphs,
salutation, date, and reference lines are flush with the left
hand margin and are not indented. The full-block style saves time
and eliminates the need for repetitious tabulation. It is the
most common letter style in current use and is suitable for a
variety of correspondence.

We wish you the best of luck in your efforts to streamline your
school's office procedures. Please let us know if we may be of
further assistance to you.

Sincerely,

Michelle Ramirez
Secretary

FIGURE 6

Full-Block Style Letter

San Francisco State University

1600 HOLLOWAY AVENUE ● SAN FRANCISCO, CALIFORNIA 94132

DEPARTMENT OF HOME ECONOMICS

September 25, 19

Miss Emily Levine, Secretary
St. Mark's School
Pittsburgh, PA 15224

Dear Miss Levine:

      In response to your request, I am typing this letter in
semi-block style. The first line of each paragraph may be indented
five or ten spaces. The typed signature is aligned with the
complimentary close, both toward the center right of the page, while
the date is situated at the extreme right of the page. The extra
operation of setting tab stops and having to reach for the tabulator
key at every paragraph is not an efficient use of the school secretary's
time; this is why we prefer to use the full-block style.

      Once again, we wish you luck with your project of
updating St. Mark's office procedures.

                    Sincerely,

                    Michelle Ramirez
                    Secretary

FIGURE 7
Semi-Block Style Letter

Days of the month should not be written as 31st, 24th, etc.

The Inside Address

The inside address is actually a duplication of the address used on the envelope. It should include all information necessary to make delivery speedy and accurate:

- Name of person to whom addressed
- Person's title or position
- Name of department (if applicable)
- Name of school or institution
- Address line and/or post office box number
- City, state, and ZIP code

Examples

Dr. Camilla Wright
Dean of Women
Administrative Building
University of Miami
1234 Pope Drive
Miami, FL 33134

Professor Harvey Fitch
Humanities Department
New York University
P.O. Box 190
New York, NY 10013

Helpful Tips

- Be sure the inside address and envelope are the same. Always double-check before inserting the letter into the envelope.
- You can use both a post office box number and street address, but the mail will be delivered to the address located directly above the city-state-ZIP code line. Be sure that you have the lines in correct sequence and that the ZIP code is correct for the delivery address.
- The term "Ms." is considered acceptable when the marital status of a woman is unknown, and many people today prefer using Ms. all the time when referring to a woman. This definitely seems to be the trend.
- It is still customary to use the masculine form of address when you are unsure of the sex of a person or when referring to a mixed group.

The Salutation

In the field of education, although the trend continues toward informality, a person is usually accorded the use of accurate title: Dr., Professor, etc. Check with the administrator to see if he or she is on a first-name basis with the recipient of the letter, and which form of address is preferred. (For further information, see ADDRESS, FORMS OF.)

The salutation and complimentary close should be compatible whether formal or informal.

Example

<u>Informal</u>   <u>Formal</u>

Dear John: Dear Mr. Jones:
Sincerely,   Sincerely,

(Signed—Paul)   (Signed—Paul E. Smith)

Paul E. Smith   Paul E. Smith
Principal   Principal

The Body of the Letter

Correspondence is usually typed single-spaced unless the letter is exceptionally short and double-spacing is needed to create a visual balance on the page. Rough drafts are double- or triple-spaced to allow space for notations and corrections. When the body is double- or triple-spaced, the paragraphs are always indented. Block style letters use a flush left margin. Semi-block or personal (informal) letters are usually indented five or ten spaces for each paragraph. When a letter is longer than one page, space it so that at least two lines of a new paragraph can fit at the bottom of the page. If less than two lines will fit, begin the new paragraph on the next page. If a letter is longer than one page, make sure that there are at least two lines of text on the last page prior to the complimentary close. Never space a letter so that the complimentary close is alone on a page.

The Complimentary Close

Be sure that the complimentary close and salutation are compatible. (See *The Salutation*.)

<u>Formal Closes</u>   <u>Informal Closes</u>

Very truly yours,   Sincerely yours,

Respectfully yours,   Yours truly,

                                              Sincerely,

                                              Faithfully yours,

                                              Respectfully yours,

                                              Cordially,

Identifying Initials

These initials indicate who dictated the letter and who typed the letter, and are useful within the school as a reference. If the same person dictates and signs the letter, it is necessary to use only your initials in lower case. If the person who signs the letter did not dictate it, indicate the dictator's initials in upper case, a colon, then yours in lower case: JM:cf.

Enclosures

When correspondence contains enclosures, this is indicated by typing "Enclosure(s)" or "Enc." flush with the left margin one or two lines below the identifying initials. If there is more than one enclosure, it may also be indicated as Enclosure-2, or Enclosure-4, etc. If the enclosures are to be returned, indicate that. For example, Enc. academic report—please return.

Additional sheets to be mailed with a cover letter are usually stapled together, but are not stapled to the letter. Fold the enclosure, fold the letter, slip the enclosure into the last fold of the letter, then place both into the envelope.

Carbon Copy

When a copy is sent, indicate as follows:

Sincerely,

Paul E. Smith
Principal

cf
c.c. John Jones   (this indicates that a carbon is being sent, and to whom)

Blind copy notations are made on the upper left of the letter carbons. In this case, the addressee is not informed that copies are being sent.

Second or Continuation Sheets

If a letter is more than one page in length, additional pages are written on the same stock, but on paper without the letterhead. This continuation paper should be comparable to the first page in color, size, and quality. It is standard to indicate the addressee or subject plus page number on continuation sheets about six spaces down from the top edge of the paper:

Example

Mr. John Jones   2.

                                OR

Board of Directors Meeting
June 1, 19xx   2.

Attention Of

If a letter is addressed to the school first and to the attention of a particular person second, it indicates that the letter is not personal and may be opened by an appropriate employee:

Example

The Rhinegold School of Business
Dr. Dennis Ryan, President
1234 Vista Brava Avenue
Novato, CA 94169

Interoffice or interschool memos are usually headed as follows:

Example

> TO: Mary Smith, Chairman, English Department
> James Jones, Chairman, Social Studies Department
> FROM: Peter Banks, Vice Principal
> SUBJECT: Student Behavior
> DATE: September 8, 19xx

Pre-Mailing Checklist

1. Is the letter proofread and free of errors?
2. Is the letter signed?
3. Are all correspondence pages included and numbered?
4. Are enclosures included?
5. Do the inside address and envelope match?
6. Have you made sufficient copies?
7. Have you sent copies to the right people?
8. Is the postage correct?

Tips for Writing School Letters

If you are responsible for answering or initiating correspondence, here are some points to keep in mind:

– Get to the point quickly but courteously. Most people are very busy and do not have time to wade through pages of print to find the purpose of a letter. Do not be curt, but state your reason for writing in the first few lines of the first paragraph.

– Try to avoid the use of "I" when writing on behalf of the school. It is better to substitute such terms as "the school," "the students," "the fac-

ulty,'' or ''the administration.'' This gives the impression that the remarks are based on existing policy or group decisions and do not merely
represent your personal opinions.

— Use the second paragraph to provide supporting facts for the main points
made in the first paragraph.

— It is helpful to consider the expected response of the recipient of the letter
and to gauge the letter accordingly. Are you making a request? Providing
information? Making an explanation? Whatever your purpose, always be
courteous even though you may have to be firm.

— Reread the letter. Have you made your point clear? Try to avoid repeti-
tion, as it becomes tedious. If there are particularly complicated instructions or requests, ask someone else on the staff to read the letter before
it is sent to make sure that your points are clear.

— Check for correct grammar and punctuation.

— Avoid slang terms, clichés, contractions, and terms that you do not fully
understand.

— Proofread for content and correctness. Have you written what you intended? Is the tone of the letter appropriate to the situation?

— Always keep a copy of all outgoing correspondence.

— If the letter is lengthy, use the closing paragraph to summarize and tie
together any loose ends. In a short letter, stop when you have made your
point, and go directly to the complimentary close.

— Either sign the letter yourself if this meets with your administrator's
approval:

> Sincerely,
>
> Mary E. Smith
> Secretary to the Principal

or sign for the principal by signing his or her name and using your initials
underneath the signature:

> Sincerely,
> (Signed Paul Jones + your initials)
>
>
> Paul Jones
> Principal

DAMAGE REPORTS   In the case of fire, water damage, damage from such natural disasters as earthquakes or tornadoes, or damage from vandalism or theft, a report will need to be filled out and sent to the central office or to the insurance carrier. This should be done within twenty-four hours of the discovery of damage. The report should include:

- Date and time of the incident
- Description of the damage
- Name of the person discovering the damage or reporting the fire
- Name of the person who contacted the police or fire department
- Name of the police officer or chief fireman who answered the call
- An itemized list of equipment that was stolen or damaged including serial numbers if possible
- Approximate cost of damage or loss
- Any other pertinent data such as bodily injury

Reports of this nature should be kept for at least two years after the claim is settled.

DELAYED ORDERS   Delayed orders are a common, if irritating, fact of life. There is often little you can do to prevent delays because the causes are usually beyond your control. Lost orders, shipping strikes, and orders shipped to the wrong location, are all too common, but if you keep accurate records of your orders and maintain a tickler system to remind yourself when orders are due to arrive, you can call the vendor if goods are delayed. This can be important. Often, a vendor will not be aware of the delay for quite some time, but the sooner you are able to notify him of the delay, the more likely you are to receive prompt attention. When you place an order, jot down the expected delivery date on your calendar or reminder file. If you do not receive a notification of delay from the vendor or shipper, and your goods have not arrived on schedule, send him a reminder of the order in writing. If an item has been placed on back order for future delivery, make a note of it. In the case of orders placed for teachers, be sure to notify them of any delays so that they can modify their plans.

DELIVERIES, RECEIVING AND VERIFYING Here are some suggestions to make the sometimes tedious task of dealing with delivery people more pleasant and more efficient:

Always keep copies of orders placed.

When a delivery arrives, look for damage and check the packing slip against your order before you sign for the shipment. Sometimes delivery people will try to pressure you into signing for a shipment before you check it. This is not a good idea, since your signature can signify acceptance of the goods *as delivered,* not necessarily as ordered. Remember, though, that delivery people have to keep to a schedule, so be considerate about detaining them unnecessarily. It should take only a few moments to check the packing slip against your copy of the original order, and to spot any obvious damage to containers. If you have doubts, or if the delivery person refuses to wait, make a note along with your signature, indicating unusual conditions. For example, ''1 carton damaged—contents not examined,'' then the signature.

DESK, ORGANIZATION OF To organize your desk efficiently, the three prime areas for consideration are: (1) incoming materials, (2) work in progress, and (3) outgoing materials. The desk top is a work area and should be left clear for current work. In order to keep your desk surface clear, you should have designated areas for the masses of paper that will cross your desk on a daily basis. Here are some suggestions for keeping your work surface clear:

- Organize your desk drawers for your specific needs. Keep your stationery, forms, and personal items in boxes or files inside your drawers where they are easily accessible but out of the way.
- Keep a file for work in progress which can be kept in your file cabinet when not in use.
- Develop efficient work habits. Keep things in the same place so that you

can find them quickly. Develop a routine that you can stick to. It will save time and increase productivity.

– Gather all materials needed before beginning a job.

– Keep telephone books off your desk but within easy reach.

– Arrange a specific area for incoming and outgoing mail. A stack of file baskets kept on one corner of your desk can serve this purpose if you do not allow them to become junk storage areas. Do not allow materials to pile up.

DICTATION EQUIPMENT   There has been great progress made in dictation equipment in the past few years. Micro dictation equipment has revolutionized the whole concept of machine dictation. No longer does the person dictating need to be tied to an office. Your administrator can use this portable equipment while traveling, while at home, or at any other convenient time. More conventional units with hand-held microphones are still available, and both types of units are often compatible.

Dictaphone Corporation's line of Dictamation equipment offers many of the latest features in dictation devices. For example, the MessageMaster is a desk top unit that doubles as a telephone message center. A digital readout informs the user of the precise number of telephone calls received and the machine permits previewing of each call for priority messages. Also offered is an LED visual display controlled by microprocessors in which the top line of the display shows where each letter begins and ends, and the bottom line pinpoints special instructions for the typist.

Another available feature offered by Dictaphone is AfterThought, which permits changes and insertions even in midsentence without erasing. The Travel Master II, via microprocessor technology, provides a cueing function that lets the secretary know the exact location of letters on the cassette, as well as any special instructions.

Such features can increase productivity and make your job more pleasant. If, however, you must plod on with less than the latest equipment, here are some suggestions for getting the job done as efficiently as possible:

Tips for Giving Dictation

– The person doing the dictating should let you know at the beginning of the tape:

the type of product needed (first draft, finished letter),

the number of copies needed,

any special notations such as blind copies, extra wide margins, unusual spacing.

- Unusual names should be spelled out clearly.
- The address should be provided if not already on file.
- Clear enunciation is essential, particularly in the case of statistics such as test scores and the like.
- It is also helpful if the person dictating is in the habit of providing correct punctuation by saying "comma," "period," etc., or by clearly indicating punctuation by vocal inflection.
- The person dictating should speak more slowly than during normal conversation.
- The tape should be played back to check for errors or changes before giving it to you for typing.

If your administrator is not in the habit of following these procedures, a few tactful suggestions from you might prove very useful in increasing your productivity, speed, and efficiency.

DRAFTS, PREPARATION OF   A rough draft is the rapid rough typing of material to get it down on paper. It should follow the finished format as closely as possible, but don't worry too much about strikeovers or corrections at this point. If you are using white paper, type the words "rough draft" in the upper right-hand corner so your work will not be mistaken for finished copy. You might use colored paper to type rough drafts. First drafts are usually triple-spaced to give the writer plenty of space for editing. Successive drafts may be double- or triple-spaced. The first tentative copy is also double-spaced to permit space for refinement and further editing. It is often photocopied for clearance or comments by others before the final copy is typed. The final copy may then be single-spaced or double-spaced depending upon its use. Works being submitted for publication are always double-spaced.

DRUG ABUSE   When you accept a position as school secretary you are in essence agreeing to do much more than process papers. You are also responsible for the students; perhaps not to the same extent as counselors, teachers, or the administrator, but you should care about them. It is essential for everyone who comes in contact with the students to have at least a rudimentary knowledge of street drugs and their effects. While your job may be only to refer drug abuse matters to a counselor or to the administrator, you should be familiar with the appearance of illicit drugs, symptoms of their abuse, and slang drug terms in common use. It is quite surprising how much incorrect information relating to drug use circulates around schools. Do not depend on others to know the facts; know them yourself. The National Clearinghouse for Drug Abuse, the National Clearinghouse for Alcohol Information, the United States Department of Health, and the National Council on Alcoholism, as well as the Drug Enforcement Administration of the United States Department of Justice have provided invaluable aid in the compilation of the information that follows.

Basic Facts About Drugs

·Drugs are chemical substances that produce physical, mental, emotional, or behavioral changes in the user. Drug abuse comes about when drugs are used for other than medicinal purposes. Even the use of prescription drugs or over-the-counter products can result in drug abuse, if these products are used in an inappropriate way or contrary to package directions. Drug addiction or drug dependence is physical or psychological dependence on any given drug. The ability of drug users to become so accustomed to a drug that larger and larger doses are required to get "high" or to produce the desired effect is termed "drug tolerance."

There are probably as many reasons for taking drugs as there are drug dependent personalities. Some of the most popular reasons are: "It makes me feel good"; escape from daily problems; an "easy" solution to problems; experimentation; a wish for instant euphoria; "Everybody does it. I don't want to be different."

"You pays your money; you takes your chances," the old saying goes. This is certainly true with any drug, whether off the street or out of a nice neat drugstore package. Any drug is potentially hazardous depending on how it is taken and on the user's particular chemical makeup. Even aspirin, cough medicines, throat lozenges, and diet pills can be extremely dangerous when used improperly or in improper combinations. *Always* check with the pharmacist before combining any medications.

If a child is to receive regular medication at school, when prescribed by a physician, the medicine is often kept with the school nurse, or if no nurse is present, with the school secretary. If you are the one responsible for distributing a child's medication, it is a good idea to check with the issuing pharmacist to see if there are any special foods or other drug combinations that should be avoided with the particular medication being given. It takes only a moment or two to check and be sure, and you could save yourself much trouble should something go awry. If you are the one distributing the medication, you can (and probably will) be held responsible should anything go wrong.

Drug Abuse Prevention

Drug abuse prevention begins by helping young people develop personal values. The main responsibility for this lies with the parents. The school can only reinforce values learned at home. If young people between the ages of eight and twenty can be prevented from abusing drugs, they will probably not develop a drug problem later. As a school secretary, you can work with teachers and administrators to guide and help young people in making the difficult choices they face while growing up. Know the facts about drugs and help the students understand the dangers of drug abuse, both to them personally and to society as a whole. Do not preach, moralize, or use scare tactics. Be a good listener and try to provide helpful factual information. If it becomes necessary, do not hesitate to call in the administrator, parents, or other persons who can help to deal with a drug problem. If young people are provided with alternative activities and feel a sense of belonging to a functional whole, they are less likely to turn to drugs for escape or recreation. If you are interested, perhaps you could help in extracurricular activities, or sponsor leisure activity groups.

Common Street Drugs Explained

Marijuana

Marijuana or "pot," "weed," "grass," is a hemp plant whose botanical name is *cannabis sativa*. It grows wild and is also cultivated in many parts of the world. Marijuana contains 419 chemicals, but the prime mind-altering chemical is delta-9-tetrahydrocannabinol or THC. This ingredient determines the potency. The flowering tops of the plant contain the highest concentration of THC.

Hashish or "hash" is the resin from the plant tops and contains five to ten times more THC than crude marijuana. The THC concentrations of marijuana can depend on the particular plant, climate, soil, and harvest time.

The most desired product is Sinsemilla, prepared from the unpollinated female cannabis plant and sometimes these "Thai sticks" from Southeast Asia find their way to the U.S. markets. (Thai sticks are marijuana buds bound onto short sections of bamboo.)

It is estimated that at least forty-one to forty-seven million Americans have used marijuana. The highest use rate is among the eighteen to twenty-five-year-old group, although there are known users as young as eight. Some people respond negatively to marijuana and experience acute panic reactions, fear of losing control, or fear of going crazy. The symptoms usually disappear within a few hours. Research has verified that marijuana does not cause physical dependence but can result in a "burnout." This slang term refers to users who have smoked consistently over a long period of time and have become dull, slow, and inattentive. They are sometimes so unaware of their surroundings that they do not even respond when friends speak to them. "Space cadets," as those who are "burned out" are often called, do not consider themselves to be burned out. Their condition may or may not reverse if they give up the drug.

A real danger of marijuana use by young people is its likely interference with the process of growing up. Research shows that extensive use can lead to impaired thinking, poor reading comprehension, and poor verbal and math skills. Young people need to have experience in making decisions, learning to deal with successes and failures, and learning to formulate their own values. By escaping into a marijuana euphoria, the person may never learn the psychological skills of maturity necessary to become a content, successful, and responsible adult.

Facts About Marijuana

- Recent research has shown that marijuana may interfere with the body's immune system and its ability to fight infection.
- Marijuana use can severely impair driving ability as it effects judgment, care, and concentration.
- Most people are introduced to marijuana (and other drugs) by their friends and acquaintances, not by some shadowy pushers lurking on the school grounds.
- Not enough research has been done to conclusively prove whether marijuana is more detrimental than alcohol.
- Marijuana should never be used during pregnancy or nursing. THC can be transmitted to the fetus, thereby causing risks of miscarriage or birth defects, and THC can affect the baby through the mother's milk.
- Research indicates that adolescent males and females may be rendered infertile by excessive use of marijuana. Chronic users (male) have lower testosterone (male sex hormone) levels and young women often have defective menstrual cycles.
- Marijuana increases the heart rate as much as fifty percent, and should not be used by people with heart conditions.
- Research shows that smoking five "joints" (marijuana cigarettes) a week is more harmful to the lungs that smoking six packs of regular cigarettes a week.

Marijuana Slang Terms

Acapulco gold	a powerful strain of marijuana with a golden tinge of color
Bong	a water pipe sometimes used to smoke marijuana
Burnout	a state of apathy and perceptual deadness resulting from excessive habitual use of marijuana
Buzz	drug-induced euphoria; a high
Colombian	a potent strain of marijuana
Dime	a quantity of street drugs that sells for $10
Dope	drugs
Duster	a cigarette made from tobacco or other leaves and sprinkled with PCP (angel dust)
Ganja	a powerful form of marijuana obtained from the flowering tops and leaves of the plant
Grass	marijuana
Hashish	a powerful form of marijuana made from the resinous secretions of the cannabis plant which are collected, dried, and compressed into balls, cakes, or sheets
Hash oil	a form of marijuana which is extracted or distilled
Head shops	stores that sell paraphernalia and other drug-related items. These shops are completely legal in many states.
High	drug-induced euphoria or intoxication
Hit	a drag from a marijuana cigarette
Joint	a hand-rolled marijuana cigarette
Killer weed	marijuana or other leaves such as mint or parsley that have been treated with PCP
Loaded	being really high
Nickel	a quantity of street drugs selling for $5
Ounce	a standard measurement for marijuana
Paraphernalia	drug apparatus, gadgets, and equipment usually sold in head shops
Pot	marijuana
Roach	the small butt end of a joint left after smoking
Roach clip	a tweezer-like gadget used to hold the roach so that it can be smoked down further than if held by the fingers
Rolling papers	cigarette papers used in making a joint
Scales	paraphernalia used to weigh drug quantities
Smoking stones	paraphernalia used to hold joints
Space cadet	a habitual marijuana user who has become burned out
Spaced out	a drug-induced state of losing touch with one's surroundings
Stash	a place used to store illicit drugs

Stoned	high
Supergrass	marijuana treated with PCP
Toke	the inhalation of marijuana or hashish smoke
Water pipe	a device used to smoke marijuana, that filters the smoke through water
Weed	marijuana

Marijuana, Summary of Effects

Cannabis sativa	produces	marijuana
		THC
		hashish
		hash oil

Dependence: physical dependence unknown; moderate psychological dependence

Effect: lasts two to four hours
euphoria, relaxed inhibitions, increased heart rate, reddened eyes, increased appetite, disoriented behavior (at least in novice users)

Overdose: anxiety, paranoia, inability to concentrate, slowed movements, time distortion

Side Effects: insomnia, hyperactivity, decreased appetite

Phencyclidine (PCP or Angel Dust)

According to a consensus of drug treatment experts, PCP poses greater risks than any other illicit drug currently in use. PCP was first developed in the late 1950s as a surgical anesthetic for humans. However, because of its unpleasant side effects such as delirium, agitation, and visual disturbances, PCP was soon used only as a veterinary anesthetic and tranquilizer.

Low doses of PCP can result in a floaty euphoria and sometimes a numbness of the extremities (the anesthetic properties). Larger doses can produce agitation, extreme excitement, muscle rigidity, loss of concentration, loss of memory, delirium, feelings of isolation, fear of dying, convulsions, speech impairment, and perceptual changes. One of the most frightening and socially dangerous aspects of PCP users is violent and bizarre behavior. PCP seems to scramble the brain's internal stimuli, thereby severely altering how the user perceives his environment. Driving and sometimes even walking can be impossible tasks for PCP users. More PCP users die from accidents caused by their erratic behavior than from the direct effect of the drug.

PCP users who indulge in moderate to high doses can experience schizophrenia-like psychosis lasting for days or weeks. During these episodes their behavior may range from being excited, incoherent, and aggressive, to being withdrawn, depressed, and uncommunicative. They may become paranoid and feel persecuted.

Because of the anesthetic qualities of PCP, users often feel little or no pain. This, coupled with their violent and bizarre behavior and feelings of invulnerability, makes it a formidable task to try and subdue someone on PCP.

Most PCP on the streets has been illegally but easily synthesized in bootleg laboratories. It has such a bad reputation on the street that it is often sold under other names which are thought to be less dangerous, such as mescaline, LSD, or THC. When you buy from the streets you can never be sure just what you will get. Most kids are introduced to PCP through friends and schoolmates. PCP comes in many forms: powdered (angel dust); tablets; crystals; and pills (P-C pills, hogs). The dust is usually smoked after being mixed with marijuana, parsley, or mint leaves. This is the favorite method of use since the user has better control of the powdered form than of pills. A user experiences numbness, slurred speech, lack of coordination, a sense of strength, and invulnerability.

To recognize a PCP user, look for a blank stare, rapid and involuntary eye movements, and an exaggerated gait. The user may also experience auditory hallucinations, image distortion, and mood disorders, as well as violent hostility.

PCP is a frightening and dangerous drug and even worse, its use is on the increase among young people. More and more hospital emergency rooms and drug crisis centers are treating PCP cases, and the increase in violent crimes by adolescents may be linked to PCP use.

If you suspect that a student is under the influence of PCP, do not attempt to deal with the situation alone. Get help from security guards, the administration, or police. It sometimes takes as many as four trained police officers to subdue a violent PCP user.

Hallucinogens (Psychedelic Drugs)

Hallucinogenic drugs may be natural or synthetic, but both distort the perception of reality. Under the influence of hallucinogens, the pupils dilate and body temperature and blood pressure rise. Perception is so altered that a user may "see" sound and "hear" colors, as well as experience a variety of visual hallucinations. Feelings of depersonalization and isolation may become so severe that suicide is an ever-present danger.

Long after hallucinogens have left the body, the user may experience "flash-backs." These are fragmentary psychedelic experiences such as the intensification of color, the movement of a stationary object, or the confusion of one object with another. Recurrent use results in tolerance, and while there is no evidence of physical dependence, psychological dependence is possible.

There are many natural and synthetic hallucinogens currently in use:

– LSD (a synthetic)
– mescaline (from the peyote cactus)
– psilocybin (from a Mexican mushroom)
– morning glory seeds
– DMT, DOM (STP), PMA, and MDA (synthetics)

LSD (LSD-25, Lysergide)

Lysergic acid diethylamide is derived from a fungus (ergot) and was first produced in 1938. In 1943, a chemist accidentally took some LSD and its hallucinogenic effects were discovered when he took the first "trip" or drug-induced psychedelic experience. He experienced vertigo, intensification of light, and visual hallucinations that lasted for about two hours. Since its chemical structure relates to a chemical which is naturally present in the brain, LSD was used in research to study the effects of psychosis. LSD was very popular in the 1960s and was adopted by those who sought a mind-expanding experience. Its popularity then waned, but it is now becoming popular once again.

LSD is usually sold in the form of tablets, thin squares of gelatin (window panes), or impregnated paper (blotter acid). During the 1960s it was used on anything and everything from sticks of gum to oranges, thereby allowing easy distribution at group gatherings, rock concerts, or "happenings."

Mescaline and Peyote

Mescaline is the active ingredient of the peyote cactus, and is derived from the buttons or fleshy parts of the plant. The Indians of northern Mexico have used peyote buttons for centuries as part of their religious rites. Peyote is usually ground into a powder and taken orally, but mescaline can also be produced synthetically. Mescaline hallucinations can last from five to twelve hours.

Psilocybin

Psilocybe mushrooms, like peyote, have been used for centuries by Indian tribes. When they are eaten, these "sacred" or "magic" mushrooms affect perception much the same way that LSD or mescaline does. The active ingredients of psilocybin and psilocyn can now be made synthetically.

The Synthetic Hallucinogens

Many chemical variations of mescaline and amphetamines have been synthesized. DOM (4-methyl-2, 5-dimethoxy-amphetamine) was synthesized in 1963 and introduced into the drug culture of San Francisco's Haight-Ashbury district in 1967. (It was soon called STP after the motor oil—"Serenity, Tranquility, and Peace.") Other synthetics soon followed, including DOB (4-bromo-2, 5-dimethoxy-amphetamine), and MDA (3, 4-methylenedioxyamphetamine). They differ from one another in the speed with which they work, and their ability to produce hallucinations. They are usually taken orally, and are rarely injected. Because they are produced in bootleg laboratories, they are seldom pure and the doses may vary considerably. They can be extremely dangerous because of these variables. There were many deaths in the late 1960s because of contaminants in STP.

Stimulants

Stimulants or "uppers" produce an increase in alertness and activity. They include cocaine, amphetamines (found in many diet pills), caffein (that's right, coffee, tea, cocoa, and cola drinks are mild drugs!), and nicotine in cigarettes. Some stimulants are available right in the drugstore. Nicotine, appetite-control pills (amphetamines), and "pep-up" pills (high doses of caffein) are available to almost anyone. Amphetamine, methamphetamine, dextroamphetamine, and cocaine are readily available on the street and through school friends. An amphetamine user can become dependent and even small doses can be toxic to some people. Users can experience these symptoms:

- anxiety   - paranoia
- restlessness   - hallucinations
- panic   - convulsions
- cardiac disturbances   - coma

Long-term use can result in brain damage and even death. When a user injects amphetamine or "speed," it becomes more dangerous, is more quickly absorbed into the system, and opens the way for infections from nonsterile equipment. "Speed freaks" (users burned out on amphetamines) experience amphetamine psychosis. (This was quite common in the drug cultures of the sixties.)

A chronic amphetamine user can be recognized by a rash similar to measles, damaged gums, teeth, and nails, and very dry lifeless hair.

The user usually gets a temporary sense of exhilaration, super energy, needs little or no sleep, and has a loss of appetite. For these reasons, stimulants are often misused or abused by college students cramming for exams, and by many athletes in competition. If "speed" is injected, a "flash" or "rush" occurs which is a sudden feeling of hyperactivity, exhilaration, and energy. Long-term use, however, results in "crashing"—a period of unpleasant depression. This unpleasant side effect spawned the "crash pads" of the sixties, places to go until the feeling wore off. Heavy users may inject amphetamines every few hours. Physical exertion increases the hazards of stimulant use since it affects the cardiovascular and temperature-regulating systems of the body. It is especially dangerous to use amphetamines while participating in physical activities such as sports competitions. Fatalities have been known to occur at such times among performing athletes.

Cocaine

Cocaine is a natural stimulant, taken from the leaves of the coca plant which has been cultivated and used by the natives of the South American Andes for centuries. The natives chew the leaves of the coca plant for refreshment and relief from fatigue. Pure cocaine was extracted in the 1880s and was used as an anesthetic in eye surgery and surgery of the nose and throat because of its ability to limit bleeding. Cocaine is distributed as a white cyrstalline powder, usually cut to half-strength by adding such sugars as lactose, inositol, and mannitol, or by adding anesthetics such as lidocaine. Cocaine is usually "snorted" through the nose, or sometimes injected directly into the bloodstream. It has become a very popular recreational drug and has earned the reputation of being safe from side effects. Actually, it has a high degree of psychic dependence, necessitating larger and larger doses at shorter and shorter intervals. Some of the unpleasant effects of cocaine are:

- anxiety
- extreme irritability
- toxic psychosis similar to paranoid schizophrenia
- tactile hallucinations so severe that users may injure themselves while trying to remove imaginary insects from under their skin
- death from respiratory failure as a result of overdoses

The Depressants (Sedatives)

Sedatives are drugs that depress the central nervous system. They calm the nerves and produce sleep, and are also called tranquilizers and sleeping pills. There are three main categories: barbiturates, nonbarbiturates, and benzodiazepines. Barbiturates can cause dependence and withdrawal can be more severe than heroin withdrawal.

The barbiturates (barbs, downers, reds) are the most commonly abused and misused category; pentobarbital (Nembutal), secobarbital (Seconal), and amobarbital (Amytal). These are also all legitimately used as sedatives or sleeping aids. The most commonly used nonbarbiturates are: glutethimide (Doriden), meprobamate (Miltown), methyprylon (Noludar), ethchlorvynyl (Placidyl), and methaqualone (Sopor or Quaalude). These are often medically prescribed as sleeping pills.

Benzodazepines are prescribed to relieve anxiety, and their rate of abuse is increasing. Diazepam (Valium) and chloridiazepoxide (Librium) are the most common drugs of abuse in this category.

Sedatives can kill. Barbiturate overdose is responsible for nearly one-third of all drug-induced deaths. Accidental deaths may occur when a user unintentionally takes an additional dose because of drug-induced confusion or impaired judgment. *Sedatives mixed with alcohol intensify the effect of both and can be fatal.*

Sedative users are people who have trouble dealing with stress or anxiety, or have insomnia. Heroin users often take sedatives to supplement or sometimes to substitute for heroin. Stimulant users take sedatives to offset the jittery feelings produced by stimulants. Others take sedatives as an escape method.

Most sedatives used on the street come from legitimate prescriptions that are misused, or from fake prescriptions. They can be obtained from unattended medicine cabinets, from friends, or from the street market.

Narcotics

When used in medicine, narcotics are extremely effective for relieving intense pain. When administered medically, narcotics are given orally or by intramuscular injection. Illicit users may smoke narcotics or use subcutaneous (skin popping) or intravenous (mainlining) methods. The opiates include opium and its derivatives morphine, codeine, and heroin. Methadone is a synthetic chemical with a morphine-like action. Narcotics cause physical and psychic dependence, and are extremely dangerous to the user. The risks are greater for a user who injects (shoots up) than for one who does not, because of the speed with which the narcotic enters the body, and the probable use of nonsterile equipment. (For example, if a user injects a dose of pure heroin, and has not yet built up enough tolerance to handle that large a dose, death can result in minutes after the injection.) Skin abcesses, inflamed veins, and lung congestion are fairly common among users, as is serum hepatitis from using nonsterile equipment.

While under the influence of narcotics, a user may experience contracted pupils and reduced vision, decreased physical activity, and drowsiness. Large doses may induce sleep, nausea, vomiting, or respiratory difficulties.

When an addict stops using narcotics, withdrawal begins within four to six hours. The full range of withdrawal symptoms includes shaking, sweating, vomiting, running nose and eyes, muscle aches, chills, abdominal pains, and diarrhea. The intensity of the symptoms depends on the degree of addiction. The synthetic narcotic methadone has been used to treat narcotics addicts in maintenance programs; the addict is given reduced doses of the drug daily to relieve the craving for heroin and to prevent withdrawal symptoms. Methadone itself causes dependence, however, and is under strict control although it too is available illegally on the street.

The Inhalants

This group of readily available chemicals can be extremely hazardous. Inhalants are breathed in order to get high. Anything in an aerosol can is a candidate for abuse including spray paint, vegetable oils, and hair spray. Other bottled fumes that are inhaled include gasoline, transmission fluid, glues, paint thinners, nail polish remover, household cleaners, and amyl nitrite (poppers) (these are capsules of heart medicine which are popped open and inhaled to get a high). It is currently thought that there may be a link between poppers and Kaposi's sarcoma, the so-called "gay cancer." Toluene, once used extensively in typing correction fluid, is the prime chemical agent in inhalants that produces the desired effects. Room deodorizers have become especially popular chemicals of abuse, and they are perfectly packaged for the job. Children between the ages of seven and seventeen are the biggest users of inhalants, probably because they are so easy to obtain.

The dangers from inhalants include impaired vision, inability to think clearly, loss of memory, drastic weight loss, violent behavior, bone marrow damage, irregular heartbeat leading to heart failure, death by suffocation when fumes are inhaled from a paper bag, and sudden death.

Glossary of Slang Terms   See FIGURE 8.

DRUG	SLANG	FORM	TYPE OF DRUG
Amphetamine	white crosses greenies speed footballs uppers pep pills whites dexies hearts wake-ups beans bennies roses oranges Black bird Black Beauties Black Cadillacs crystals crank crink amped cris cristian bombidos co-pilots bottles jugs b-bomb turn abouts chicken powder lightning nuggets dynamites splash sparkle plenties cross tops peaches marathons cross-roads bumble bees thrusters meth	capsule pill liquid powder tablet lozenge	Stimulant
Barbiturate	downers block busters reds barbs blues blue birds blue devils blue heaven blue bullets blue dots candies softballs seccies seggies Christmas trees Mexican reds green dragons yellow jackets yellow bullets red bullets goof balls devils nebbies nimbies peanuts pink lady phennies	pills capsules tablets liquid injection	Depressant or Sedative

FIGURE 8

Glossary of Drug Slang

DRUG	SLANG	FORM	TYPE OF DRUG
Cocaine	coke Cecil coconut Big C Corrine flake Bernice jam sniff bernies lady snow snow rock white frisky powder incentive dream girl gold dust star dust paradise Carry Nation heaven dust nose candy uptown toot	powder (sniffed, snorted, or injected)	Stimulant Local anesthetic
Hashish	hash kif Black Russian quarter moon soles	resin (smoked)	Relaxant or hallucinogen in large doses
Heroin	horse junk H Harry scat smack scag stuff cat chick big H thing Mexican mud doojee duji dogie crap brown sugar Chinese red brother	powder (sniffed or injected)	Narcotic
Inhalants	poppers snappers huffing sniffing	aerosols, solvents	

FIGURE 8, *continued*

DRUG	SLANG	FORM	TYPE OF DRUG
LSD (d-lysergic acid diethylamide)	acid sugar cubes big D ghost hawk-25 beast coffee blue heaven California sunshine orange mushrooms chocolate chips mellow yellows window panes paper acid trips	tablet	Hallucinogen (psychedelic)
Marijuana	grass pot dope hemp weed herb tea Mary Jane Acapulco Gold Colombian Panama Red Panamanian gold Zacatecas purple Mexican green broccoli bush gage dry high greta Texas tea yesca sweet Lucy	dried leaves	Relaxant or hallucinogen in large doses
Mescaline	mesc beans butoons cactus moon peyote mescal mescal buttons	tablet capsule	Hallucinogen
PCP (phencyclidine)	hog angel dust crystal cyclone PeaCe Pill bad grass super grass elephant killer weed DOA	powder crystals tablet	Veterinary anesthetic

FIGURE 8, *continued*

Drug Information Organizations

The following organizations can provide you with materials on drug abuse, alcohol, and tobacco. You can write to them for useful information.

National Clearinghouse for Drug
Abuse Information
5600 Fishers Lane, Room 10A-56
Rockville, Maryland 20857

or

Box 1635
Rockville, Maryland 20850

National Clearinghouse for Alcohol
Information
9119 Gaither Road
Gaithersburg, Maryland 20760

or

Box 2345
Rockville, Maryland 20850

Technical Information Center
Office on Smoking and Health
5600 Fishers Lane, Room 1-16
Rockville, Maryland 20857

Addiction Research Foundation
33 Russell Street
Toronto, Ontario, Canada MS52S1

Alcohol and Drug Problems
Association of America
1101 15th Street, N.W., Suite 204
Washington, D.C. 20005

Alcohol, Drug Abuse, and Mental
Health Administration
Office of Communications and
Public Affairs
5600 Fishers Lane, Room 6C15
Rockville, Maryland 20857

Center for Multicultural Awareness
2924 Columbia Pike
Arlington, Virginia 22204

Do-It-Now-Foundation
National Media Center
Box 5115
Phoenix, Arizona 85010

Drug Abuse Council
1828 L Street, N.W., 12th floor
Washington, DC 20036

Education Film Library Association
17 West 60 Street
New York, New York 10023

Mental Health Materials Center
Human Services Education Resource
System
419 Park Avenue South
New York, New York 10016

National Association of State Drug
Abuse
Program Coordinators
1612 K Street, N.W., Suite 900
Washington, DC 20006

National Audiovisual Center
National Archives and Records
Service (GSA)
Washington, DC 20409

National Clearinghouse for Mental
Health Information
National Institute of Mental Health
5600 Fishers Lane, Room 11A-33
Rockville, Maryland 20857

National Drug Abuse Center for
Training and Resource Development
656 Quince Orchard Park
Room 617
Gaithersburg, Maryland 20760

NORML
2317 M Street, NW
Washington, DC 20037

Prevention Branch
Division of Resource Development
National Institute on Drug Abuse
5600 Fishers Lane, Room 10A-30
Rockville, Maryland 20857

Prevention Materials Institute
Box 152
Lafayette, California 94549

Public Affairs Pamphlets
381 Park Avenue South
New York, New York 10016

Pyramid Project
39 Quail Court, Suite 201
Walnut Creek, California 94596
or

7101 Wisconsin Avenue, Suite 1006
Washington, DC 20014

Following is a list of state agencies that can give you information about the various drug abuse prevention, treatment, and rehabilitation programs within the State:

ALABAMA

Drug Abuse Program Section
Division of Alcoholism and Drug
Abuse
Department of Mental Health
145 Molton Street
Montgomery, Alabama 36104

ALASKA

Office of Drug Abuse
Department of Health & Social
Services
Pouch H-01D
Juneau, Alaska 99801

ARIZONA

Drug Abuse Programs
Division of Behavioral Health
Services
Department of Health Services
2500 East Van Buren
Phoenix, Arizona 85008

ARKANSAS

Office of Drug and Alcohol Abuse
Prevention
Department of Social &
Rehabilitation Services
1515 Building
1515 West 7 Street
Little Rock, Arkansas 72203

CALIFORNIA

California Department of Health
Substance Abuse Division
Room 1592, 744 P Street
Sacramento, California 95814

COLORADO

Alcohol & Drug Abuse Division
Department of Health
4210 East 11 Avenue
Denver, Colorado 80220

CONNECTICUT

Connecticut Alcohol and Drug
Council
Department of Mental Health
90 Washington Street
Hartford, Connecticut 06115

DELAWARE
Bureau of Substance Abuse
Governor Bacon Health Center
Cottage No. 8
Delaware City, Delaware 19706

FLORIDA
Bureau of Drug Abuse Prevention
Division of Mental Health
Department of Health &
Rehabilitation Services
1323 Winewood Boulevard
Tallahassee, Florida 32301

GEORGIA
Alcohol and Drug Abuse Section
Division of Mental Health &
Retardation
Department of Human Resources
618 Ponce De Leon Avenue, NE
Atlanta, Georgia 30308

HAWAII
Alcohol and Drug Abuse Branch
Department of Health
1270 Queen Emma Street,
Room 404
Honolulu, Hawaii 96813

IDAHO
Bureau of Substance Abuse
Division of Community
Rehabilitation
Department of Health and Welfare
LBJ Building, Room 327
Boise, Idaho 83720

ILLINOIS
Dangerous Drugs Commission
300 North State Street, 15th floor
Chicago, Illinois 60610

INDIANA
Division of Addiction Services
Department of Mental Health
5 Indiana Square
Indianapolis, Indiana 46204

IOWA
Iowa Drug Abuse Authority
615 East 14 Street
Des Moines, Iowa 50319

KANSAS
Drug Abuse Unit
Department of Social and
Rehabilitation Services
Biddle Building
2700 W. 6 Street
Topeka, Kansas 66608

KENTUCKY
Alcohol and Drug Abuse Branch
Division for Prevention Services
Bureau of Health Services
Department of Human Resources
275 East Main Street
Frankfort, Kentucky 40601

LOUISIANA
Bureau of Substance Abuse
Division of Hospitals
Louisiana Health and Human
Resource Administration
Weber Building, 7th floor
Baton Rouge, Louisiana 70801

MAINE
Office of Alcoholism and Drug
Abuse Prevention
Bureau of Rehabilitation
32 Winthrop Street
Augusta, Maine 04330

MARYLAND

Drug Abuse Administration
Department of Health & Mental
Hygiene
Herbert O'Connor Office Building
201 W. Preston Street
Baltimore, Maryland 21201

MASSACHUSETTS

Division of Drug Rehabilitation
Department of Mental Health
190 Portland Street
Boston, Massachusetts 02114

MICHIGAN

Office of Substance Abuse Services
3500 North Logan Street
P.O. Box 30035
Lansing, Michigan 48909

MINNESOTA

Drug and Alcohol Authority
Chemical Dependency Division
Department of Public Welfare
402 Metro Square Building
St. Paul, Minnesota 55101

MISSISSIPPI

Division of Drug Misuse
Department of Mental Health
1001 Lee State Office Building
Jackson, Mississippi 39201

MISSOURI

Division of Alcoholism & Drug
Abuse
Department of Mental Health
2002 Missouri Boulevard
Jefferson City, Missouri 65101

MONTANA

Addictive Diseases Division
Department of Institutions
1539 11 Avenue
Helena, Montana 59601

NEBRASKA

Nebraska Commission on Drugs
P.O. Box 94726
State Capitol Building
Lincoln, Nebraska 68509

NEVADA

Bureau of Alcohol & Drug Abuse
Rehabilitation Division
Department of Human Resources
505 East King Street
Carson City, Nevada 89710

NEW HAMPSHIRE

Office of Drug Abuse Prevention
3 Capital Street, Room 405
Concord, New Hampshire 03301

NEW JERSEY

Division of Narcotic and Drug
Abuse Control
Department of Health
541 East State Street
Trenton, New Jersey 08609

NEW MEXICO

Drug Abuse Agency
Department of Hospitals &
Institutions
113 Washington
Santa Fe, New Mexico 87501

NEW YORK

Office of Drug Abuse Services
Executive Park South
Albany, New York 12203

NORTH CAROLINA

North Carolina Drug Commission
Box 19324
Raleigh, North Carolina 27609

NORTH DAKOTA

Division of Alcoholism and Drug
Abuse
Department of Health
909 Basin Avenue
Bismarck, North Dakota 58505

OHIO

Ohio Bureau of Drug Abuse
Division of Mental Health and
Mental Retardation
2929 Kenny Road, Room B207
Columbus, Ohio 43221

OKLAHOMA

Division of Drug Abuse Services
Department of Mental Health
P.O. Box 53277, Capitol Station
Oklahoma City, Oklahoma 73105

OREGON

Programs for Alcohol and Drug
Problems
Mental Health Division
Department of Human Resources
2575 Bittern Street, NE
Salem, Oregon 97310

PENNSYLVANIA

Governor's Council on Drug and
Alcohol Abuse
Riverside Office Center
Building No. 1, Suite N
2101 North Front Street
Harrisburg, Pennsylvania 17110

RHODE ISLAND

Rhode Island Drug Abuse Program
Department of Mental Health and
Retardation and Hospitals
303 General Hospital
Rhode Island Medical Center
Cranston, Rhode Island 02920

SOUTH CAROLINA

South Carolina Commission on
Alcohol and Drug Abuse
3700 Forest Drive
P.O. Box 4616
Columbia, South Carolina 29240

SOUTH DAKOTA

Division of Drugs and Substance
Control
Department of Health
Joe Foss Building
Pierre, South Dakota 57501

TENNESSEE

Alcohol and Drug Abuse Section
Department of Mental Health
501 Union Street, 4th floor
Nashville, Tennessee 37219

TEXAS

Drug Abuse Division
Department of Community Affairs
Box 13166, Capitol Station
Austin, Texas 78711

UTAH

Division of Alcoholism and Drugs
554 South 300 East
Salt Lake City, Utah 84111

VERMONT

Alcohol and Drug Abuse Division
Department of Social and
Rehabilitation Services
State Office Building
Montpelier, Vermont 05602

VIRGINIA

Department of Mental Health/Mental
Retardation
Division of Substance Abuse Control
Commonwealth of Virginia
P.O. Box 1797
Richmond, Virginia 23214

WASHINGTON

Office of Drug Abuse Prevention
Community Services Division
DSHS, OB-43E
Olympia, Washington 98504

WEST VIRGINIA

Division of Alcoholism and Drug
Abuse
Department of Mental Health
1800 Washington Street, East
Charleston, West Virginia 25305

WISCONSIN

Bureau of Alcohol & Other Drug
Abuse
Division of Mental Hygiene
Department of Health and Social
Services
One West Wilson Street, Room 523
Madison, Wisconsin 53702

WYOMING

Drug Abuse Programs
State Office Building West
Cheyenne, Wyoming 82001

Drug abuse is on the increase in all segments of our society, from the "straight" people on diet pills and tranquilizers, to children as young as seven years old. One of the best defenses against drug abuse is factual information. So many students who pop pills as easily as candy have very little information about the chemicals which they thrust into their bodies. While you may not have a great effect in making changes in the drug abuse problem, you can try by keeping abreast of the latest information and being ready with factual answers when they are needed.

DUPLICATING MACHINES Also see PHOTOCOPYING. Schools are known for their outdated equipment, so you may have to work with duplicating machines that you would never find in business. Here is a breakdown of the most common types found in schools:

Hectograph Duplicators

There are two basic types of hectograph duplicators, gelatin method and spirit method. The gelatin process is seldom used anymore. It is an outdated messy process requiring the preparation of a special master paper which is typed on with special ribbon or written on with special ink. The finished sheet is then placed face down on a prepared moist gelatin surface and the reverse image is transferred to the gelatin. Paper is then applied to the gelatin to receive the finished image. The machines used in this process may have a flat bed or rotary cylinder. One advantage of the gelatin process is the ability to produce copies in several colors by using different inks or carbon sheets. Two-hundred clear copies are all that can be expected from one master.

In the spirit method, the master copy is typed or written on a carbon-backed sheet and is then fastened to a rotary drum. As the paper passes through the machine, a special fluid is brought into contact with the master sheet and transfers the image to the final copy. Master sheets may be saved and reused. Additions can easily be made to a master and errors or changes can be corrected by scraping the carbon from the back of the typed master. (A single-edge razor blade or a scalpel works well.) The masters of this process are often referred to as "dittos." Spirit duplicating machines may be operated by hand cranking, or may be fully automatic.

Mimeograph Process   Also see STENCILS.

The mimeograph process is also known as the stencil method. The fiber or plastic (mylar) master stencil is cut by using a typewriter set to be used without the ribbon, or by using a special stylus for handwriting. The stencil is then placed face down on the drum section of the mimeograph machine which is covered with an inked pad. The cuts in the stencil allow the ink to pass through, transferring the image to paper, which is in turn passed under the rotating drum. Stencils can be stored and reused indefinitely. This process makes about 5,000 clean copies per stencil. Corrections are made by applying mimeograph correction fluid over the mistake, then retyping.

The mimeograph process is one of the most common forms of duplicating processes found in schools. While the machines may vary slightly, the method of operation is fairly standard for this type of equipment. Following are guidelines for operating a typical mimeograph machine:

1. Check the ink supply. A reservoir inside the cylinder holds the ink supply. The pad is inked by tipping the reservoir. To check the ink supply, turn the cylinder until the ink cap is up. Unscrew the cap and measure the ink supply with the ink measuring rod. Add half a can of ink at a time until the dipstick indicates the correct level. To ink the pad, turn the cylinder until the ink filler cap is in a three o'clock position. Pull the inking lever and turn the lever to the right. Hold it down while turning the hand wheel clockwise. This will rotate the cylinder and allow the ink to flow to the pad. When the pad is sufficiently inked, release the lever and return the cylinder to the normal position.

2. Load the paper on the feed table.

   Set the retainer pads for the length of the paper being used.

   Lower the feed table by moving the lowering lever.

   Set the left-hand rail for the width of the paper being used.

   Move the right-hand rail as far right as possible.

   Press the rubber retainer pads to hold the paper in place.

Place one ream of paper on the feed table so that the stack is against the far left retainer pad.

Adjust the feed rolls over the margins of the paper.

Raise the table so the top of the paper stack is about ⅛ inch above the metal plate.

3. Set the copy counter for the desired number of copies.

4. Attach the stencil to the cylinder.

Open the clamps and remove the protective cover from the cylinder.

Hold the stencil at the bottom edge with the backing sheet side toward you and attach the stencil stub to the stub hooks. Close the clamp.

Separate the stencil from the backing. Tear off and discard the backing.

Turn the cylinder slowly while laying the stencil smoothly over the ink pad. Ease out any wrinkles.

Open the side and end clamps. Lay in the stencil and close the clamps.

When blockout material is used on the cylinder, it is not necessary to close the side or bottom clamps to hold the stencil in place. This saves time and is less messy

5. Set the guides on the receiving tray for the length and width of the paper being used.

6. Run copies.

Switch the machine to the ON position.

Move the feed lever to the ON position.

The automatic counter will shut off the feed when the required number of copies has been made. When finished, turn the machine to the OFF position.

7. Remove the stencil and discard it, or place it in a special cover if you wish to retain it. Replace the protective cover on the machine cylinder.

Hints

Tape a copy to the front cover of the stencil holder if you are planning to retain a stencil. This will enable you to easily identify the stencils kept on file.

Most of the inks used in this type of process can be removed from clothing if you spray it with hair spray while still wet, then blot and rinse with clear, cool water. It is best to check the fabric with a little hair spray in an inconspicuous spot to be sure that no discoloration or damage will occur.

Offset Process

The offset process used to be done by chemically fixing the copy onto a metal plate. Currently, either a specially typed master form or the xerography method is used to make the master copy. The impression is inked and pressed against a rubber sheet which then transfers the image to a copy sheet. This operation is done by a powered machine. Thousands of copies can be produced by this method, and the masters can be stored and reused.

Raised Image Process

There are many techniques for producing raised image printing. However, the master copy is made by a typesetting machine such as those used in the printing process. Work requiring this type of process is usually sent out to a printer for setting.

EDUCATIONAL ORGANIZATIONS

American Association for Gifted
Children, Inc.
15 Gramercy Park
New York, NY 10003

American Association of
Community and Junior Colleges
One Dupont Circle, N.W.,
Suite 410
Washington, DC 20036

American Association of School
Administrators
1801 N. Moore Street
Arlington, VA 22209

American Association of University
Women
2401 Virginia Avenue, N.W.
Washington, DC 20037

American Camping Association
Bradford Woods
Martinsville, IN 46151

American Council on Education
One Dupont Circle, N.W.
Washington, DC 20036

American Library Association
50 E. Huron
Chicago, IL 60611

American Montessori Society
150 Fifth Avenue
New York, NY 10011

American Personnel and Guidance
Association
1607 New Hampshire Avenue,
N.W.
Washington, DC 20009

Arizona Association of Independent
Academic Schools, Inc.
4832 E. Weldon
Phoenix, AZ 85018

Association for Childhood Education
International
3615 Wisconsin Avenue, N.W.
Washington, DC 20016

Association of American Colleges
1818 R Street, N.W.
Washington, DC 20009

The Association of American
Universities
One Dupont Circle, Suite 730
Washington, DC 20036

Association of California School
Administrators
1575 Old Bayshore Highway
Burlingame, CA 94010

Association of Colleges and
Secondary Schools
Barber-Scotia College
Concord, NC

Association of Colorado Independent
Schools
4000 East Quincy Avenue
Englewood, CO 80110

Association of Military Colleges and
Schools of the United States
P.O. Box 1309
Alexandria, VA 22313

California Association of
Independent Schools
1510 Monte Vista
Santa Barbara, CA 93108

The College Board
888 Seventh Avenue
New York, NY 10019

Council for Advancement and
Support of Education
One Dupont Circle, Suite 530
Washington, DC 20036

Council for American Private
Education
1625 Eye Street, N.W.
Washington, DC 20006

Council for Basic Education
725 Fifteenth Street, N.W.
Washington, DC 20006

The Council for Exceptional
Children
1920 Association Drive
Reston, VA 22091

Council for Religion in Independent
Schools
107 S. Broad Street
Kennett Square, PA 19348

Cum Laude Society
4 Liberty Square
Boston, MA 02109

Educational Records Bureau
100 Worcester Road
Wellesley, MA 02181

Educational Testing Service
Princeton, NJ 08541

European Council of International
Schools
19 Claremont Road
Surbiton, Surrey KT6 4QR, England

Friends Council on Education
1507 Cherry Street
Philadelphia, PA 19102

International Association of
Counseling Services
1607 New Hampshire Avenue,
N.W.
Washington, DC 20034

International Schools Association
Palais Wilson 20
1211 Geneva 14, Switzerland

National Association for Foreign
Student Affairs
1860 19 Street, N.W.
Washington, DC 20009

National Association for Creative
Children and Adults
8080 Springvalley Drive
Cincinnati, OH 45236

National Association for the
Education of Young Children
1834 Connecticut Avenue, N.W.
Washington, DC 20009

National Association of Elementary
School Principals
1801 N. Moore Street
Arlington, VA 22209

National Association of Independent
Schools
4 Liberty Square
Boston, MA 02109

National Association of Teachers
Agencies
1825 K Street, N.W., Suite 706
Washington, DC 20006

National Catholic Educational
Association
One Dupont Circle, N.W.
Washington, DC 20036

National Society for the Study of
Education
5835 Kimbark Avenue
Chicago, IL 60637

New England Association of Schools
and Colleges, Inc.
131 Middlesex Turnpike
Burlington, MA 01803

New York State Association of
Independent Schools
33 Warder Drive
Pittsford, NY 14534

The Religious Education Association
409 Prospect Street
New Haven, CT 06510

The Secondary School Admission
Test Board
Box 2610
Princeton, NJ 08540

Western Association of Schools and
Colleges
1614 Rollins Road
Burlingame, CA 94010

EDUCATIONAL PUBLICATIONS

AMERICAN EDUCATION
U.S. Office of Education
Washington, DC 20202

AMERICAN FORESTS
1319 18 Street, N.W.
Washington, DC 20036

AMERICAN JOURNAL OF
SOCIOLOGY
University of Chicago Press
11030 Langley Avenue
Chicago, IL 60628

THE AMERICAN SCHOLAR
1811 O Street, N.W.
Washington, DC 20009

AMERICAN SOCIOLOGICAL
REVIEW
American Sociological Association
1722 N Street, N.W.
Washington, DC 20036

THE AMERICAN TEACHER
American Federation of Teachers
1012 14 Street, N.W.
Washington, DC 20005

ANIMAL KINGDOM
N.Y. Zoological Society
Zoological Park
Bronx, NY 10460

THE ANNALS
The American Academy of Political
and Social Science
3937 Chestnut Street
Philadelphia, PA 19104

ANTIOCH REVIEW
Box 148
Yellow Springs, Ohio 45387

ARCHAEOLOGY
Editorial & Business Office
Archaeological Institute of America
53 Park Place
New York, NY 10007

BOOK REVIEW DIGEST
H.W. Wilson Co.
950 University Avenue
Bronx, NY 10452

BOYS' LIFE
The Boy Scouts of America
North Brunswick, NJ 08902

CHILDHOOD EDUCATION
3615 Wisconsin Avenue, N.W.
Washington, DC 20016

THE CLEARINGHOUSE
Heldref Publications
4000 Albemarle Street, N.W.
Washington, DC 20016

THE CREATIVE CHILD AND
ADULT
National Association for Creative
Children and Adults
8080 Springvalley Drive
Cincinnati, OH 45236

CURRENT BIOGRAPHY
H.W. Wilson Co.
950 University Avenue
Bronx, NY 10452

CURRENT HISTORY
4225 Main Street
Philadelphia, PA 19127

EDUCATION
1362 Santa Cruz Court
Chula Vista, CA 92010

EDUCATION AND TRAINING OF
THE MENTALLY RETARDED
The Council for Exceptional
Children
Mental Retardation Division
1920 Association Drive
Reston, VA 22091

THE EDUCATION DIGEST
Box 8623
Ann Arbor, MI 48107

EDUCATION INDEX
H.W. Wilson Co.
950 University Avenue
Bronx, NY 10452

THE EDUCATIONAL FORUM
116 Ramseyer Hall
Ohio State University
Columbus, Ohio 43210

EDUCATIONAL RECORD
American Council on Education
One Dupont Circle
Washington, DC 20036

THE ELEMENTARY SCHOOL
JOURNAL
University of Chicago Press
11030 Langley Avenue
Chicago, IL 60628

ENGLISH JOURNAL
1111 Kenyon Road
Urbana, IL 61801

ETC.: A Review of General
Semantics
P.O. Box 2469
San Francisco, CA 94126

EXCEPTIONAL CHILDREN
The Council for Exceptional
Children
1920 Association Drive
Reston, VA 22091

THE EXCEPTIONAL PARENT
P.O. Box 4944
Manchester, NH 03108

FOREIGN AFFAIRS
58 East 68 Street
New York, NY 10021

FRONTIERS, Magazine of Natural
History
Academy of Natural Sciences of
Philadelphia
19 and Parkway
Philadelphia, PA 19103

THE GEOGRAPHICAL REVIEW
American Geographical Society
Broadway at 156 Street
New York, NY 10032

THE GIFTED CHILD
QUARTERLY
National Association for Gifted
Children
217 Gregory Drive
Hot Springs, AR 71901

THE GUIDEPOST
American Personnel and Guidance
Association
1607 New Hampshire Avenue,
N.W.
Washington, DC 20009

HARVARD EDUCATIONAL
REVIEW
Longfellow Hall
13 Appian Way
Cambridge, MA 02138

INDEPENDENT SCHOOL
National Association of Independent
Schools
4 Liberty Square
Boston, MA 02109

INSTRUCTIONAL PSYCHOLOGY
P.O. Box 5630
Milwaukee, WI 53211

JOURNAL OF EDUCATION
765 Commonwealth Avenue
Boston, MA 02215

JOURNAL OF EDUCATIONAL
RESEARCH
P.O. Box 1605
Madison, WI 53701

JOURNAL OF EXPERIMENTAL
EDUCATION
P.O. Box 1605
Madison, WI 53701

THE JOURNAL OF GENERAL
EDUCATION
The Pennsylvania State University
Press
University Park, PA 16802

JOURNAL OF HIGHER
EDUCATION
Ohio State University Press
2070 Neil Avenue
Columbus, OH 43210

MATHEMATICS TEACHER
National Council of Teachers of
Mathematics
1906 Association Drive
Reston, VA 22091

THE MODERN LANGUAGE
JOURNAL
National Federation of Modern
Language Teachers Association, Inc
University of Nebraska
Omaha, NE 68182

NATIONAL GEOGRAPHIC
17 and M Streets, N.W.
Washington, DC 20036

NATIONAL GEOGRAPHIC
WORLD
17 and M Streets, N.W.
Washington, DC 20036

NATION'S SCHOOLS REPORT
Capitol Publications, Inc.
2430 Pennsylvania Avenue,
Suite G-12
Washington, DC 20037

THE NEW REPUBLIC
1220 19 Street, N.W.
Washington, DC 20036

PEABODY JOURNAL OF
EDUCATION
George Peabody College for
Teachers
Nashville, TN 37203

PERSONNEL AND GUIDANCE
JOURNAL
American Personnel and Guidance
Association
1607 New Hampshire Avenue,
N.W.
Washington, DC 20009

THE PROGRESSIVE
408 West Gorham Street
Madison, WI 53703

PSYCHIATRY: Journal for the
Study of Interpersonal Processes
William Alanson White Psychiatric
Foundation
1610 New Hampshire Avenue,
N.W.
Washington, DC 20009

QUARTERLY REVIEW OF
LITERATURE
26 Haslet Avenue
Princeton, NJ 08540

READING IMPROVEMENT
1362 Santa Cruz Court
Chula Vista, CA 92010

RELIGIOUS EDUCATION
409 Prospect Street
New Haven, CT 06510

THE ROUND TABLE
18 Northumberland Avenue
London, WC2 N5BJ, England

SATURDAY REVIEW
1290 Avenue of the Americas
New York, NY 10019

SCHOOL REVIEW
University of Chicago Press
11030 Langley Avenue
Chicago, IL 60628

SCHOOL SCIENCE AND
MATHEMATICS
P.O. Box 1614
Indiana University of Pennsylvania
Indiana, PA 15701

SCIENCE ACTIVITIES
Heldref Publications
4000 Albemarle Street, N.W.
Washington, DC 20016

SCIENCE NEWS
1719 N Street, N.W.
Washington, DC 20036

SCIENTIFIC AMERICAN
415 Madison Avenue
New York, NY 10017

THE SIGHT-SAVING REVIEW
79 Madison Avenue
New York, NY 10016

THE SOCIAL STUDIES
Heldref Publications
400 Albemarle Street, N.W.
Washington, DC 20016

SOCIOLOGY OF EDUCATION
American Sociological Association
1722 N Street, N.W.
Washington, DC 20036

TEACHER
77 Bedrord Street
Stamford, CT 06901

TEACHING EXCEPTIONAL
CHILDREN
The Council for Exceptional
Children
1920 Association Drive
Reston, VA 22091

THOUGHT
Fordham University Press
Bronx, NY 10458

TODAY'S EDUCATION
1201 16 Street, N.W.
Washington, DC 20036

TRAVEL
Travel Building
Floral Park, NY 11001

URBAN EDUCATION
Sage Publications
275 S. Beverly Drive
Beverly Hills, CA 90212

THE YALE REVIEW
1902A Yale Station
New Haven, CT 06520

EDUCATIONAL SUPPLIERS Check the Yellow Pages of your telephone directory for additional suppliers in your area.

Scientific Supplies

Edmund Scientific
101 E. Gloucester Pike
Barrington, NJ 08007
(609) 547-8900

Rascher & Betzold, Inc.
5410 N. Damien Avenue
Chicago, IL 60625
(312) 275-7300

First Aid and Medical Supplies

H. L. Moore
P.O. Box 156
New Britain, CT 06050
(203) 225-4621

A. J. Masuen Co.
11 Central Avenue, N.W.
Le Mars, IA 51031
(712) 546-4563

Audio-Visual Equipment and Materials

R. V. Butterworth, Inc.
P.O. Box 4893
Hayward, CA 94540
(415) 785-4230

6959 California Avenue
Portland, OR 97211
(503) 288-6733

5417 NE 30 Avenue
Seattle, WA 98136
(206) 938-4677

Wholesale Educational Suppliers Co.
63 South Fourth Avenue
Mt. Vernon, NY 10550
(914) 664-8200

Graphic Supplies & Equipment

Hartco Products Company, Inc.
357 W. Pearl Street
West Jefferson, OH 43162
(614) 879-8315

Institutional Supplies

Belmont Jobbing & Supply
2775 Shermer Road
Northbrook, IL 60062
(312) 564-3850

Photo & Sound
Corporate Headquarters
116 Natoma Street
San Francisco, CA 94105
(415) 421-0410
(locations in 7 states)

Northeast AudioVisual Inc.
548 Donald Street
Bedford, NH 03102
(603) 668-5511

EMERGENCY PROCEDURES   It is hoped that you will never need to use the information in this section, but it could save your life as well as the lives of students and other school personnel. It is far better to know emergency procedures that you will never use than to be caught in an emergency without knowing what to do. While some of the information given here may seem to cover areas outside the realm of the school secretary, it is possible that you may have to use it, especially if you work in a small school or a rural area. Here, then, is what to do in case disaster strikes, based on the advise and recommendations of the Federal Emergency Management Agency and the American Red Cross.

General Guidelines

Most disasters strike without warning, so it is essential to follow these rules:

- KEEP CALM

  This can mean the difference between life and death. When people panic they behave in an irrational manner. History shows numerous tragic incidents of death and injury during disasters that could have been prevented if people had not panicked.

- THINK

  Do not rush into any action without taking a moment to assess the situation.

- LEARN YOUR AREA'S WARNING SIGNALS

  Most communities have some type of emergency outdoor warning system such as a siren. For example, a three- to five-minute steady blast often means that you should turn on your radio or television for emergency information. It is a good idea to check with your local Office of Emergency Services before disaster strikes.

- TRY NOT TO USE THE TELEPHONE

  Learn to rely on your battery-operated radio instead of the telephone during emergencies. Telephone lines should be kept clear for reporting emergency events to local authorities. If you tie up telephone lines to get information, you could prevent vital calls from being received and thereby worsen the situation.

- KEEP EMERGENCY SUPPLIES ON HAND

  In any major disaster your supplies of food, water, and medical aids will be severely limited. Prepare well in advance and keep a stock of supplies. Some school districts follow excellent emergency procedures, while others are quite lax in this area. Discuss with your administrator the need to be prepared. If the responsibility for arranging emergency supplies or procedures falls to you, take care of it. The more you know about emergencies and how to cope with them, the better your chances for survival. You will then be alive to help others who may not have been so prudent.

Emergency Supplies Checklist

- Water stored in unbreakable plastic containers
- Food canned or sealed, that does not require cooking or refrigeration
- First aid kit
- Blankets
- Flashlights or lanterns with operational batteries and spares

- Radio that is battery-powered, with extra batteries
- Emergency toilet
- Fire extinguishers (know how to operate them in advance)
- Chlorine bleach for purifying water, or water purification tablets

Water Supply

Water is an even more important consideration than food. An average adult requires at least one quart of water per day. You can estimate your emergency water supply needs by multiplying this amount by the number of people in your school. For example, a school population of 300 would require 75 gallons of water per day. Latest studies indicate that under no circumstances should water be rationed to make it last. It is safer to drink as needed than to ration. If you have no stored water available, there are still sources available within most buildings such as the hot water tank, the flush tanks (not bowls) of toilets, and the pipes of the plumbing system.

To make suspicious or contaminated water safe to drink, add one of the following: (1) water purifying tablets (obtained at drug stores) at the ratio of four tablets per gallon; (2) liquid chlorine household bleach, provided the label says it contains *hypochlorite* as its *only* active ingredient at the ratio of eight to ten drops per gallon; (3) two percent tincture of iodine at the ratio of twelve drops per gallon. If water is cloudy or foul-smelling, double these amounts.

Emergency Toilets

In major disasters the sewer lines will probably be damaged. So that you do not further contaminate the water supply, it is safest to use emergency toilets consisting of watertight containers with tight-fitting lids, such as garbage cans. Each time the emergency toilet is used, pour in a small amount of disinfectant such as chlorine bleach to reduce bacteria and odor. After each use, replace the lid. The contents of the container should be buried one or two feet deep to prevent the spread of disease by rats and insects.

Earthquakes

Many schools in earthquake-prone areas hold regular earthquake drills in which the students are taught to take cover and protect themselves from flying debris. (We who live in California are quite accustomed to earthquake activity, but this can sometimes be a detriment to our safety as we tend to overlook potential dangers and the havoc that earthquakes can cause.)

If you work in a school with a large student population, the role of the school secretary in earthquake emergency procedures will probably be quite small—you may only need to look out for yourself. If, however, you are a secretary in a small school, the burden of responsibility could fall squarely on your shoulders. If an earthquake strikes during school hours when the administrator is off the premises, you will more than likely be the person to whom students and faculty alike will turn for guidance, since you and the administrator are often permanently linked in people's minds. Here, then, are some basic emergency procedures that you should know in case of an earthquake.

Earthquakes hit without warning. So far, no reliable methods of earthquake prediction have been discovered. Although experiencing the movement of the earth beneath your feet can be a frightening experience, earthquakes themselves seldom cause death or injury. However, the movement of the earth can cause buildings to topple or debris to fall. Most casualties result from such falling objects, fires, and explosions caused by rupturing gas lines and automobile gas tanks.

What to Do When an Earthquake Hits

1. KEEP CALM.

   Do not panic. If you take proper precautions, you will most likely be unharmed. There is a story of a Westerner who was visiting Tokyo. While he was eating in a restaurant with a group of Western and Oriental friends, a massive earthquake struck. As the building began to sway, the Westerners screamed and ran in panic while one of the Oriental men in the group sat calmly throughout the experience and resumed eating as soon as the movement of the earth stopped. His tremendous calm and acceptance of nature so influenced one of the Westerners that he questioned the Oriental, only to discover that he was a Zen master. The Westerner spent the next six years in Japan studying Oriental philosophy in an attempt to achieve such peace of mind. Most of those who panicked and ran were injured; those who remained or calmly took cover were unharmed.

2. STAY WHERE YOU ARE.

   If you are outdoors, stay there. Move away from buildings and utility wires. Stay in open, clear spaces if possible.

   If you are indoors, stay there. Take cover under heavy furniture such as a desk or table. Avoid glass, windows, and outside doors. If there is no large furniture, brace yourself under the door of an *inside* (preferably support wall) door. After you have reached a place of safety, cover your head with your arms.

Most injuries occur while trying to run from one place to the next. STAY WHERE YOU ARE.

3. DO NOT USE OPEN FLAMES.

   Do not light candles, matches, cigarette lighters, or other open flames. Gas lines may have been ruptured during the quake and open flames can cause explosions.

4. EXTINGUISH FIRES IMMEDIATELY.

   The fire department may not be able to help you in the aftermath of a major earthquake. The basic rules of firefighting are:

   a. Remove the fuel.

   b. Remove the air (smother the fire).

   c. Douse the fire (with water or an extinguisher). Try to save your water supply in an emergency. You will need it to survive.

   In *electrical fires, shut off the electricity first.* Then douse the flames with water or blankets, or use an extinguisher suitable for electrical fires. *Do not attempt to extinguish an electrical fire with water unless you have shut off the source of the electricity.*

   In *oil or grease fires,* try to shut off the source of whatever is burning, then smother it with sand, earth, or blankets. *Do not use water on grease or oil;* it will cause the flames to spread. For small grease fires, salt or baking soda may be used.

   In *gas fires,* shut off the gas supply. (Make sure you know where the gas and electric shutoff valves are located.) Then use water or smother the flames.

5. In the small school, the school secretary is sometimes called upon to chaperone students on outings, or drive injured students to the doctor. If you are in a car when an earthquake strikes, stay in the car. If you decide to proceed after the main quake, remember that there are usually aftershocks—watch out for power lines. *Never approach downed electrical lines.*

What to Do After the Earthquake

1. Check for injuries. Do not move the seriously injured unless they are in further immediate danger.

2. Check water, electricity, and gas lines for damage. Since severe aftershocks may still occur, shut off the valves even though the lines may be unharmed.

3. Check sewage lines. If they are damaged or you are unsure, prevent further flushing of toilets and use emergency toilets.

4. Check any chimneys for damage as fire could result.

5. Evacuate severely damaged buildings. Aftershocks could cause the building to collapse.

6. Do not listen to rumors. Do not spread rumors. Speculation causes panic.

7. Keep telephone lines clear. Listen to your radio for instructions.

8. Stay away from hazardous areas.

9. Prepare yourself and the students for additional aftershocks.

10. Check to make sure all students are accounted for by calling the roll or checking with the teachers.

11. Begin emergency survival procedures as already outlined.

12. Hold all children at school until called for by the parents or until you nave *written permission* to release them.

Floods

It is unlikely that you will be in school when a flood hits, as flood warnings are issued when rainfall or melting snow reaches a high enough level to cause rivers to overflow, and schools are usually closed. If, however, school is in session when a flood warning occurs, the school may have to be evacuated, or in some cases you may actually be stuck at school until the flood waters subside. Just in case, here are some emergency procedures to follow:

1. Know in advance how high the school ground is above possible flood level. When the warnings are broadcast, you can then know whether or not your school is a likely candidate for flooding.

2. Have emergency supplies readily available and know where they are kept.

3. Know where sandbags, plastic sheeting, and other such materials are stored. Never place sandbags around the outside walls of a building at the basement level to prevent flooding. The pressure of seeping water can cause severe structural damage. Instead, let the water flood the basement level. This will equalize pressure on the outside of the building and avoid structural damage to the foundations.

4. If there is time, arrange to have valuable equipment moved to upper floors of the school.

If you receive *evacuation* warnings:

1. Follow the instructions of local authorities.
2. Make sure all students are accounted for and arrangements have been made for their disposition. Make sure that you have *written parental permission* before releasing minors during an emergency.
3. Make sure the building is secure before leaving.
4. Travel with caution. Do not wait too long so that you are marooned. If parents cannot be located in time to pick up their children, they may have to stay with you or other school personnel. Check with the administrator and use common sense. This is a potential life and death emergency.

If you have been caught at school during the flood, when the flood is over:

1. Do not eat food that has been contaminated by flood waters.
2. Be sure water is safe to drink. Purify it when in doubt.
3. Cut off all sources of electricity—*carefully. Do not handle live electrical equipment in wet areas.*
4. Use *only* battery-powered flashlights or lanterns.
5. If possible, report broken power lines and utilities to the police, fire department, or other appropriate agencies.
6. Keep listening to your radio for instructions and further warnings.

If you should be out of doors with students when a flash flood warning is relayed:

1. Stay away from natural streams and water channels.
2. Head for the high ground.
3. Stay calm, and follow emergency procedures.

Hurricanes

A *hurricane watch* means that a hurricane is threatening coastal or inland areas. It does *not* mean a hurricane is imminent. A *hurricane warning* is issued when it is expected to strike within twenty-four hours. If you are at school when a hurricane is imminent, here's what to do:

1. Stay calm.
2. Take an attendance list to keep track of students.
3. Listen to your radio for the latest bulletins.
4. Keep in close contact with your administrator and help in any way you can.

5. Board up windows to prevent injuries from flying glass.

6. Make sure outdoor objects are secure and will not be carried through windows.

7. Make sure your emergency supplies are ready.

8. Check batteries in your equipment.

9. If there is not time to dismiss school, stay inside wherever you are.

10. Remain indoors during the hurricane. Travel is extremely dangerous.

11. Do not be fooled by the eye of the hurricane. If the storm center passes directly over you, there will be a brief lull of a few minutes to half an hour. After this lull, or passing of the eye, the rest of the hurricane will hit with full force—stay inside.

When the hurricane is over:

1. Stay inside until local authorities let you know it is safe to leave.

2. Keep tuned to your radio for instructions.

3. Stay away from potentially dangerous areas.

4. Avoid loose or dangling wires.

5. Report broken utility lines to police or fire departments.

6. Take precautions to prevent fires.

7. Familiarize yourself with emergency flood procedures as hurricanes can cause severe flooding.

Tornadoes

A tornado is an extremely violent storm with high-speed whirling winds. The tornado funnel cloud spins like a top and may sound as loud as a roaring train. Tornadoes frequently accompany hurricanes. When a tornado warning is issued—take notice immediately.

1. Go to a storm cellar.

2. Stay away from windows.

3. If there is no cellar, take shelter in interior hallways on the lowest floor. *Stay out of auditoriums and gymnasiums.* Their structure makes them extremely unsafe during tornadoes.

4. If you are outside, take cover and lie flat in the nearest ditch, ravine, or depression in the ground.

5. When the tornado has passed, check for injuries and damage; then follow appropriate emergency procedures.

Severe Storms

Severe storms are a common winter hazard in certain areas of the country. They are something you simply learn to live with, but keep safety precautions in mind, be aware of weather conditions, and make use of radio, television, and newspapers to stay alert to potential storm hazards. Here is some information about severe storms that will better enable you to cope with the situation.

A *blizzard* is the most dangerous of winter storms. A *severe blizzard warning* means that you can expect winds of forty-five miles per hour at least, with temperatures lower than ten degrees.

A *heavy snow warning* can mean an expected snowfall of four inches or more in a twelve-hour period.

As with other emergency weather conditions, it is possible that severe winter storms could strand you at school for an indefinite period. If this should happen, here are some guidelines to follow:

1. Use heating fuel sparingly. Dress warmly and turn down thermostats to conserve fuel.
2. The school should be closed off so that you and other personnel or students are centrally located in a confined area where you can conserve energy.
3. Make sure that there are emergency supplies and that you know their location. Do not rely on someone else's knowledge. Often in emergencies, people become befuddled and forgetful because of stress.
4. Bring to your confined area:
   food and medical supplies
   emergency backup heaters
   extra blankets
   flashlights and batteries
   radio
   simple tools
   fire extinguishers
   water supply
5. Keep extra warm clothes at school if you live in an area that is subject to severe winter storms. You may need them in an emergency.

Tidal Waves

If you live in an earthquake area near the ocean, tidal wave activity is a very real possibility. A tidal wave (tsunami) is actually a series of waves caused by sudden shifts in the ocean floor. If you are outdoors, perhaps chaperoning or traveling with students near the ocean, be aware of these safety pointers:

1. While not all earthquakes spawn tsunamis, many do. If you are in a coastal area when there is an earthquake, be prepared for a tidal wave.

2. If you can, get to high ground away from the ocean.

3. Remember, a tsunami is a *series* of waves, not just one giant wave. Stay clear of the area until local authorities inform you that danger is passed.

4. If you are at the ocean and the water line suddenly recedes, evacuate the area immediately—a tidal wave could be imminent.

5. Depend on your local authorities for information and follow emergency procedures.

Fires

Your local fire department will handle fires in the normal course of events. At most, you would be required to activate the fire alarm and contact the fire department. In an emergency such as a natural disaster or nuclear attack, however, local authorities may not be immediately available. Here are some guidelines for preventing and handling fires under emergency conditions:

To Prevent Fires

1. Make sure that papers and flammable items are not permitted to accumulate. Files and papers should be housed in metal file cabinets. The storing of "dead files" in cardboard boxes or containers is a fire hazard and should be discouraged.

2. Do not overload electrical circuits. Check your typewriter and equipment cords for fraying. Have the cords repaired or replaced as needed. Make sure extension cords are of adequate size to carry the electrical load.

3. Any flammable liquids such as duplicating machine supplies, machine oil, etc., should be stored in closed *metal* containers.

4. Do not place books or papers on heaters.

5. Keep a fire extinguisher nearby and *know how to use it.*

If the Fire Has Begun

1. If it is a small fire, attempt to extinguish it by
   a. taking away the fuel,
   b. smothering it,
   c. cooling it with water or an extinguisher.
2. If the fire is too large to control, evacuate the area and take an attendance list with you to check for missing students.
3. Fires can spread rapidly. Take no chances: lives are more valuable than property.
4. Remember not to use water on grease or electrical fires.

Nuclear Attack

This section is included after much deliberation and vacillation. At first glance, it may seem farfetched and remote from the realm of the school secretary, but after some reflection about our unstable world condition, it seemed reasonable to include it.

In the case of a nationwide attack, people close to the blast area would be killed or severely injured; people a few miles away would be damaged by heat and light from the blast and fallout; people who were outside the immediate area would not be affected by the blast but would still be subject to fallout.

In case of an attack, you would need protection from:

1. the blast,
2. initial radiation,
3. heat, fire, explosions,
4. radioactive fallout.

If fallout shelters are available in your community, familiarize yourself with their locations. The less you are exposed to fallout, the less radiation damage you will receive. A fallout shelter can be any space, provided the walls and roof are thick enough (concrete, brick, thick lumber) to absorb the dangerous gamma rays. In many communities, schools serve as fallout shelters. Public fallout shelters may be identified by the standard yellow and black fallout shelter signs.

Most communities have adopted standard warning signals in case of enemy attack. An *attack warning signal* is a three- to five-minute *wavering sound* made by sirens, or a series of *short blasts on whistles,* horns, or other equipment. These warning signals mean that a real enemy attack has been detected and that immediate protective action should be taken.

The *alert signal* is used by some communities to warn of an impending *natural disaster* or *other emergency*—this is a three-to-five-minute *steady blast* on sirens, whistles, or horns.

What to Do if You Hear a Signal

1. The school population should immediately take cover in the nearest fallout shelter or protective environment (unless government authorities have given other instructions).
2. Turn on your battery-operated radio and tune to the station that is broadcasting official emergency information. Follow the instructions given.
3. If there is no time to get to a shelter, improvise. (See section "How to Improvise a Fallout Shelter.")
4. Do *not* use the telephone. Depend on radio or television broadcasts for information. The telephone lines must be kept clear for official calls.
5. If there is a sudden bright flash, *take cover immediately*. If you protect yourself *within a few seconds*, you might avoid serious damage from the intense heat and blast. Never look at the flash: you could be blinded.

Where to Take Cover

1. The most sheltered and protected part of a building
2. A tunnel or subway (if outdoors)
3. A cave or outcrop of rocks (you may be on a field trip)
4. Under a parked car or bus
5. Under heavy furniture

After taking cover, lie on your side in a curled up position. Cover your head with your arms and hands.

After the blast and heat waves have passed, get to a shelter right away to protect yourself from radioactive fallout. If you have been exposed to radiation, a thorough washing with soap and water is recommended if possible.

How to Improvise a Fallout Shelter

If there is no time to get to a permanent fallout shelter, you may have to improvise. The basement or storm cellar would be the best choice, or the most protected interior area closest to the ground.

An improvised shelter will need shielding materials as protection from radioactive fallout. Following is a list of possible shielding materials:

- concrete blocks
- bricks
- sand
- doors
- large heavy furniture
- boxes or cartons filled with sand (fill them after you move them into place)
- stacked lumber
- stacked building materials

The shielding material should be positioned to cover as much of the wall, floor, and ceiling space as possible. Be sure to cover windows. Then, follow the general instructions under EMERGENCY PROCEDURES.

EMOTIONAL CRISES   On occasion you may have to deal with people who are in a state of emotional upheaval. They may be severely mentally ill or temporarily unstable because of a sudden trauma. If a person's behavior seems strange or threatening:

- Stay calm.
- Get help immediately. Inform the administrator, police, ambulance, or other relevant agencies.
- While waiting for help to arrive, do not antagonize the person. Remain calm. Your mood can easily be transferred to another person who is already upset. If you seem agitated, you can make it worse.
- Do not involve yourself with the person any more than is absolutely necessary. You could do more harm than good. Wait for trained personnel to arrive, but be prepared to protect yourself if necessary.

EMPLOYMENT

Applications

In large school districts, hiring is usually done at a central location by a specific employment department. In small or private schools, however, the administration is responsible for hiring and firing. If you are responsible for helping to process employment applications, here are some suggestions:

- Applications may be solicited by advertising or search committee processes or may arrive unsolicited in the form of a letter accompanied by a résumé. If the application arrives as a standard school employment application form, scan it to be sure that all the necessary blanks are filled out before giving it to the administrator. If the case of unsolicited employment requests, staple the résumé to the letter and give both to the administrator.
- When the position is filled, it is customary for small institutions to notify

candidates by mail that there is no longer a vacancy. This is often done with a form letter.

- The secretary may be responsible for completing and gathering the following information and placing it in the new teacher's file:
  - Signed employment contract
  - Credential number or certified copy of credential
  - Health forms
  - Benefit forms such as insurance and retirement
  - Tax withholding forms
  - Transcripts of college records
  - Various personnel forms as necessary
  - Emergency information card
  - Evidence of chest X-ray for tuberculosis clearance if necessary
  - Fingerprint card if required

Termination

Usually, either a letter of resignation or explanation is included in the employee's file. All other forms pertaining to the employee can then be gathered and filed together in that person's folder. It is helpful to mark the date of termination, a forwarding address, and any other pertinent information, on the inside cover of the folder in case you need it for future reference or employment verification. The fold is then ready to be filed in the inactive personnel file.

ENROLLMENT

Employee Enrollment

The forms used for personnel enrollment will vary from school to school. There are, however, some standardized categories:

The Application Form

This may be a simple single-page form containing basic employee information such as name, address, telephone, social security number, and a brief résumé; or it may be an elaborate multipage snap-out data processing form that will be analyzed and/or stored by computer.

W-4 Form

This government form is to be filled out by all employees and indicates the number of legal deductions to be considered when figuring the payroll.

Medical Insurance Applications

Most plans require that the applicant fill out a form indicating age and past medical history as well as dependents and/or beneficiaries. Some plans also require a physical examination.

Life Insurance Application Form

If your school offers this option, a form will need to be filled out by the employee and a beneficiary will need to be designated.

Retirement Application Form

Some schools require that an applicant be employed for a specific number of months prior to being eligible for a retirement plan. Many independent schools belong to TIAA (Teachers Insurance and Annuity Association), which offers retirement and life insurance plans at group rates to independent schools and colleges. One big advantage of this plan is that the participant can transfer it to any other participating school or college.

Student Enrollment

1. Make up a separate file for each student. The file package should include:
   - a copy of the application,
   - a copy of the tuition contract (if applicable),
   - previous school records,
   - current medical records,
   - current test data,
   - applicable financial aid data,
   - applicable correspondence,
   - other data such as I-20 forms for foreign students.
2. Inform the student or parent of any required immunizations or X-rays for tuberculosis.
3. Make sure that any applicable tuition contracts have been turned in and that all monies have been paid.
4. Have the student (or parent if the student is a minor) sign a release form and obtain a transcript from the previous school.
5. Have any required state, county, or city forms filled out and send them to the appropriate agency.
6. If financial aid is requested, direct the student to the financial aid officer or provide the necessary forms.
7. Give the student a copy of his or her schedule.

8. Arrange for a locker and make sure the number is recorded.

9. Arrange for student orientation. This may be done in groups, or individually, depending on the size of your school and the age of the students. At the elementary level it works well to have a classmate act as a guide to show the new student around.

10. Place the student on the official roll register.

11. Make up a student address record. A speedy and accurate method for keeping student address records is to type them on 3×5 cards, which can then be kept in a file box or file register. The cards can be easily changed or replaced.

12. Be sure you have a student emergency card on file. This will give permission from the parent for medical assistance if the student is a minor. If the student is not a minor, it still gives information on whom to notify in case of emergency, and can note any drug allergies or medic alert warnings.

13. Notify the teachers. At the beginning of the term, you will provide them with class lists If a student enters at midterm, give the teachers a transfer slip.

Student Forms Used

Figures 9, 10 and 11 show sample forms commonly used in attendance/enrollment procedures.

EXCHANGE OF SUPPLIES OR EQUIPMENT If an item must be returned or exchanged, following these simple procedures can aid in promoting a smooth transaction:

— If there are manufacturer's or shipper's instructions regarding the return of merchandise, read them carefully and follow the instructions to the letter. This can speed up your request.

— Always include a letter of explanation with the returned merchandise, and remember to keep a copy on file.

— Be precise in your requests. What is wrong with the order as received? Do you want an exchange? If so, give complete details. Do you want a refund? A credit? Be specific.

— Avoid being rude or snide in your correspondence or conversations, even though you may be frustrated by incorrect orders. If you are polite, specific, and keep accurate records, your returns or exchanges should cause you little difficulty.

DUE DATE
FOR APPLICATION:

_____

APPLICATION FOR ADMISSION

Applicant's name_____
                      Last   First   Middle
                      (Please underline name by which applicant is to be called)

Home address_____
                No.   Street

_____ Telephone:_____
   City   State   Zip

Date of birth_____ Birthplace_____
              Month   Day   Year

Applying for grade_____ beginning September, 19_____ Present Grade _____

Present school_____
                  Name   Street   City   State

Please list schools attended:

             Name of school   Location   Dates attended

_____

_____

Father's name in full: Mother's name in full **including** maiden name:

_____   _____

Living?_____   Living?_____

Occupation_____   Occupation_____

Name, address, phone of business firm: Name, address, phone of business firm:

_____   _____

_____   _____

Name and location of school: Name and location of school:

High School_____   High School_____

College_____   College_____

Graduate School_____   Graduate School_____

Paternal Grandparents   Maternal Grandparents
of Applicant:_____   of Applicant:_____

Address:_____   Address:_____

Name and address of guardian if other than parent:

_____

FIGURE 9

Sample application form for elementary school

132

TRANSCRIPT OF RECORD

The _____ School will need the below information from your child's present school before we can process her application. Please indicate below that parent authorization is granted and send this form to her school.

I hereby authorize _____
                              (name of present school)

to release all records for _____
                                    (child's name)

to The _____ School.

_____   _____
Date   Parent Signature

The purpose of this form is for furnishing The _____ School with information that will help our Admissions Committee. We appreciate the information that you furnish us.

TRANSCRIPT OF RECORD

1. This certifies that _____ attended

the _____ school from _____ 19 ___

to _____ 19 ___ and is now in grade _____

2. Please rate the candidate's personal characterisitcs according to the following:

	Attitude	Industry	Dependability	Seriousness of purpose	Influence on others	Emotional stability
1. Exceptional						
2. Excellent						
3. Good						
4. Fair						
5. Poor						

3. Has the candidate attended school regularly? _____ If not, why? _____

4. Extra-curricular activities and special interests _____

5. Principal's recommendation:

6. Have all financial obligations been met promptly and in full? _____

_____   _____   _____
Date   Name   Title

FIGURE 10

Sample request for transcript form

133

Applicant's Name_____
(Please Print)   Last   First   Middle

    The student named above has applied for admission to The _____ School and has given your name as a reference. The Admissions Committee would be most appreciative if you would furnish the information requested below. Concrete illustrations are particularly helpful. Perhaps a limited knowledge of the applicant will prevent you from commenting on all of the topics listed below. Use your own judgment.

1. How long have you known the applicant, and in what specific relationship?

2. Character (honesty, sense of responsibility, potentiality for leadership, respect for authority, emotional stability)

3. Personality (manners, friendliness, individuality, sense of humor, maturity)

4. Study habits (initiative, industry, motivation, imagination, originality)

5. Social relationships (peers, adults)

6. Interest and proficiency in non-academic activities both in and out of school (clubs, sports, hobbies, jobs)

FIGURE 11

Sample reference request form used in admissions

134

FACULTY

Orientation of New Teachers

The administrator will usually handle orientation for new teachers at the beginning of the year, probably at a faculty meeting before the opening of school. However, you should be prepared to answer any questions or give directions if asked to do so. In the administrator's absence, or at his request, you may be responsible for orienting new or substitute teachers. Here are some suggestions:

1. Provide the new faculty member with a folder containing the following items:
   - Bell schedule or list showing lengths of periods, lunch breaks, recess
   - Attendance sheets for taking the roll
   - Simple map of the school layout showing restrooms, classrooms by number, cafeteria, and important offices
   - Lesson plan or list of duties
   - List of school regulations and discipline procedures
   - Fire drill instruction or emergency procedures
   - Report sheet for reporting activities to the regular teacher (in the case of substitutes)

2. Give the teacher any necessary keys or lock combinations.

3. Let the teacher know that you will be glad to answer questions or give explanations of the data contained in the folder.

4. If you can introduce the new teacher to another teacher who will be working close by, it will make him feel more at ease.

5. The new teacher or substitute should also be introduced to the principal or department chairman, if they have not already met, who may wish to carry out the orientation procedures instead.

Faculty Records

Faculty records are usually considered confidential. If employment verification is requested by credit companies, they will usually ask for the starting date of employment and sometimes a salary verification. Many schools prefer not to give out salary or other personal information without the consent of the staff member in question. Faculty records kept on file typically contain:

- a résumé
- college transcripts
- copies of teaching credentials or certificates
- medical information

- emergency information
- payroll information
- attendance records

Working with Faculty

A teacher's primary responsiblity is to the students, but in the performance of a teacher's duties a tremendous amount of paper work is generated, some of which will fall to you. Your responsibilities may include: typing minutes of meetings, faculty bulletins and reports, orienting new teachers, locating lost items, making copies, instructing teachers in the use of office or audio-visual equipment, and answering an endless list of questions. Here are some guidelines to help you work effectively with the faculty:

Budgeting Your Time

First, thoroughly discuss with the administrator which duties are yours and which are the teachers'. Then, based on your discussion, type up a list of duties that you will do for teachers, and a list of duties that the teachers will have to do for themselves. Keep these lists available for reference if questions should arise regarding responsibility.

Make notes on the frequency of work to be done for teachers—monthly, daily, weekly, at random.

When dealing with extras (requests that are not on your list), (1) consider the amount of time necessary to perform the task; (2) consider whether the teacher really needs your help or is sloughing off his responsibilities onto you; (3) consider whether this will become a habitual experience if you agree to do it once; (4) consider if you do a task for one teacher can you or do you want to do it for all teachers? Do not play favorites. Word spreads quickly and you will soon find it unpleasant to work with disgruntled faculty members.

How to Say "NO" Without Making Enemies

There will be times when you must refuse to do work or to spend time on a project. However, you will not wish to alienate a faculty member or create an unpleasant working relationship. In this case, give a reasonable explanation of why you cannot do the project. Do not simply say, "I'm too busy." Let the teacher know why you are too busy. Say something such as "I'd really like to help you out, but I'm working on a deadline to finish these Academic Committee Reports," or "I'm sorry I can't help you now, but the report cards must be finished by tomorrow." Teachers can relate to overwork and are usually quite understanding if you are pleasant and honest with them.

Dealing with Faculty Problems

Most faculty problems arise from poor communication. By the time information has been filtered through board, parents, students, or administration, it sometimes bears little resemblance to the original form. There may be little that you can do to alleviate this misinformation, but you can strive to promote a friendly atmosphere in which people will feel free to ask questions and air grievances before a situation becomes explosive. To promote this climate you can do the following:

- Never gossip. You will hear many facts and many rumors in your position. Repeat none of them. If possible, try not to listen to idle gossip—it wastes your time and it can cause a great deal of damage.
- Be friendly. Show interest in others without prying into their personal lives. Do not, however, let your office become a social center.
- Smile. It will not only brighten someone else's day but since smiling uses fewer facial muscles than frowning, you will age less visibly.
- Learn names. People usually feel that if you care enough to learn their names, you must care enough to consider them as people instead of mere numbers.
- Strive to be cooperative, flexible, tactful, discreet, honest, loyal, patient. This may seem an impossible order to fill (and on some days it definitely will be), but it's something to work toward.
- Refer major problems to the administrator. Do not give opinions on faculty disputes. Stay out of the line of fire as much as possible.

FEDERAL AND STATE REPORTS   A book could be written on this subject alone, but for the purposes of this entry there are only a few things to keep in mind:

- Government reports abound in many areas of education including accreditation, medical, funding, and demographic statistics.
- Almost all government reports, while requiring lengthy and detailed re-

sponses, provide lengthy and detailed instructions. If you read the instructions carefully, work slowly and carefully, and have accurate records to which you refer, you should have few if any problems.

– More often than not, the administration will handle the major reports. The school secretary may only need to gather information from the files and type up the final draft.

FILING   The filing system is the heart of any school, around which all other functions revolve. In order for all facets of the school to run smoothly, the filing system must (1) meet the needs of the particular school; (2) be maintained accurately as to active and inactive files; and (3) be conveniently located. This section will provide you with tips on how to set up or reorganize your school's system, how to maintain an efficient system, and how to make filing equipment work for you. If you should require more detailed information, you could refer to a booklet published by the National Association of Educational Secretaries, 1800 North Moore Street, Arlington, VA 22209, entitled *File It Right and Find It,* which goes into great detail about filing systems in educational institutions.

Changing the System

Before making any radical changes in your school files consider these points:

– Does the current system meet your needs? Can you locate active and inactive files easily and quickly? Is the system simple enough to be practical? Is the current system too time-consuming?

– Do you have the authority to change the present filing system or will you need clearance from the administration or supervisor? If you work in a large school with centralized files and its own specialized records management personnel, you will have to stay within the confines of an established system. If, on the other hand, you work in a small institution and are chiefly responsible for the files, you will have more leeway to rearrange them to suit your needs.

– What do you like about the present system? Make a list.

– What do you dislike? Make another list. Would you like easier retrieval? Better equipment? More efficient coding systems? More space?

– After you have made your lists you will be in a better position to realistically assess the situation.

– Can you do all the reorganization yourself or do you need help?

– Will the rearrangement require new or additional filing equipment? Are there sufficient funds in the budget to allow for more or better equipment?

– Will the administrator mind any upheaval caused by the reorganization?

– Try to anticipate the pluses and minuses of redoing the system, then discuss it with your administrator before proceeding. Some administrators like to "play in the files" rather than leaving you in charge. If you rearrange the system, but the administrator continues to use the old method, you could have a real mess on your hands. Be sure this is clarified before you begin any reorganization.

Basic School Categories for Files

Following are some basic subject categories designed for a medium-sized school. This is only a suggested outline and you will need to adapt the categories to suit your particular needs and requirements.

ACCIDENT REPORTS
– personnel
– student

ACCREDITATION
– agencies
– reports

ADMINISTRATIVE
– Board of Directors (or School Board)
– committees
– election of officers
– meetings and minutes
– policies and procedures

ADMINISTRATOR'S FILES
– correspondence
– engagements and invitations
– expenses
– social organizations
– speeches
– travel arrangements

AWARDS
– endowments
– honor roll
– scholarships

BUILDINGS AND GROUNDS
– architect's plans and blueprints
– bids and contracts

– building codes
– building inspection
– construction and maintenance
– keys and locks
– permits

CALENDARS
– administrative
– faculty
– general

EQUIPMENT
– audio visual
– classroom
– office
– physical education

FINANCIAL
– bank statements
– bills
– bookstore
– budgets
– cash receipts
– contracts
– payroll records
– tax records

FORMS
– include a sample of every form used in the school with a notation as to where the main supply is kept

GENERAL CORRESPONDENCE

GOVERNMENT AGENCIES

- federal
- state
- local

INSURANCE

- accident
- automobile
- bonding
- equipment
- fire
- theft
- tuition refund

INSTRUCTIONAL MATERIALS

- adult education
- apprentice programs
- audio-visual education
- business education
- camps
- child care
- driver training
- first aid and safety
- handicapped students
- master class schedule
- suppliers

MAILING LISTS

- administration
- alumni (filed by year of graduation)
- educational associations
- libraries
- press associations
- officials
- parent teacher organizations
- personnel
- professional organizations
- service organizations
- students

- textbook publishers
- welfare agencies
- youth groups

ORGANIZATIONS

- business
- civic
- education
- parents
- professional
- school staff
- social

PERSONNEL

- absences
- applications
- contracts
- credentials and certificates
- evaluations
- medical records
- pension and retirement
- procedures and policies
- recommendations
- salary schedules
- substitutes

PROGRAMS AND EVENTS

- assemblies
- fund drives
- productions
- seminars

PUBLICATIONS

- articles
- bibliographies
- brochures
- bulletins
- catalogs
- clippings
- handbooks
- library books
- magazines

- publishers
- textbooks
- yearbook

STUDENTS

- admissions
- alumni
- attendance
- behavior
- cumulative record
- employment
- enrollment
- graduation
- medical records
- placement
- recommendations
- schedules
- testing data
- transcripts
- transfers
- withdrawals
- work permits

STUDENT ACTIVITIES

- band
- clubs
- dance programs
- drama programs
- graduation programs
- student government
- tickets

SUMMER SCHOOL

- enrollment
- fees
- schedules

TRAVEL

- accommodations
- bus routes
- field trips
- permissions
- transportation

Improving Efficiency

Everyone has his or her favorite way of working. Over the years you have probably developed ways to improve speed and efficiency when filing but here are some suggestions you may find helpful:

- Place your file cabinets in a well-ventilated, well-lit, easily accessible area.
- Decentralized files are often the most convenient, so that each staff member has pertinent information readily available.
- Select durable file folders. Some of the new plastic folders have a long life, are available in colors for easy color coding, and slip easily in and out of file drawers.
- Decide either on staggered tabs or tabs flush left or right, whichever you prefer to work with. Try to keep the tabs uniform as it is easier to deal with them. Personally, I prefer tabs flush left (because I am right handed) since you do not have to waste time making sure that staggered tabs are always in sequence, and it is easier to locate and pull files.

- File materials promptly so that they do not get lost. If you must postpone your filing, keep a special file folder marked "For Filing" and place materials in it immediately until you have time to file them in the proper location.

- Code each article in pencil with its proper destination before placing in the "For Filing" folder. This speeds up the filing process later.

- Place the most current items at the front of each file folder where they will be more readily accessible.

- Reserve about one-fourth or one-fifth of each file drawer and leave this space empty to allow for rapid retrieval and rearrangement.

- Store necessary filing supplies in one of these empty file drawer spaces. Some articles you might wish to keep within easy reach are:

additional folders	extra file labels
transparent tape for	records retention schedule
mending tears	pen and pencil
staple remover	rubber cement
stapler	blank standard size paper
additional staples	
scissors	

- Before filing, tape torn pages, remove paper clips or pins, and staple pages together as needed.

- When filing small notes or clippings, first paste them to a standard size sheet of paper so that they will not get lost.

- If a folder is stuffed with papers, make up an additional folder for the extra papers, broken down numerically, alphabetically, or chronologically. For example:

Correspondence 1	(numerically)
Correspondence 2	
Student Enrollments A–L	(alphabetically)
Alumni—Graduated 1963	(chronologically)

- If material is to be temporarily removed from a file, insert a sheet in its place with the following information: "Removed from file on (date) by (name of person removing)." Follow with a brief description of the article removed.

- Reserve one file drawer for storage of temporary records and records that need to be reviewed for active/inactive status. As you have time during the school year, you can then work on these files at your leisure, or you can wait until the quieter summer months to deal with them.

- Before placing an inactive file in the morgue, indicate on the label the time span covered by the file: "Receipts, September 19– to June 19–."
- Give careful consideration to materials before you place them in the permanent file. Are they really necessary? Review files often and remove obsolete matter promptly.

Coding Systems

There are many ways of coding for filing—by alphabet, by number, or by color. If you choose to use the alphabetical or numerical systems, you would assign a letter or number to each file category that you wish to encode. However, one of the most effective and easy ways is to use color coding. All you have to do is decide on your basic color categories and how you wish to arrange your files. For example:

Blue	male student files
Yellow	female student files
Red	faculty files
Green	administrative files
Pink	staff files (other than faculty)
Orange	general (business and miscellaneous)
Purple	taxes or legal matters

After you have decided on your color categories, you can then proceed either to use standard file folders and color key the file labels to your categories, or you can use the newer colored plastic file folders, which are more durable and easier to see quickly.

Once your basic color categories are set up, you can then break down your code even further by using colored spots to designate your retention schedule. Get some small colored self-adhesive labels. They are available in dots or small squares. Code each file folder tab with the appropriate color and write the beginning year of the file's life in the colored spot. For example:

white dot	retain	one year or less
blue dot	retain	two to four years
yellow dot	retain	at least seven years
red dot	retain	permanently

By writing the year of the file's beginning in the dot, you will know when it is time to review the file. At the proper time you can then either destroy the file or move it into the next category by placing a new colored dot over the old one. This system can be adpated to any way that suits you best.

You might also consider setting up a similar system for your correspondence files. The system can be simplified for correspondence by marking the proposed retention in pencil in the upper right-hand corner of the correspondence prior to filing. Then, each summer or as you review the files, you can discard obsolete materials.

Developing a Records Retention Schedule

Each school record has a different life span. Correspondence, attendance, personnel, and government records vary greatly in how long they must be retained. In order to keep your files accurate and efficient, and to prevent the accumulation of papers from becoming overwhelming, it is important to establish a records retention schedule according to your school's specific requirements. To begin, any school's records can be broken down into three basic categories: (1) student-related items; (2) administrative and personnel items; (3) all other items. All legal matters and any other items which are to remain in a permanent file should be written on high-quality paper stock and stored in fireproof file cabinets or in a fireproof vault. If a permanent file must be replaced by a more recent version (perhaps a more recent policy statement, for example), be sure you know the ground rules for disposition of the old file. Is it your school's policy to retain such files indefinitely for reference? Will you simply substitute the new file for the outdated one?

Before destroying any permanent record, it is a good idea to get an administrator's signature authorizing you to do so. All you need to do is type a brief statement, have it signed, then place it in a file marked "Permanent Records— Obsolete." The statement could read as follows: "(Name of file) destroyed on (date) by the authorization of (name of administrator)" followed by the authorized signature. By doing this, you cannot be held responsible later if it is found that the file should have been retained. It is also an excellent record to have if you need to search for lost files.

As you proceed with your records retention schedule you will need to confer with your administrator to determine the amount of time that each record should be kept. Then make up a chart showing the categories and length of retention time. Keep a copy for yourself and keep one in your file storage drawer for reference when sorting files.

FILING EQUIPMENT, TYPES OF   It is estimated that twenty-five to forty percent of labor time related to filing is spent in looking for misplaced files. Part of this problem can be solved by having a workable filing system that suits your school's particular requirements. Another solution can be found in having one competent person ultimately responsible for the files. In either case, proper equipment plays a large role in maintaining efficient filing systems. Basically, there are five types of filing equipment:

- Vertical files (conventional type)
- Lateral cabinets with suspension drawers for drop filing
- Open-shelf filing
- High density filing with double or triple depth and movable aisle systems
- Automated files

Select the equipment that is appropriate for your system from your suppliers' catalogs.

FILMS, EDUCATIONAL   Most film companies will rent films to educational institutions at a reduced rate if the film is to be used in the classroom. If a school rents a film for a film festival or other public showing, the regular rate usually applies. You can obtain catalogs from the film distributors simply by writing or telephoning your request to them. Some companies provide order forms in the catalog, while you will need to make up your own form for others. The following information should be included in your film order:

- School name and address
- Purchase order number and/or your name
- Name of the film
- Film catalog number
- Price of the film
- Dates that you wish to rent the film and alternate dates if possible. If you order films several months in advance, your school will be assured of the best selection, but remember not to schedule films during vacation periods.

Each distributor's catalog provides detailed ordering instructions and information.

Krasker Memorial Film Library

Boston University
565 Commonwealth Avenue, Boston, MA 02215
Tel: 617/353-3272

ORDER BLANK

Ship to:

_____

_____

_____

_____

Phone #: _____

Films will be _____ Picked up _____ Shipped.

Send Confirmations to _____ Shipping Address _____ Billing Address.

Bill to:
(if same as shipping address, leave blank)

_____

_____

_____

Purchase Order #: _____

Customer # (if known): _____

Please enter our rental order for the following films:

LEAVE THIS COLUMN BLANK	COMPLETE FILM TITLES (refer to catalog)	DATE WANTED 1st CHOICE	2nd CHOICE

Authorized Signature _____ Date _____

(use reverse side if necessary)

FIGURE 12

Sample film order form

146

Distributors (listed by state)

ARIZONA

Central Arizona Film Cooperative
Arizona State University
Tempe, AZ 85281
(602) 965-7564

CALIFORNIA

Paramount Non-Theatrical
5451 Marathon Street
Hollywood, CA 90038
(213) 462-0700

Audio-Brandon Films (West Coast)
1619 North Cherokee
Los Angeles, CA 90028
(213) 463-1131

UCLA Media Center
Instructional Media Library
405 Hilgard Avenue/Royce Hall
Los Angeles, CA 90024
(213) 825-0755

Warner Bros. Inc.
Non-Theatrical Division
4000 Warner Boulevard
Burbank, CA 91522
(213) 843-6000

Westcoast Films
25 Lusk Street
San Fransciso, CA 94107
(415) 362-4700

University of California
Extension Media Center
2223 Fulton Street
Berkeley, CA 94720
(415) 642-0460

Universal Education & Visual Arts
Universal Kinetic Division
155 Universal City Plaza
Universal City, CA 91608
(213) 985-4321

National Aeronautics and Space
Administration (NASA)
Ames Research Center
Moffett Field, CA 94035
(415) 965-5000

Walt Disney
Western Film Library
6904 Tujunga Avenue
N. Hollywood, CA 91605
(213) 763-0150

Churchill Films
662 North Robertson Boulevard
Los Angeles, CA 90069
(213) 657-5110

COLORADO

Educational Media Center
University of Colorado
Stadium Building
Boulder, CO 80309
(303) 492-7341

DISTRICT OF COLUMBIA

NASA Headquarters
Code FAM
Washington, DC 20546
(202) 755-8366

National Geographic Society
Educational Services
Department 79
Washington, DC 20036
(Sales and Information)
(301) 948-5926

FLORIDA

Instructional Media Center
Division of Instructional Research
and Service
Florida State University
Tallahassee, FL 32306
(904) 644-2820

Modern Talking Picture Service
5000 Park Street North
St. Petersburg, FL 33709
(813) 541-7571

ILLINOIS

Northern Illinois University
Media Distribution Department
Altgeld Hall, Room 114
De Kalb, IL 60115
(815) 753-0171

The Roland Collection
1825 Willow Road
Northfield, IL 60093
(Excellent collection of films
on art.)
(312) 446-4153

INDIANA

Purdue University
Audio-Visual Center
Stewart Center
West Lafayette, IN 47907
(317) 749-2833

IOWA

AVC Media Library
Audiovisual Center
The University of Iowa
Iowa City, IA 52240
(319) 353-5885

MASSACHUSETTS

Boston University
Krasker Memorial Film Library
765 Commonwealth Avenue
Boston, MA 02215
(617) 353-3272

NEBRASKA

Modern Sound Pictures Inc.
1402 Howard Street
Omaha, NE 68102
(402) 341-8476

NEW JERSEY

Karol Media
East 36A Midland Avenue
Paramus, NJ 07652
(201) 262-4170
(National Geographic Film Rentals)

Time-Life Films
P.O. Box 644
Paramus, NJ 07652
(201) 843-4545

NEW YORK

Films Incorporated
440 Park Avenue South
New York, NY 10016
(212) 889-7910

(Several locations serving different
states. Contact for information.)

Association Films — Executive Offices
866 Third Avenue
New York, NY 10022
(212) 935-4210

Audio-Brandon Films (East Coast)
34 MacQuesten Parkway South
Mount Vernon, NY 10550
(914) 664-5051

Eye-Gate Media
146-01 Archer Avenue
Jamaica, NY 11435
(212) 291-9100

OHIO

AV Services
Kent State University
Kent, OH 44242
(216) 672-3456

OKLAHOMA

United Films
1425 South Main
Tulsa, OK 74119
(918) 583-2681

Audiovisual Center
University of Oklahoma
Stillwater, OK 74074
(405) 624-7216

PENNSYLVANIA

Clem Williams Films
2240 Noblestown Road
Pittsburgh, PA 15205
(412) 921-5810

UTAH

Audiovisual Services
Brigham Young University
290 Gerald R. Clark Building
Provo, UT 84602
(801) 378-1211

University of Utah
Educational Media Center
207 Milton Bennion Hall
Salt Lake City, UT 84112
(801) 581-6112

WASHINGTON

Audio-Visual Services
B-54 Administration Building AC-30
University of Washington
Seattle, WA 98195
(206) 543-2714

WISCONSIN

Audiovisual Center
University of Wisconsin
Florence Wing Communication Center
1705 State Street
La Crosse, WI 54601
(608) 784-6050

Other Sources of Film Loans and Rentals

Foreign consular offices, listed in the telephone directory.

United States Departments of the Army, Navy, and Air Force.

Major museums that have collections of films and slides that can be rented or borrowed.

Audio-Visual Guidebooks

Educator's Guide to Free Films, published by Educator's Progress Service, Inc., Randolph, WI 53956

Film Programmer's Guide to 16mm Rentals, published by Reel Research, Box 6037, Albany, CA 94706

Index to 16mm Educational Films, University of Southern California National Information Center for Educational Media, 3716 South Hope Street, Los Angeles, CA 90007

Faculty Newsletter

It can be very helpful to the faculty if you make up a monthly film newsletter. This is just a reminder of the films scheduled to be shown for that month plus the name of the teacher who will show the film and the subject area. The film newsletter gives faculty members an opportunity to share rental films and can reduce overall costs.

Free Loan Films

Major corporations and some government agencies offer free loan films and educational materials. To order them it is generally necessary to send a request on the school's letterhead. Just be sure that your ordering information is accurate and that you fulfill any "courtesy requirements"; some firms require you to fill out a postcard rating the free-loan materials. This is usually done by the person showing the film or using the materials.

How to Set Up and Maintain a Film Log

If you are responsible for ordering films, you will need to keep track of their arrival, departure, and possibly the payment of resulting invoices. Here is a simple method that works.

- Make up a film log on standard $8\frac{1}{2} \times 11$-inch lined paper that you can keep in a binder. Use these headings and make up a separate sheet(s) for each month:

TEACHER   FILM TITLE   SHOW DATE   ARRIVED   RETURNED

  Be sure to block out vacation dates on each page.
- When you place a film order, enter the film title and the person who will show the film in your log on the appropriate page.
- List the show date (the date on which the film is due to be shown). Films may arrive as much as a week early.
- When the films arrive, mark the date of arrival in the "Arrived" column. Then notify the teacher that the film is available.
- When you return a film, write the mailing date in the "Returned" column. If a film is lost or misplaced in shipment you can quickly determine the date it was sent back.
- If films are cancelled or unavailable, just cross them off your list.

FINANCIAL AID RECORDS   Student loans, scholarships, and work-study programs all require that extensive financial and personal data forms be filled out in order to apply. These files are confidential. They often contain information of a highly personal nature including such items as:

- detailed income data
- detailed expenses
- outstanding loans
- credit ratings
- lists of personal and real property owned
- inheritances or trust fund data
- lists of dependents

This type of information may be asked either of the student or the parents, depending on the age of the student.

FIRE DRILLS Fire drills are usually held on a monthly basis at random times which are either determined by the administrator, you, or the visiting fire chief. Although drills should be held without warning, try to schedule them for times that will cause the least disruption. It would be unnecessary, for example, to schedule a fire drill during exam week or during the performance of a school play. Some students find it funny to pull fire alarms during the school day. Obviously, this procedure should be severely discouraged, but if a false alarm is turned in, allow the drill to proceed as normal and follow the set routine. In addition to initiating the fire drill, you may be required to help keep exits clear and keep traffic moving smoothly, to check bathrooms, close office doors, and signal reentry into the building. It should be standard procedure that someone (probably you) takes an attendance list of the entire school outside of the building during each drill. In case of a real fire, this list could help identify missing persons. The janitor is usually responsible for making sure that fire alarm bells and fire extinguishers are in proper working order. However, be sure you know how to operate them in case of real emergencies. (See also EMERGENCY PROCEDURES.)

FIRST AID, BASIC INFORMATION A basic knowledge of first aid is helpful, if not essential, to the secretary of the smaller school where there is no nurse. Good training is available through courses and books produced by the American Red Cross, and if you are in a position where extensive first aid treatment is a regular part of the job, it may be wise to avail yourself of Red Cross training.

This section is written to refresh your memory about basic first aid techniques and/or to supply you with information that at the very least can help you comfort and aid, and at the most, perhaps save a life.

Accidents and Injuries

The school secretary acting as nurse may be called on to deal with a wide range of cuts and bruises—thankfully, most of them minor. Older or adult students can take care of minor injuries themselves and need only to be directed to the first aid kit. Children will probably need supervision and care.

Remember when dealing with children that your reaction to an injury can have a lasting effect on them. If you show fear or panic, your emotions will be transferred to them and you may soon have to deal with hysteria as well as the injury. The injured child is frightened. Be reassuring; acknowledge the injury. (Do not play down the pain or discomfort as it will only make the child cry louder in an attempt to show you that he really is hurt.) Most of all, be calm. A few reassuring words and a calm disposition will do more for the child than any other first aid treatment that you can dispense.

Here is a list of typical minor injuries that children may bring to you during the day.

Cuts and Lacerations

1. Reassure and comfort the child.

   Children know very little about how their bodies work and most seem fascinated by new knowledge about themselves. When a child is crying or fussing as you are cleansing a wound, explain why you are cleaning the wound and how wonderful the body is in being able to heal itself, etc. You will need to gear your story to the particular age of the child and the situation, but the storytelling usually calms him down, and you can use the opportunity to teach him how to care for his own injuries.

2. Assess the situation. Is this a deep wound that might require stitches or professional medical help? If you think it is, apply direct pressure to stop the bleeding, and get help in contacting the parents or in taking the child for medical treatment. If the cuts or scratches are minor, you can treat them yourself.

   IMPORTANT: If a child has a deep cut along the shaft of a finger and cannot flex the finger, a tendon may have been severed. Contact the parent and/or get medical help immediately.

3. Expose the wound by removing any clothing covering it. Knees are favorite areas of injury, so you will need to remove pants or stockings to clean the area. Some children may be a little squeamish about taking off their clothes in front of you, but here again, reassurance coupled with a businesslike attitude on your part usually solves this problem quickly.

4. Thoroughly cleanse the wound with soap and water. This may cause some stinging, and tears and fussing may follow. Remain calm but firm, and continue to cleanse the wound. It is important to remove all foreign particles from the area.

   If an antiseptic is used, hydrogen peroxide may be swabbed over the wound area. It is as useful as any other over-the-counter product used in the cleansing process and children love to watch it "bubble."

5. Once the wound is thoroughly cleaned, let it air dry. Do not blow on the wound to speed up drying or allow the child to, as this will blow mouth bacteria onto the wound. Make sure the child does not touch the wound; this can also introduce bacteria into the area.

6. After the wound area has dried thoroughly, you are ready to bandage it. Usually, if the wound has been well cleansed, no antiseptic is necessary (they are not very effective, and some such as iodine actually destroy body tissue). A sterile gauze pad may be taped over the area, or a plastic strip bandage may be used.

Infected Pierced Ears

There are now many young children with pierced ears. It is quite common for a child to be sent to the nurse with swollen and inflamed ear lobes. In most cases, the child has the earring fastened too tightly, and the excessive pressure on both sides of the ear lobe causes a reduction in blood supply to the area; it becomes and stays infected. Instruct the children to fasten their earrings further back on the earring post. This will prevent further swelling and can also prevent them from losing their earrings. (When the earring is worn too tightly, the extra pressure might cause a spring-like action that causes the clasp to fly off and consequently the earring gets lost.)

Torn Nails

Torn nails are very painful. A child who comes to you with a freshly torn nail will be in considerable pain, probably crying, and very upset.

1. Comfort the child.
2. Hold the finger with a clean cloth, applying pressure if necessary to stop the bleeding. Let the child know that you are just going to look at the finger.
3. Examine the area carefully. If the tear is small, or in a straight line, just cleanse it and bandage it. The nail will eventually grow out, but may need to be taped until it has grown out sufficiently to be clipped off. If the nail is hanging off, the piece of nail should be removed. A quick jerk will usually take care of it, or the child may prefer to remove the torn

nail tip himself. Then, cleanse it and bandage it. If the whole nail has been torn off or is severely damaged, it is best to contact the parent for further instructions.

Injury to the Eye Area

Do not take chances with eyes—eyesight is very precious. Get medical help immediately:

1. If there is a direct injury to the eye.
2. If the surrounding area has been injured and the eye is bloodshot.
3. If the injury to a surrounding area has caused blurred vision or double vision.
4. If there is pain in the eye.
5. If there is a foreign body which you are unable to remove by flushing the eye with water.
6. If chemical substances have gotten into the eye. In this case, immediately flush with water and keep flushing until medical help is available.

Mouth Injuries

Superficial bleeding inside the mouth can be controlled by having the child rinse with water, then suck on an ice cube. No further treatment is necessary. Severe bleeding should be referred to a physician as sutures may be necessary.

Human Bites

While playing or fighting, it is not uncommon for children to bite each other. Since the human mouth contains a great deal of bacteria, all human bites have a high probability of infection. Cleanse the wound, but do not bandage a human bite wound. Bandaging this type of wound can encourage bacterial growth. Notify the parents so that they can keep an eye on the wound, and check on the child's tetanus booster.

Animal Bites

A child may be bitten by an animal on the way to school and come in to tell you about it, or the bite may come from an animal used in science or other classes. Cleanse and bandage the area and notify the parents. The possibility of rabies and tetanus must be dealt with and parents should be informed of the situation.

Slivers and Splinters

Splinters are foreign objects that become embedded in the skin, carrying bacteria and perhaps infection. Splinters should be removed immediately with clean tweezers. Sometimes, soaking the area for a few moments aids in splinter removal. Following removal, thoroughly cleanse the area.

Stuck Rings and Other Wonders

Children do not seem to realize that fingers come in many sizes. The lure of a glittering object is sometimes overwhelming, and it is not until the object is firmly fixed on the finger that the child suddenly realizes it is indeed stuck. Most rings can be removed by the following method:

1. Lubricate the finger with soap, petroleum jelly, or oil. Gently manipulate the ring and it will usually slip right off.

2. If it is still stuck, the child might have caused the finger to swell while trying to remove the ring before coming to you. In this case, place the finger in ice water, or surround it with ice water for a few moments to reduce swelling. Slide the ring to the part of the finger where it is the most loose and massage the finger from the tip toward the hand in an attempt to move the swelling past the stuck object. After a few minutes, lubricate again and once more gently try removal again. Pulling, tugging, and other rough treatment will only cause further swelling.

3. If the object is still stuck, it may have to be cut loose. It is wise to contact the parent at this point.

Small children also love to stuff things up their noses. A remarkable array of objects can come to rest in the child's nasal passage—bits of paper, erasers, paper clips, food, chalk, beads, art supplies, and on and on. The child may have a nosebleed or a nasal discharge, or part of the object may be hanging out of the nostril. If you can easily remove the object, do so. Otherwise, contact the parents immediately.

Ears are another favorite spot for storing objects. If a child has a foreign object in the ear, do not try to remove it yourself; you may damage the ear's delicate inner workings. Contact the parents and get medical help.

Once you have removed an object from an unwanted spot, be cautious about returning it to the child; it may well wind up right back in the same nose, ear, etc. (I usually confiscate marbles, erasers, paper clips, and the like and return valuable objects directly to the parent with a word of caution.)

Sprains and Strains

Sprains and strains occur quite frequently as a result of physical activity. Strains are injuries to muscular areas or tendons as a result of overstretching or pulling. Sprains are usually injuries in which ligaments in or around the joint are torn.

If a child is brought to you with a possible sprain or strain, elevate the area and apply an ice pack for thirty minutes or so. Often this is all that is necessary and the child will be fine. If, after the application of an ice pack, there is not much improvement and the pain, swelling, discoloration or immobility are still evident, contact the parents and/or seek medical help.

Broken Bones

Broken bones and fractures are one and the same. Fortunately, they are generally rare during school hours. Sprains and strains are far more common. If a fracture is suspected, do not move the student, since you could cause further damage. Contact the parents and/or get medical help right away. Just for your information, here is a summary of the different types of fractures:

1. Simple Fracture. In this case, the bone is broken through but remains aligned. The bone will be immobilized in a cast, but setting or manipulation is not usually required.

2. Displaced Fracture. Here, the broken bone segments are out of alignment and will require setting before casting.

3. Hairline Fracture. Here, the bone is cracked like a piece of porcelain. This can be a difficult fracture to determine, since it may not even show up on X-rays. While no setting is required, the area is still immobilized in a cast.

4. Greenstick Fracture. In this type of fracture, only a portion of the bone is broken; the break does not go clear through the bone. It is quite common in children, and requires immobilization in a cast.

5. Impacted Fracture. Here, the fragmented ends of the bone are jammed together, resembling cars in a head-on collision. Setting and applying a cast are required.

6. Compound Fracture. In this instance, the fragmented end of bone can protrude through the skin. Compound fractures are very serious injuries requiring immediate professional medical aid.

If you are unsure whether or not an injury is serious, assume that it is serious and make appropriate medical and parental contact.

Bleeding

DIRECT PRESSURE ON THE WOUND = BLEEDING STOPPED

(ninety-five percent of the time)

If a student is injured and is continuing to bleed, apply a clean cloth or sterile gauze padding to the area, grasp it firmly, and apply direct pressure to the wound for several minutes. Do not remove the pressure to look at the wound until at least fifteen minutes have passed; otherwise you can disturb the clotting process and start the bleeding again.

After a few minutes, check the wound. In most cases the bleeding will have stopped. If there is still bleeding, continue pressure for another ten or fifteen minutes. If, after the second attempt, there is still bleeding, get professional medical aid.

The direct pressure method is suitable for most wounds of the extremities. However, in the case of continued bleeding of the throat, eye, or abdomen, do not apply pressure, but seek professional help immediately.

After the bleeding has stopped, you can cleanse the wounded area and determine whether simple bandaging is sufficient, or whether to get further medical treatment.

In many states or school districts, children are required to have certain immunizations and shots before enrolling in school. If a child suffers a deep cut or puncture wound, however, a tetanus shot or booster may be in order. To be on the safe side, it is best to contact the parent in such cases, so that they may make an informed decision.

Burns

The most likely types of burns in a school situation are minor burns from cooking classes, or chemical spills that will require only rudimentary first aid treatment. However, it is prudent to be aware of the degrees of severity of various burns so that you can evaluate a burn with accuracy. Here is a breakdown of burn severity by degrees:

First-Degree Burns

SYMPTOMS: Redness of the skin (as in sunburn)

Pain

No blisters

EFFECTS: Most first-degree burns are harmless and will easily heal without complications. If, however, a first-degree burn should cover large areas of the body, it can be dangerous, and medical help should be sought immediately.

TREATMENT: Immediate immersion in cold water. This makes the burned area feel better quickly, and actually stops further destruction of tissue. In the case of a very small burn, this may be all the treatment necessary. Larger burns may benefit from a dressing of sterile gauze and an antibacterial ointment.

Second-Degree Burns

SYMPTOMS:	Redness and blistering
EFFECTS:	Significant tissue damage has occurred.
TREATMENT:	Take no chances. Unless the second-degree burn is very small (less than dime-sized) get professional help *immediately*. Burns can be very dangerous. *Small* second-degree burns may be treated in the same way as first-degree burns.

Third-Degree Burns

SYMPTOMS:	White color (tissue destroyed)
	Black color (tissue charred)
	No pain (no nerves left to carry pain impulses)
EFFECTS:	Scarring
	Possible skin grafts needed.
TREATMENT:	Get professional help immediately—no exceptions.

Frostbite

In cold climates, frostbite is not uncommon in children who play in the snow, so you should be aware of its symptoms and treatment. Ice or snow that is thrown in snowball fights can become lodged in areas of clothing around the neck or ankles and can cause hardened areas of red skin. (Severe frostbite is usually hard, white, and painless.)

Treatment: Immerse the injured area in warm water for fifteen to thirty minutes. Pain is a good sign as it shows that life is returning to the injured part. Once the area is warm, get the person to a physician. Do not rub snow into frostbite as it will only increase the damage.

NOTE: In case you are wondering why a section on frostbite is included in a school secretarial manual; I was working in a school in California and chaperoning a group of students on a ski week in Yosemite National Park. We were camping in an isolated area up in the high country. One of the students and one of the teachers had inadequate footwear, and both wound up with frostbitten toes. It was many hours before we were able to get medical help. We were all glad that I knew first aid for frostbite, otherwise they might have lost their toes. You can never be sure what situations you will encounter—be prepared.

Choking

Choking is most commonly caused by an obstruction in the throat which prevents the victim from breathing properly. Food, toys, and erasers are often the culprits in choking in schools. The victim is probably very frightened, so whatever you do, avoid further panic which can only worsen the situation.

1. Quickly assess the situation. If the person is beginning to turn blue, there is an inadequate oxygen supply. Get someone else to call for an ambulance while you attempt to remove the obstruction.

2. For an adult or older child, the Heimlich Maneuver is one of the most effective methods for dislodging foreign objects:
   - Grab the person from behind around the midriff area.
   - Lock your arms around the person by holding one wrist with the other hand.
   - Press into the person's diaphragm, using short, sharp thrusts.
   The object should readily dislodge.

   The Heimlich Maneuver can be easily learned with only a few minutes of instruction. Most local Red Cross chapters have a program to teach it; please care enough to be aware and take the few minutes to learn this vital life-saving technique.

3. For young children, medical opinion varies as to how much pressure their fragile chest cages can stand: the Heimlich Maneuver may be too severe for them. If the child is small, hold him upside down and strike him sharply between the shoulder blades. If the child is larger, bend him forward over your knee or over a table or chair before striking. Do not strike while the child is in an upright position, as this can drive the object further down.
   If this method fails with a younger child, and if the situation is obviously life-threatening, trying the Heimlich Maneuver is justified.

4. Once the foreign body has been removed, do not give it to the child as a souvenir. Too often, the same object finds its way back into the same undesirable location.

Fainting (Unconsciousness)

Fainting can be caused by many things. Sometimes people faint at the sight of blood or injury; some children faint in science classes when beginning animal

American Red Cross

TO SAVE A LIFE

ARTIFICIAL RESPIRATION

If victim appears to be unconscious, tap victim on the shoulder and shout, "Are you okay?"

If victim is not breathing, begin artificial respiration at once.

Tilt the victim's head backward so chin is pointing upward (Fig 1).

Fig. 1

Pinch nose closed. Place your mouth tightly around victim's mouth and blow into his mouth (Fig 2). Volume is important. Blow quickly four times.

Fig. 2

Check for the pulse at the side of the neck (Fig. 3) for five (5) seconds. If there is no pulse, and no breathing, begin CPR *if* you have been trained. Classes are available through American Red Cross

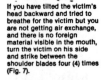

If the victim has a pulse but is not breathing, begin artificial respiration — one breath every five (5) seconds for adults.

Fig. 3

Watch victim's chest to see when it rises. Stop blowing when chest is expanded; raise your mouth; turn your head to side and listen for exhalation (Fig 4). Watch victim's chest to see that it falls; rhythmically repeat the blowing cycle.

Fig. 4

On infants or small child, tilt head slightly. Cover and seal mouth *and* nose with your mouth, and blow shallow breath once every three (3) seconds.

FIRST AID FOR CHOKING

CONSCIOUS VICTIM

A person who has a completely blocked airway *cannot breathe, cough or speak.*

Ask, "Can you speak?" If not, the victim's airway is completely blocked. Give four back blows high up between the shoulder blades. The head should be lower than the chest, if possible (Fig. 5).

If unsuccessful — stand behind victim, wrap your arms around victim's middle, just above the navel. Clasp your fist with your other hand and press into the victim's abdomen with four (4) *quick* upward thrusts (Fig. 6).

If four back blows and four thrusts do not work, *repeat* the sequence. *(Do not give up!)*

UNCONSCIOUS VICTIM

If you have tilted the victim's head backward and tried to breathe for the victim but you are not getting air exchange, and there is no foreign material visible in the mouth, turn the victim on his side and strike between the shoulder blades four (4) times (Fig. 7).

Roll the victim on his back and give four abdominal thrusts by placing the heel of one hand between the rib cage and the navel and thrusting upwards towards the head (Fig. 8).

Wipe foreign matter from the mouth with fingers (Fig. 9), and try to give breaths again. Repeat the entire sequence until successful.

Fig. 5

Fig. 7

Fig. 6

Fig. 8

Fig. 9

TO CONTROL BLEEDING

2. If bleeding continues, apply PRESSURE on the supplying artery.

1. Apply DIRECT PRESSURE and elevate

Pressure on the brachial artery

Hand pressure on the femoral artery

EMERGENCY PHONE

Doctor_____Ambulance_____Fire_____

NOTE: FOR ANY SERIOUS INJURY OBTAIN TRAINED MEDICAL HELP AS SOON AS POSSIBLE

FIGURE 13

This American Red Cross chart shows at a glance the correct procedures to follow for artificial respiration and choking.

FIRST AID AT A GLANCE

AILMENT	SIGNS AND SYMPTOMS	FIRST AID
1. **POISON**	Symptoms vary greatly. Aids to determine whether poison was swallowed: a. Information from victim or observer b. Presence of poison container c. Condition of victim (sudden onset of pain or illness) d. Burns around lips e. Breath odor f. Pupil contracted to pinpoint size	***ALL VICTIMS*** Call Emergency Rescue Squad Save label or container for I.D. ***CONSCIOUS VICTIMS*** Dilute the poison with milk or water Do not neutralize with counteragents Do *not* give oils ***UNCONSCIOUS VICTIMS*** Maintain open airway (victim on side) Give mouth-to-mouth resuscitation or CPR if necessary Do *not* give fluids, Do *not* induce vomiting ***CONVULSIONS*** Do *not* restrain victim Loosen tight clothing Watch for airway obstruction Do *not* give fluids Do *not* induce vomiting
2. **SHOCK**	1. Skin pale (or bluish), cold to touch; possibly moist or clammy 2. Victim weak 3. Rapid pulse (over 100) 4. Rate of breathing usually increases; may be shallow or deep and irregular	Keep victim lying down. Cover him only enough to keep him from losing body heat; obtain medical help as soon as possible
3. **FRACTURES** **AND** **DISLOCATIONS**	1. Pain and tenderness 2. May have difficulty moving injured part 3. Obvious deformities — swelling and discoloration	Keep broken bone ends and adjacent joints from moving, and give care for shock Call for medical help
4. **BURNS**	Skin is: 1. Red — 1st Degree 2. Blistered — 2nd Degree 3. Charred — 3rd Degree	Pain of first degree and of a small second degree burn can be relieved by excluding air. Three ways to exclude air from 1st or 2nd degree burns only: 1. Submerge in cold water 2. Apply a cold pack 3. Cover with a thick dressing or unused plastic. *DO NOT* use plastic to keep air off a burn on the face! For a 3rd degree burn, cover with dry clean cloth and call for medical help. If any burn occurs to the victim's face area, watch for possible need for artificial respiration
5. **HEART** **ATTACK**	Two principle symptoms: 1. Acute pain in chest, upper abdomen or down left arm and shoulder 2. Extreme shortness of breath	Place victim in comfortable position, usually sitting up. If not breathing, give artificial respiration. Call for medical help and give prescribed medication, if any. *DO NOT* give liquids to unconscious victims Take a CPR class, available through the American Red Cross
6. **LOSS OF** **CONSCIOUSNESS**	Unresponsive	Keep victim warm and lying down, head turned to one side. If consciousness is not regained quickly, send for medical help. If breathing stops, give artificial respiration. Never give an unconscious person food or liquids

DRUGS AND THEIR ABUSE
In case of drug abuse emergencies, it is important that the signs and symptoms of the abuse be identified by the individual providing the immediate assistance. The type of drug, plus information on the size and age of the victim and his general condition should be provided to the drug abuse center or attending physician, if possible. For further information on drugs and their abuse, call your local drug abuse center.

The following informational books and pamphlets are available at your local Red Cross chapter:

- *Drugs and Their Abuse*
- *First Aid for Poisoning*
- *First Aid for Snakebite*
- *First Aid for Foreign Body Obstruction of the Airway*
- *Heart Attack*
- *Safety and Survival in an Earthquake*
- *Standard First Aid and Personal Safety* (textbook)
- *Advanced First Aid and Emergency Care* (textbook)

FOR INFORMATION ABOUT FIRST AID AND CARDIOPULMONARY RESUSCITATION (CPR) CALL YOUR LOCAL CHAPTER

FIGURE 14

This American Red Cross First Aid at a Glance chart is an excellent tool for first aid reviews.

dissection; others may faint because of low blood sugar caused by skipping breakfast, or because of an illness or injury. Remember, drug overdoses can also cause lack of consciousness.

1. First, determine the severity of the episode. Has the person fainted, or is he truly unconscious? Pinch the person's shoulder. Loudly call his name or ask "How are you?" in an attempt to get some reaction. Sprinkling the person's face with a few drops of cold water, or *briefly* passing smelling salts under the nose may revive him. If none of these techniques work, the person is probably truly unconscious. Call an ambulance immediately.

   If a person merely feels faint, having him bend forward and place his head between his knees can send a blood supply to the brain and prevent fainting.

   Never try to give an unconscious person anything to eat or drink—you could cause choking.

2. If the person is truly unconscious, check to see if he is still breathing. Place your hand under the victim's nose to feel for breath; watch for the chest to rise and fall; listen for the sound of breathing. If there is no breath, cardiopulmonary resuscitation (CPR) is required.

   CPR training cannot be learned by reading; you will need to take a course. Call your nearest American Red Cross or American Heart Association. Most classes are either free or low-cost. It only takes about six hours of instruction to learn CPR techniques.

Heart Attack

Teachers, school staff, adult students, and drug abusers are all likely candidates for heart attacks. The symptoms of heart attacks and choking can be so similar as to be confusing. However, if the victim can speak, it's probably a heart attack. Heart attack symptoms may include shortness of breath, pale or blue skin, fear, sweating, and/or nausea. Call an ambulance or get the person to the nearest hospital.

If you are going to drive the person to the hospital, take another person with you. You should have one person to drive and one person to give CPR should the victim's heart stop before reaching the hospital. In any heart attack, the greatest risk is during the first two hours. *Get help immediately!*

Heatstroke

Sometimes in a warm, humid environment, the body's "thermostat" malfunctions and the body is unable to regulate its temperature. Heatstroke can result. The person is unable to sweat, thus unable to reduce body temperature by evaporation, and the body temperature keeps climbing higher. Permanent brain dam-age can result if the body temperature remains too high for too long a period of time. In a heatstroke victim, the skin is red, hot, and dry. (Pale, cool, or wet skin lets you know it's not heatstroke.)

Call an ambulance, and while waiting for it to arrive, cool the person as quickly as possible:

- Remove the clothing.
- Cover the skin with cold, wet cloths and change them as they become warm.
- Fan the person or place him under cool running water if possible. Do not use ice.

Poisoning

1. Stay calm and determine (if possible) what poison has been swallowed.
2. Get the poison container and call an ambulance.
3. Call your poison control center (their telephone number should be taped under your telephone) and ask for instructions.

Following is a list of emergency first aid procedures for poisoning to be used in case you cannot get immediate professional help:

1. If gas, smoke, or fumes have been inhaled, get the person into the fresh air immediately.
2. If poison or chemicals have gotten into the eye, flush it for at least fif-teen minutes with lukewarm tap water poured from a cup or pitcher. Use only water.
3. If poison has been spilled on the skin or clothing, remove the clothing and flush the skin with water. Then wash with soap and water and rinse.

After poison has been swallowed:

- Do not give table salt, mustard water, or hydrogen peroxide to drink.
- Do not give fruit juices or vinegar to drink as these may cause further burns.
- Do not give oil or mineral oil to drink.

With the current trend toward using more and more indoor plants as decorative elements in school offices, waiting areas, and classrooms, there is a danger of poisoning from plants in schools that cater to very young children. Nursery schools, in particular, should be especially careful in choosing plants, since some plants are extremely poisonous when chewed or touched. Following is a list of common poisonous plants. If you work in a school with very young children, encourage your administrator to check the plants against this list and remove any potential hazards from the school environment.

Poisonous Plants (Potentially hazardous to small children)

Common Name	Poisonous Part	Botannical Name
Bird of Paradise	fruit, seeds	strelitzia regirae
Boston ivy	all parts	parthenocissus quinquefolia
Caladium	all parts	caladium
Creeping Charlie	all parts	glecoma hederacea
Dumbcane	all parts	dieffenbachia
Emerald Duke	all parts	philodendron hastatum
Glacier ivy	leaves, berries	hedera glacier
Heartleaf	all parts	philodendron cordatum
English ivy	leaves, berries	hedera helix
Marble Queen	all parts	scindapsus aureus
Majesty	all parts	philodendron hastatum
Nephthytis or Arrowhead Vine	all parts	syngonium podophyllum albolineatum
Parlor ivy	all parts	philodendron cordatum
Pothos	all parts	scindapsus aureus
Red Princess	all parts	philodendron hastatum
Saddleleaf	all parts	philodendron selloum
Split leaf philodendron	all parts	monstera deliciosa
Umbrella plant	all parts	cyperus alternifolius

The following plants are particularly poisonous:

Castor bean	seeds	ricinus communis
Oleander	all parts	norium oleander
Poinsettia	leaves, flowers	euphorbia pulcherrima

Shock

As unpleasant as it may be, violence in schools is increasing. Gunshot or stab wounds, which would once have been unheard of on a campus, are becoming more frequent, and if the trend continues, may become a common occurrence. before too much longer. A great danger from such wounds is shock due to excessive blood loss. While you wait for the ambulance to arrive, you may need to follow these emergency procedures:

Symptoms: drowsiness or restlessness

thirst

rapid breathing

rapid pulse

pale, cool skin

The great danger in shock is brain damage due to oxygen deprivation from blood loss, so your goal is to keep as much blood as possible flowing to the brain to supply oxygen until professional help arrives.

1. Lay the person down and elevate the feet to work with gravity in sending blood toward the brain, unless you suspect a head injury. In the case of a head injury, lay the victim flat to prevent swelling of the head area.

2. Attempt to control excessive bleeding by the direct pressure method.

3. Cover the victim to keep him warm.

4. Give nothing to eat or drink. People in shock may require surgery to control bleeding and food or drink may cause a delay that could prove fatal.

Overdose of Drugs

If you suspect drug overdose (the person may be groggy with slurred speech, or may be unconscious) call for an ambulance right away and follow appropriate emergency first aid procedures as already outlined. Try and find out from the person or from friends what kind of drug has been taken. Better yet, try to get a sample to give to hospital personnel, as many street drugs are misrepresented to the user. While waiting for help, you main goals are:

1. To get a conscious person to remain conscious by throwing up the ingested drugs and lowering the risk of heavy overdose.

2. Preventing an unconscious person from oxygen deprivation or from choking on his own body fluids.

3. If the person is unconscious, lay him on his side to allow fluids to drain from the mouth. Watch for vomiting.

4. Call your poison control center for further instructions.

5. Give nothing to eat or drink.

Childhood Illness

If you are acting as school nurse, you will undoubtedly be sent an unending stream of children who feel sick. Some may be catching a cold; some may be faking, perhaps to miss an exam or a disliked class; and some may really be quite ill. Thanks to mandatory immunization programs in many states, some of the worst childhood illnesses such as measles, polio, whooping cough and diphtheria rarely occur, so the most common complaints are sore throats, stomachaches, headaches, minor insect bites, and rashes. Your local public health department will usually keep you notified of any outbreaks of contagious diseases, and you can call on them if you need advice in evaluating a potential contagious-disease situation.

Here are some tips on how to handle childhood illness in the school.

Rashes

CHICKENPOX. This is still one of the most contagious of childhood diseases. It usually occurs about two weeks after exposure. The rash begins as individual red pimple-like spots that soon turn into small clear blisters. Scabs will follow a day or two after the blisters. Successive series of pox spots appear for the first four or five days of the illness. Chickenpox is contagious from the day before the onset of the rash until all the spots have disappeared—usually five to seven days. If you suspect chickenpox, the child should be removed from the classroom, the parents notified, and the child sent home until a physician clears him to return to school.

SCARLATINA (Scarlet Fever). Scarlatina is a streptococcal (strep) throat infection accompanied by a rash. Tiny red pin dots appear over the skin giving it the appearance of a scarlet flush, and the normal bumps on the tongue get bigger and redder. Rapid treatment with antibiotics is necessary, so the parent should be notified and the child sent home until cleared by a physician.

VIRAL RASHES. There are hundreds of viral rashes that are contagious, so any child who is suspect should be removed from other children until cleared by professional medical personnel.

ALLERGIES. Allergic reactions can cause symptoms that may produce various rashes or swellings, or may duplicate symptoms of the common cold. In rare instances, allergies can prove fatal, as in the case of allergic reactions to insect bites. Since only trained medical professionals can accurately evaluate such symptoms, it is best to remove the child from the proximity of other children until the condition is diagnosed as noncontagious.

If a child receives an insect bite and develops hives all over the body, experiences shortness of breath, difficulty in swallowing, and tightening of the throat muscles, he is probably having an allergic reaction which could prove fatal. The child should be given emergency medical care. Other insect bites can be treated with ice to reduce swelling, pain, and itching.

Lice

It's a safe bet that every year there will be cases of lice in any school. Lice fall into two basic categories: crab lice which inhabit pubic hair, or in the case of children, eyelashes or eyebrows; and head lice which inhabit the hair of the head and lay eggs (nits). Lice can be removed by using prescription shampoos, but they spread easily, so the child should be sent home until effective treatment is undertaken.

Stomachaches

Stomachaches and children seem to go hand in hand. Most stomachaches are the result of indigestion or a math test. They usually pass quickly and require no more on your part than a little sympathy. The main thing to watch out for in stomachache complainers is possible appendicitis. If the pain is accompanied by fever, tenderness in the lower right (or sometimes left) side, and the pain gets progressively worse, it may be appendicitis and the parent should be notified. Appendicitis is not easy even for a physician to diagnose, so do the best you can and always play it safe by contacting the parent if you have any doubts. The parent will know whether "Johnny has those stomachaches all the time and his doctor says it's nothing to worry about," or whether to have the child checked by a physician.

Headaches

Exam week or major tests increase the incidents of headaches in most schools. If, and only if you have *written* permission, an aspirin or headache remedy given according to label directions takes care of ninety-nine percent of all headaches. The other one percent may require a call to the parent.

Vomiting

Some children can spit up on cue. Vomiting is not usually a cause for concern, unless poisoning is suspected. If the child vomits more than once, or does not feel better after resting for a few minutes, contact the parents, or in the case of suspected poisoning, follow appropriate emergency procedures.

The Abused Child

Child abuse can take many forms—physical abuse; mental abuse; or sexual abuse. The abused child often has a very poor self-image and feels that he must be at fault and must have done something bad, or, in fact, he must be bad and therefore deserving of such treatment. The abused child will seldom volunteer information about the abuse and will often try to hide it and protect the abuser because of confusion, misplaced loyalty, guilt, or shame. Repeated or unaccounted for marks, scars, and bruises should be considered suspect. Bring any such concerns to the attention of your administrator. Sometimes a child will really want you to guess what the problem is and will throw out hints in conversation. Try to be sensitive in picking up these hints, but remember also that children love to dramatize a situation. There may not be an abuse situation at all, but they may relish the attention they get from making one up.

This is a difficult area to cope with. Rely on the training and wisdom of your administrator or a professional counselor. Also, most cities have child abuse centers that can help and will investigate suspected child abuse situations.

Onset of Puberty

Hormonal changes cause much disruption in the pubescent child. Tears and tantrums, fears and fights are everyday occurrences. With the sex education program provided by contemporary schools and parents, most children are provided with adequate facts about the changes taking place in their bodies, and are prepared to accept them. A little guidance or support may be needed in the case of girls having their first menstrual periods, however, so if you are acting as school nurse, be ready to be supportive and patient. Respond honestly and factually to any questions (if you can) and keep personal prejudices to yourself.

Convulsions

Most schools have at least one or two epileptic students or staff members. While most epileptics are able to lead perfectly normal lives and control their convulsive seizures through medication, it is possible that occasional convulsions may occur, and that you will be called on to help the person. Be advised too, that young children sometimes suffer from febrile convulsions (caused by high fevers), which have nothing to do with epilepsy.

Since there has been much misinformation passed down about epilepsy and convulsions, it might be wise to try and clear up any misunderstandings. Convulsions are involuntary muscle spasms caused by sudden erratic nerve impulses coming from the brain. Epilepsy or convulsions are not in any way related to insanity. There is absolutely no reason to fear someone who is prone to convulsions. Your concern should be to protect the person from harming himself while the convulsion is in progress, and to protect him from ridicule or embarrassment following the episode. Attempt to educate the ignorant and uninformed about convulsions. A convulsion usually lasts only a few seconds, but during that time the person will twitch and thrash around and is liable to be injured from hitting his arms, legs, or head against the floor or furniture. Here are some guidelines to follow during a convulsion:

1. Do not pin the person to the floor, as this may make the seizure worse. Instead, remove potentially hazardous objects from his path.

2. Since the person stops breathing during a seizure, swallowing the tongue does not pose any particular hazard. The chances of a person doing really serious injury to himself by biting his tongue are slim compared to the damage you might do in trying to force something into his mouth, so just leave the person alone after removing hazardous objects from the area.

3. After the seizure, the person will be groggy. Lay him on his side to prevent fluids from blocking his breathing passages.

4. Do not give food or drink; this may cause choking.

5. Call for professional help.

For further information about epilepsy and how to deal with it, contact The Epilepsy Foundation of America, 1828 L Street, N.W., Washington, DC 20036.

First aid is essential for each of us to know. If, after reading this section, you still feel a little uneasy or unsure of your first aid skills, please consider enrolling in Red Cross courses—their benefits cannot be overstated. Even if you do not have an opportunity to use first aid skills on the job, they could prove to be a tremendous benefit in your personal life.

Obtaining First Aid Supplies

A trip to the local drugstore may solve most of your first aid needs, or you can order directly from a supplier. Buying supplies in bulk can save as much as seventy-five percent off the retail cost, depending on the item and the quantity ordered. A variety of first aid kits is available, or you may choose to purchase some items on an individual basis and others in bulk to suit your particular needs. For example, you may decide that a smaller quantity of eye wash and a larger amount of adhesive bandages would better suit you than that provided in kit form, or that some of the items provided in kits are unnecessary for you. Kits have definite advantages though, in that they are portable and are usually housed in dustproof and waterproof containers.

You can custom-design your own kit by purchasing in bulk the items you use most frequently and keeping them in portable metal containers such as tackle

boxes or tool kits. The following items should be included in a school first aid
kit:

- sterile bottled eye wash (this can be invaluable in the removal of foreign
  objects or in flushing out chemicals)
- 2×2 sterile gauze pads
- 3×3 sterile gauze pads
- adhesive or surgical tape
- self-adhering gauze bandage
- scissors
- tweezers
- cotton swabs
- first aid guide (Refer to FIRST AID, BASIC INFORMATION)
- sterile cotton
- aspirin or aspirin substitute (also children's aspirin if necessary)
- adhesive bandages preferably with nonstick pads in regular and extra-
  large sizes for knees
- eye pads (to keep the eye from further injury until medical help is
  available)
- three-inch gauze bandage
- antiseptic spray or cream and/or hydrogen peroxide
- elastic bandages in two- and three-inch sizes
- mouth-to-mouth breather unit for artificial respiration
- rescue blanket designed to retain body heat for shock victims
- ice packs
- snake bite kit (if necessary for your location)

FOOD, ORDERING   If your school is large enough to have a cafeteria, food
ordering is usually handled by the cafeteria staff. It may be necessary, however,
for you to order milk or juice for snack time, or to arrange for catered food in
private institutions. The procedure for this is basically the same as for ordering
any other merchandise. You will need to give the vendor precise information,
and keep accurate records of orders and deliveries.

Storage of Food

When food items are delivered, it is essential that they be given prompt attention
to avoid their spoiling. Perishable items should be placed under refrigeration im-

mediately, especially milk, other dairy products, and meat. Fresh fruits or vegetables should be left in their crates and placed on racks or shelves off the floor. Cereals and flour products must be stored off the floor so that they cannot be contaminated by water spillage. All chemicals and insecticides should be stored far away from foodstuffs. If any items that are delivered have broken seals, or packages have an offensive odor, either do not accept delivery, or report the damage to the vendor immediately.

FOOTNOTES Footnotes play an important role in academic reports and papers. They indicate the sources of borrowed facts that are included in the report.

When to Use Footnotes

1. For every direct quotation.
2. For every important statement of fact, unless all the facts in one paragraph come from the same source, in which case a single footnote is sufficient.
3. For an opinion borrowed from another writer.

How to Organize Footnotes

1. Footnotes should be numbered continuously for the entire paper or for each chapter if the report is divided into chapters.
2. Call attention to the footnote by typing the number at the end of the statement or paragraph by turning the typewriter one-half space up from the typed line. Do not use parentheses or a period following the footnote number in the text.
3. Indicate the number of the footnote at the bottom of the page. Single-space footnotes and set them off from the rest of the text by a line fifteen spaces long beginning at the left margin. The line should be a single space below the text.

Sample Footnotes

In conclusion, it is not surprising that footnotes are placed at the foot of a page.[1]

---

1. Sometimes notes are inserted between the lines at points in the text, or they may be grouped at the end of chapters.

Abbreviations Often Used in Footnotes

art. and arts., for article and articles
c., for copyright

ca., for *circa* (about a given date)
cf., for *confer* (compare, see)

chap. and chaps., for chapter and chapters
col. and cols., for column and columns
ed. and eds., for editor, edition, and editors
et al., for *et alii* (and others, other authors)
f. and ff., for the following page or line, pages or lines
fig. and figs., for figure and figures
ibid., for *ibidem* (in the same place)
1. and 11., for line and lines
loc. cit., for *loco citato* (in the place cited)

n. and nn., for note and notes
n.d., for no date, used in bibliographies
no. and nos., for number and numbers
op. cit., for *opere citato* (in the work cited)
p. and pp., for page and pages
sec. and secs., for section and sections
st., for stanza
vol. and vols., for volume and volumes
v. and vv., for verse and verses

FOREIGN STUDENTS People living in the United States who are not United States citizens are classified into four groups: immigrants, nonimmigrants, parolees and undocumented aliens. Persons in all these categories can become students in elementary and secondary schools. An immigrant has been legally admitted to the United States as a permanent resident alien and may elect to become a citizen after living in the United States for five years and passing a test. A nonimmigrant resides abroad and is a citizen of a foreign country but is in the United States temporarily, sometimes specifically to get an education.

Before any school can accept or enroll a foreign student with F-1 (nonimmigrant) status, it must complete legal steps in order to comply with Immigration and Naturalization Service (INS) regulations. First, the school or school district must be authorized to accept and enroll foreign students. This authority is granted after an application is made to the local District Director of the INS. The filing form is I-17. Once the application has been approved and the authority has been granted, the designated school official can sign the Certificate of Eligibility (INS Form I-20) which must be issued to prospective nonimmigrant students in order for them to remain in school here. The administrator will usually be required to sign the I-20 form, although you will undoubtedly be the one who fills it out.

Before a student can be issued an I-20 Form, however, three conditions must be met: (1) the student must meet the requirements of the school and must have been accepted by them based on academic qualifications; (2) the student must be proficient in English or the school must be willing to provide the student with special English language instruction; (3) the student must furnish the school with evidence from his family, sponsor, or by scholarship that he is able to meet all educational and living expenses while in the United States. Students here on an F-1 visa are not permitted to accept employment of any kind except as specifically authorized by INS regulations. A new bulletin from the INS will be forthcoming shortly, updating regulations and rules for foreign students. If you wish to get further information, contact the National Association for Foreign Student Affairs, 1860–19 Street N.W., Washington, D.C. 20009, or your local INS.

FORMS, DESIGNING   You may be asked to create new school forms or to redesign existing forms that have become obsolete. In either case there are a few things to consider. What function will the form serve? Is it really necessary or can an existing form do the job? Can an existing form be modified rather than starting from scratch? ALL the necessary data must be gathered before you begin. If you are modifying an existing form, are there problems that should be eliminated in the redesigned version? Remember to leave enough space for the desired information to be filled in. Most people find it extremely frustrating to be faced with a one-inch line when asked to give information that will require several lines. If the form is to be professionally printed, check with your printer and see if he has any tips about the weight of the paper, carbonless paper, or other information that can help to make the redesigned form as efficient as possible.

GALLEY PROOFS Galley proofs are sheets of paper that show the lines of type just as they have been set by the typesetting machine. They are usually issued for jobs at least booklet size in length. Single-page jobs, cards, and forms usually require a proof of the job as it will look when completed.

GRAMMAR, USAGE TIPS Following is a glossary of words that are commonly confused or misused. They are arranged alphabetically for quick reference.

a	Use "a" before all consonant sounds, "h" (if it is pronounced), "w," and a long "u." For example, a tree, a hospital, a wintry day, a unicorn
an	Use "an" before all vowel sounds except long "u," and before words beginning with silent "h." For example, an elephant, an honorary degree
accept	to receive, or an affirmative reply
except	excluding
	He graciously *accepted* the commission.
	They were all on time *except* you.
affect	to change
effect	the result of change
	The illness has *affected* his entire life.
	Obesity is the *effect* of overeating.
allusion	an indirect reference

illusion	a fantasy; a deceptive image
	In his recent speech, he made *allusions* to Freud's theories.
	It has often been said that dreams are reality and reality **an** *illusion*.
all ready	everyone is prepared
already	previously
	Are you *all ready* to go?
	I have *already* done that.
altar	a dais for worship
alter	to change
	She placed flowers on the *altar* for the wedding.
	A beard can really *alter* a man's appearance.
amount	total (used with singular)
number	individual items (used with plural)
	She carries a large *amount* of excess weight.
	The *number* of people was smaller than expected.
as	See "like."
beside	alongside; by comparison with
besides	in addition to; furthermore; other than
	The flower lay *beside* the dish.
	There will be many others in attendance *besides* you.
born	brought into existence
borne	(past participle of bear); to have undergone
	She was *born* in April.
	He has *borne* the consequences with dignity.
brake	a device for stopping a machine or vehicle
break	to shatter or burst
	The car's *brakes* were faulty.
	The earth tremor caused the vase to *break*.
capital	chief; principal; wealth or money; the top part of a column or pillar; the chief city of a state or country
capitol	the main government building
	capital city, capital gains, capital of a column, investment capital

Congress meets in the *Capitol* Building in Washington, D.C., which is the *capital* of the United States.

choir	a group of singers
quire	24 or 25 sheets of paper (1/20 of a ream)
cite	to refer to; to summon
site	a plot of ground; location
sight	the act of seeing

He *cited* passages from the Bible in which Christ restored the *sight* of the blind at a local *site*.

coarse	rough; vulgar; unrefined
course	path; direction; part of a meal

She served *coarse* peasant bread with the first *course* of the meal.

complement	that which completes; a set
compliment	praise; congratulations

On the color wheel, red and green are *complementary* colors.

I have received many *compliments* on my new dress.

console	(verb) (con sole′) to comfort
console	(noun) (con′sole) an ornamental bracket; a table; a cabinet
consul	a government official
council	a group gathered for consultation
counsel	advice; a lawyer

The *council* met to receive *counsel* from the attorney.

desert	(verb) to abandon
	(noun) an arid wilderness
dessert	(noun) a deserving reward or punishment; the sweet course of a meal
emigrate	to move to another region
immigrate	to arrive in a new region
fewer	of small number (use with items that can be counted)
less	a smaller amount (use with amounts)

This year there are *fewer* members.

After tax deductions my salary is *less* this year than last.

formally	prim; conventional; traditional
formerly	in the past
imply	to indicate or hint; suggest
infer	to draw a conclusion by reasoning from facts or evidence (Use in the same way as conclude; for informal usage you may substitute "gather.")
	Are you *implying* that I stole that money?
	Am I to *infer* that he is a thief?
its	belonging to (possessive)
it's	contraction of it is or it has
	I gave the dog *its* supper.
	It's going to rain.
later	subsequently
latter	the last mentioned (as opposed to former)
	I will see you *later*.
	Of the two comments, I agree with the *latter*.
lay	to place or put
lie	to recline
	His coat *lay* on the sofa.
	I am going to *lie* down for a while.
lead	(verb) to show the way
lead	(noun) a metal; pencil lead
led	past tense of to lead
like	a preposition that introduces a prepositional phrase
as	a conjunction that introduces a subordinate clause
	Like and as are *not* interchangeable.
	Martha delivered her speech *as* she was taught.
	That secretary seems *like* a nice person.
loose	(adjective) free; unbound
lose	(verb) to mislay
miner	a person who works in a mine digging ore
minor	lesser in rank; under legal age
moral	(adjective) referring to character or the choosing between right and wrong

morale	(noun) enthusiasm or willingness to endure hardships; state of mind
passed	(adjective) qualified; fulfilled a requirement
passed	(verb) past tense of to pass; gone by; ended
	The *passed* exam was actually more difficult than the one he failed. (adjective)
	He *passed* the test with flying colors. (verb)
past	(adjective) a time or condition gone by; over
past	(noun) the history of a person or group
peace	freedom from war or strife
piece	a fragment or part
personal	private; of a person
personnel	employees; persons engaged in work
plain	clearly understood, evident
plane	flat, level, even
principal	chief, main; head of a school
principle	a fundamental truth
stationary	not moving
stationery	paper and envelopes
than	used with expressing comparison
then	a point in time
	I like this better *than* that.
their	possessive form of they
there	at a particular place
they're	contraction of they are
to	in the direction of (also used with infinitive verb form)
too	also; as well
two	the number between one and three
waist	the area between ribs and hips
waste	refuse, trash
whether	used to introduce an indirect question
weather	the condition of the atmosphere (rain, snow, etc.)
	She wanted to know *whether* I would help.
	The *weather* is lovely today.

who   (nominative case) use this pronoun in the subject position

whom   (objective case) use this pronoun in the object position

GRAPHICS

Glossary of Common Terms

accordion fold	in binding, a term which describes a fold that opens like an accordion
against the grain	folding paper at right angles to the grain
agate line	a measurement for depth of columns of space
airbrush	a pressure gun device used to apply pigment by spraying
ascender	that part of a letter which rises above the main body, as in "d"
backbone	the back of a bound book, also called the spine
bad break	an incorrect word division
basis weight	the weight in pounds of a ream (500 sheets) of paper cut to a specific standard size for that grade
binders' board	a grade of board used in making the covers of cased books
bleed	extension of a printed image beyond the border or trim edge of a page
blocking out	eliminating undesirable portions by opaquing the image
blowup	an enlargement
body	a term referring to the viscosity or covering power of ink
body type	the kind of type used for the main text of a book as opposed to headings
boldface type	heavier than the surrounding type
bond paper	a grade of paper suitable for correspondence; it is strong, durable and permanent
book paper	a grade of papers used in graphic arts, suitable for book printing
break for color	to separate different color parts

brownprint	a brown-colored proof photograph
case	the covers of a hardbound book
chalking	dusting caused by improper drying of ink
cold type	a direct impression method of typesetting
collate	assembling of sheets for binding
continuous tone	a photograph that contains all the tones from black to white
contrast	the gradations between highlights and shadows
copy	the material that is to be reproduced in printing
copyfitting	fitting the content of a piece into a given area
crop	to eliminate portions of copy
cut	a photoengraving
deckle edge	the untrimmed feather edge of paper
descender	the part of a letter extending below the main body, as "q"
display type	type set larger than the text to attract attention
dummy	a preliminary drawing or layout showing positions as they will appear in the final reproduction
em	the square of a type body
embossing	impressing an image in relief to get a raised surface
expanded type	greater width than normal; also called extended type
face	the printing surface of type
facsimile	the exact reproduction of an item, sometimes abbreviated "fax"
felt side	the smoother side of paper best for printing
folio	the page number
font	the complete assortment of type of one size and face
galley	the metal tray used to hold type
galley proof	a proof of set type as it is in the galley before being made up into pages
grain	the direction in which the fibers lie within the paper
halftone	a reproduction whereby the image is formed by dots of various sizes
italic	letters that slope forward and are used for emphasis

justify	to space uniformly to the correct length
kraft	paper or board made from unbleached wood pulp
laid paper	paper patterned with a grid of parallel lines giving a ribbed look
ledger paper	a type of paper used in record keeping
letterspacing	the spacing between each letter
line copy	copy suitable for reproduction as is without using a screen
logotype or logo	the name of a company or product formed into a special design and used as a trademark
lower case	small letters as opposed to capitals
M	the abbreviation for one thousand
matte finish	dull finish without gloss
mechanical	a pasteup or layout
newsprint	paper made from wood pulp and most commonly used in printing newspapers
opacity	a property of paper which minimizes the ability to show through
overlay	a transparent covering over copy on which additional information, instructions, or copy is placed
overprinting	double printing of an area
perfecting press	a process that prints both sides of the paper at once
pica	a printer's measure in which one pica equals ⅙ of an inch
point	a printer's measure of type sizes; 72 points to an inch
ream	500 sheets of paper
scaling	determining the proper size for an item that is to be reproduced
score	an indentation made to expedite folding
self-cover	a cover that is the same weight paper as the text pages
serif	the cross lines of letters, as in "t"
sizing	a paper treatment which makes it resist liquid penetration
spiral binding	a book bound with spiral wires that are set into holes along the binding edge

stock	the paper or board that is to be printed
text	the body of copy as opposed to headings
tissue overlay	a thin sheet of tissue applied over artwork for protection or used as an overlay
watermark	a name or design impressed on the paper during manufacture
widow	a single word by itself in a line which cnds a paragraph; not good typesetting

Graphics Layout Tips

— To prevent rulers and bottles from sliding, glue strips of sandpaper on the bottoms.

— To keep wet ink and drawings from smearing while drying, make a "clothesline file." Hang some string in an unobtrusive place and clip the drawings to the string with clothespins.

— Keep your fingers off artwork by holding the piece by the edges. Do not cough or talk over the artwork as it may run or stain.

— Mark every piece of artwork with the school's name and address on the back so that it will not get lost at the printer.

— To protect artwork when mailing, lay it between two sheets of corrugated cardboard that are slightly larger than the original.

— Use an old telephone book or catalog as a backup for brushing on glue or rubber cement. If you get glue smudges on the page simply tear it off and discard it. The next clean page is ready for use.

— You can dry mount a layout with rubber cement as follows:

    (1) Spread rubber cement over the back of the illustration after placing it face down on a clean surface;

    (2) Spread rubber cement over the area where it is to be placed and positioned;

    (3) When both cemented areas are dry, carefully set the illustration onto the background and apply gentle pressure. Cover the artwork with a clean piece of paper before applying pressure.

— When working with photographs, never write instructions on the back of the photo with ink or felt tip pen as it may bleed through and stain the other side. If the subject of a photo is not easily recognizable, indicate which is the top and bottom of the photo on the back in pencil.

- You can achieve harmony in a design by:
  (1) Keeping the caption and text style the same.
  (2) Centering all elements for a symmetric balance. (If you wish to achieve an asymmetric image, it is still important to balance the composition.)
  (3) Choosing colors that work well together.
  (4) Maintaining a balance between light and dark areas of the design.

- For ease in carrying brushes or pens, fold a stiff card into a pocket. Stretch two rubber bands around it and slip in the pens or brushes.

- To revive an old brush that is misshapen, dip it into a water-soluble glue (such as white glue) and work the hairs between your fingers until they are reshaped. Then hang the brush to dry for a day or so. When it is dry, wash it and remove the glue. It should now have its original shape again.

- If a ballpoint pen still has ink but will not write, try holding a match or cigarette tip to it for a minute or so; sometimes the heat will make the ink flow again.

- If you spill rubber cement, first stand the container upright to prevent further spills. Then take two small stiff cards and scoop up the spill. If the cement is clean, you can return it to the bottle; otherwise, deposit it into an old can, carton, or envelope, and discard it. The remaining residue of rubber cement can easily be rubbed off most surfaces once it is dry.

GRAVURE   Gravure is an example of intaglio printing, which is the opposite of relief printing. In this case, the image area is recessed rather than raised. It is costly to make gravure plates but the reproduction quality is excellent. Large color jobs such as catalogs usually use the gravure process. Steel-die engraving uses an etched copper plate to form the image.

GUIDANCE RECORDS   Guidance or counseling folders are often maintained separately from the students' other records, in or near the office of the school guidance counselor. Upon the student's graduation or leaving the school, the guidance folder is added to the student's cumulative file. Guidance folders will often include the following:

- I.Q. (intelligence quotient) test scores
- Psychological test data

- Vocational test data
- Copies of report cards or transcripts
- Attendance information
- Behavior reports
- Medical data

As with all student records, guidance records are confidential. No information may be released without the written consent of the student (if adult) or the parent (if the student is a minor).

HEALTH DEPARTMENT, REPORTING OF DISEASE TO It is usually required that certain communicable diseases be reported to the health department. Figure 15 gives a listing of diseases that should be reported to your local health department. However, it is wise to check with the department in your area for current information. Figure 16 provides you with information on the

Amebiasis
Anthrax
Botulism
Brucellosis (Undulant Fever)
Chancroid
Cholera
Coccidioiomycosis
Conjunctivitis, Acute Infection of the New born (Gonorrheal Ophthalmia, Ophthalmia Neonatorum, and Babies' Sore Eyes in the first 21 days of life)
Dengue
Diarrhea of the Newborn
Diphtheria
Disorders Characterized by Lapses of Consciousness
Dysentery, Bacillary (see Shigella Infections)
Encephalitis, viral
Food Poisoning (other than Botulism)

German Measles (Rubella)
Gonococcal Infections
Granuloma Inguinale
Hepatitis, Infectious (A)
Hepatitis, Serum (B)
Hepatitis, unspecified
Leprosy (Hansen's Disease)
Lymphogranuloma Venereum (Lymphogranuloma Inguinale)
Malaria.
Measles (Rubeola)
Meningitis, Viral
Meningcoccal Infections
Mumps
Paratyphoid Fever, A, B and C (see Salmonella Infections)
Pertussis (Whooping cough)
Plague
Poliomyelitis, Paralytic
Psittacosis
Q Fever
Rabies, Human or Animal
Relapsing Fever

Rheumatic Fever, Acute
Rocky Mountain Spotted Fever
Salmonella, Infectious (exclusive of typhoid fever)
Scarlet fever
Shigella Infections
Smallpox (Variola)
Streptococcal Infections, hemolytic (including Scarlet Fever & Streptococcal Sore Throat)
Syphilis
Tetanus
Trachoma
Trichinosis
Tuberculosis
Tularemia
Typhoid fever, cases and carriers
Typhus fever
Viral Exanthem in Pregnant Women
Yellow Fever

FIGURE 15

If a member of your school contracts any of the above-mentioned communicable diseases, it should be reported to your local health department immediately. It is always wise to keep in touch with them for current information and reporting requirements.

DISEASE	PATIENT		CONTACT (2)	
	Minimal Period of Exclusion	Special Requirements for Re-admission	Period of Observation (3)	Other Prophylactic Measures
Chickenpox	Seven days after blisters appear.	None.	Three weeks.	None.
Conjunctivitis, epidemic (pink-eye)(4)	Duration of illness.	None.	Three days.	None.
Diphtheria (1)	Duration of illness.	Authorization by Health Department	Household: (In home) until authorized to return by Health Department (5). Classroom: Five days.	Booster if five years or more since last.
Hepatitis, Infectious	Seven days after onset.	None.	Seven weeks.	Household: Refer to physician for decision concerning gamma globulin. Classroom: None.
Measles	Seven days after rash appears.	None.	Two weeks.	Refer to physician for decision concerning gamma globulin.
Meningococcal (1) disease, including meningitis	Duration of illness.	Authorization by Health Department	Five days.	Household: Refer to physician. Classroom: None.
Mumps	Nine days after onset, or until swelling subsides, if less.	None.	Three weeks.	None.
Poliomyelitis	Seven days or for duration of fever.	None.	Three weeks.	Under age 18 years, give booster if five years or more since last.
Rubella	Duration of illness.	None.	Three weeks.	None.
Salmonella, shigella and typhoid	Duration of illness.	Authorization by Health Department	Three weeks, for typhoid, Three days for other (2).	To be determined by Health Department.

Scabies (4)
Impetigo
Ringworm:
  Skin
  Scalp
Pediculosis
	Until under medical treatment.	Unhealed lesions must be covered, including scalp.	Variable.	None.

Smallpox *	Duration of illness.	Authorization by Health Department	Until vaccination or re-vaccination read as positive by physician.	Vaccination or re-vaccination required of all contacts, all ages.
Streptococcal disease, including scarlet fever	Duration of illness.	None.	Three days.	None.
Tuberculosis	Duration of illness.	Authorization by Health Department	Variable. May include skin-testing and chest X-ray.	Refer to a physician for evaluation.
Whooping cough	Duration of cough.	None.	Two weeks.	None.

*Smallpox has been officially declared eradicated from the world as of May 1980. Routine smallpox immunization is no longer recommended.

NOTES:

1. For diphtheria, meningococcal disease, and the salmonella-shigella-typhoid group, a "carrier state" may persist in a recovered patient, or in a household contact. These apparently healthy carriers (of the disease organism) must be individually evaluated by the Health Department for school exclusion, re-admission or working in the school cafeteria.

2. Household contacts are considered intimate; classroom contacts are more casual and, for some diseases, are less likely to produce illness in the contact. Hence, the varied recommendations. For the salmonella-shigella-typhoid group, "contact" also includes persons who may have ingested contaminated materials in same meals or prepared by same food handlers as patient, even if at different times or places. Susceptibility of contact (a person not previously immunized or having had the disease) should be evaluated and considered.

3. Period stated refers to time since onset of last case in classroom. If fever or other early signs of illness appear in contacts, disease in question must be ruled out.

4. Reportable only if outbreak of multiple cases.

FIGURE 16

This chart provides a quick reference in identifying the periods of exclusion from school for common communicable diseases.

187

MEDICAL TERMS

Bordetella pertussis	Bacterium that causes pertussis (whooping cough)
Clostridium tetani	Bacterium that causes tetanus
Corynebacterium diphtheriae	Bacterium that causes diphtheria
Diphtheria	A very serious disease which can affect people in different ways. It can cause an infection in the nose and throat which can interfere with breathing. It can also cause an infection of the skin. Sometimes it causes heart failure and paralysis. About 1 person out of every 10 who get diphtheria dies of it.
Epidemic parotitis	Mumps.
GG	Gamma globulin; sometimes used as synonym for ISG or MIG.
ISG	Immune serum globulin; formerly given with live attenuated measles vaccine to forestall serious reactions.
Measles (Rubeola)	The most serious of the common childhood diseases. Usually it causes a rash, high fever, cough, runny nose, and watery eyes lasting 1 to 2 weeks. Sometimes it is more serious. It causes an ear infection or pneumonia in nearly 1 out of 10 children who get it. One child out of every 1,000 who gets measles has an inflammation of the brain (encephalitis). This can lead to convulsions, deafness, or mental retardation. One child in every 10,000 who gets measles dies of it.
MIG	Measles immune globulin; formerly given with live attenuated measles vaccine to forestall serious reactions.
Mumps	A common disease of children. Usually it causes fever, headache, and inflammation of the salivary glands, which causes the cheeks to swell. Sometimes it is more serious. It causes a type of meningitis in about 1 child in every 20 who gets it. More rarely, it can cause inflammation of the brain (encephalitis). This usually goes away without leaving permanent damage, but it can cause deafness.
Pertussis (whooping cough)	Causes severe spasms of coughing which can interfere with breathing. It also often causes pneumonia. Convulsions, brain damage, and death may occur, most often in very young infants.
Poliomyelitis	A contagious viral disease that, in its severe form, can cause permanent paralysis. It is caused by three types of virus that live in the noses, throats and, especially in the intestinal tracts of infected people. Type I virus is the most frequent cause of illness and paralysis. Virus Types II and III are milder and do not usually cause outbreaks. Polio occurs most often in children between the ages of one and sixteen.
Rubella (German Measles, 3-day measles)	A common disease of children and may also affect adults. Usually it is very mild and causes a slight fever, rash, and swelling of glands in the neck. The sickness lasts about 3 days. Sometimes, especially in adult women, there may be swelling and aching of the joints for a week or two. Very rarely, rubella can cause inflammation of the brain (encephalitis) or cause a cut to bleed longer than normal. If a pregnant woman gets rubella, there's a good chance that she may have a miscarriage or that the child will be born crippled, blind, or with other defects.
Rubeola	Measles, 10-day measles, red measles.
Tetanus (lockjaw)	Results when wounds are infected with tetanus germs, which often grow in dirt. The bacteria in the wound make a poison which causes the muscles of the body to go into spasm. Six out of every 10 persons who get tetanus die of it.

FIGURE 17

This is a guide to commonly used medical terms that you may encounter when dealing with illness in the school.

GLOSSARY OF VACCINES AND MEDICAL TERMS

Attenuvax *	live further attenuated measles vaccine
Biavax *	mumps and rubella vaccine
Cendehill *	rubella vaccine
Cendevax *	rubella vaccine
Diplovax *	trivalent oral polio vaccine
DTP or DPT	diphtheria and tetanus toxioids and pertussis (whooping cough) vaccine
DT	diphtheria and tetanus toxoids
Edmonston B	live attenuated measles vaccine
Enders	live attenuated measles vaccine
HPV-77 or HPV-77-De5	rubella vaccine
IPV	inactivated polio vaccine
Infagen *	DPT vaccine
Lirugen *	live further attenuated measles vaccine
Meruvax *	rubella vaccine
M-M-R *	measles, mumps, and rubella vaccine
MOPV	monovalent oral polio vaccine
Moraten *	live further attenuated measles vaccine
M-R-Vax, M-R *	measles and rubella vaccine
Mumpsvax *	live attenuated mumps vaccine
MuR *	mumps and rubella vaccine
M-Vac *	live attenuated measles vaccine, Edmonston B strain
OPV	oral polio vaccine, monovalent or trivalent
Orimune *	trivalent oral polio vaccine. A monovalent oral polio vaccine was also marketed under this name.
Pfizer-vax Measles K *	inactivated measles vaccine
Pfizer-vax Measles L *	live attenuated measles vaccines, Edmonston B strain
Quadrigen *	inactivated polio vaccine combined with DTP vaccine
RA 27/3	rubella vaccine
Rubeovax *	live attenuated measles vaccine, Edmonston B strain
Sabin	oral polio vaccine, monovalent or trivalent
Salk	inactivated polio vaccine
Schwarz	live further attenuated measles vaccine
Td	tetanus and diphtheria toxoids (vaccine), "adult" type (used in children also)
Tetanus Toxoid, T	tetanus toxoid
TOPV	trivalent oral polio vaccine
Tri-Immunol *	DTP
Triogen *	DTP
Tri-Solgen	DTP
TVS	Trivalent Sabin

* Brand Name

FIGURE 18

This glossary of vaccines will help you understand immunization records more thoroughly, and will aid you in the recording of medical data.

duration and usual period of exclusion from school for common communicable diseases. It is a good idea to keep in close contact with your health department. They can give you valuable information and help in dealing with disease reporting, epidemics, immunization requirements, and communicable disease control. Figure 17 explains commonly used medical terms that will be helpful when dealing with illness in school. Figure 18 is a glossary of vaccines; this will aid you in understanding and recording medical data.

I

ILLUSTRATIONS, PREPARATION OF See also GRAPHICS, GLOS-SARY OF COMMON TERMS The first draft of artwork or illustrations is called the *rough layout*. Many changes or additional layouts may be made before the *finished layout* or *comprehensive* is prepared. The comprehensive is a finished piece that leaves no doubt as to what the printed product will look like. A *dummy* is then made of the proposed pieces. Once the dummy has been approved, the artist can then put together all the elements and prepare for reproduction. Artwork printing in the school is usually limited to logos for letterhead stationery, brochures, programs, and announcements. You will usually need to provide the graphic artist or printer with only a rough sketch or a verbal description of an idea and he will then prepare a rough layout for you.

The professionals will take care of *scaling* (changing the size of the original without changing the dimensions) and *cropping* (eliminating or reducing certain areas). The *pasteup* or *mechanical* is the final product which is then sent for reproduction.

When discussing illustrations with a printer it is helpful to understand the trade jargon. *Line* copy refers to type, diagrams, charts, and ink drawings. *Continuous tone* images may be photographs or rendered (drawn) illustrations. For reproduction purposes, continuous tone images must be converted to a series of dots or *halftones*. The human eye "fills in" the spaces between the dots and we think we see a complete image. An example of this is a blow-up of a newspaper photo which shows the dots clearly. Sometimes you might have to prepare simple illustrations for the printer. If so, here are some guidelines to help you:

  – Make the original 1½ times the size of the desired finished size. Defects will be reduced as the size is reduced.

- Keep the drawing in proportion to the size of the finished page.
- Use black ink or black press-on tape (available in art supply stores in a variety of widths) for marking lines.
- Shading is usually done on a tissue overlay.
- If you need help with an illustration, perhaps the art teacher or an artistic student can help.

IMPRINTING MACHINES   The most common use for imprinting machines in schools is for addressing envelopes, labels, or tags. Basically, there are three types of methods using the imprint process:

1. <u>Spirit Hectograph Master Cards</u>. These master cards are made with the aid of a ditto or hectograph machine. The image on the card is transferred to documents by means of a special fluid. About 250 imprints can be made from each card.

2. <u>Stencil Cards</u>. Small pieces of stencil mylar are mounted in cardboard frames, rather like photographic slides. The copy is typed or written on the stencil.

3. <u>Metal Plate Method</u>. Metal plates are embossed with the imprint information and are then run through a special machine that transfers the printed image via an inked ribbon.

With most of these methods, various accessories enable you to custom design a system to suit your school's particular requirements. Some of the newer stencils can be used a minimum of 10,000 times and still maintain a clear copy. The plates or cards for addressing machines may be kept in alphabetical order, or by subdivision groups suitable for different purposes—by grade, by geographic area, by subject area, and so on.

Some imprint machines have the capability of choosing the correct plates for a particular mailing. You simply key in the correct information to the machine and it skips over plates that are not covered by the instructions.

INK USED IN PRINTING   Inks are composed of three main parts: solid pigments from which the color is derived; fluid vehicles in which the pigment is suspended; chemical compounds such as driers. Four basic terms are applied when discussing printing inks:

1. <u>Body</u>. This is the consistency of ink, sometimes called the viscosity. It is the body that determines how freely ink will flow.

2. <u>Length</u>. This is the ability to form filaments. Long inks flow readily but form long filaments, which are not desirable for use with high speed presses. Short inks are the consistency of butter and can gum up equipment. Each type of equipment has its own best type of ink.

3. <u>Tack</u>. This is the stickiness of the ink. Offset inks must be tacky to print sharp images. In color printing, inks with a variety of tackiness are used so that one color will trap the next.

4. <u>Drying</u>. Drying is an important consideration when discussing printing inks, because the finished piece cannot be handled until the ink is completely dry. So the drying qualities of an ink relate to the speed of the job as well as to other factors.

Basic Ink Types

Letterpress Inks

These are usually paste form inks of moderate tack. Newsprint inks dry by penetration into the surface of the paper. Heat-set inks dry by evaporation.

Offset-Lithographic Inks

These inks are formulated to print from plane surfaces. One of the strongest inks; usually of intense colors; gloss or matte.

Gravure Inks

Rapid-drying fluid inks which must be free of particles that could scratch the engraved cylinder or plate.

Specialty Inks

- High Gloss Inks. These appear glossy when dry and contain extra varnish. The more resistant the surface of the paper, the glossier the ink will appear. These are available for both letterpress and offset.
- Quick Setting Inks. These dry almost on contact and have a fair gloss.
- Metallic Inks. This type of ink employs metallic powders such as aluminum or copper which give a metallic luster.
- Moisture Set Inks. These are almost free from odor and are ideal for food packaging printing.
- Magnetic Inks. These were developed to increase the speed and efficiency of handling bank checks as they can be read by electronic equipment.
- Scuff-Resistant Inks. These are excellent choices for packaging and mailing containers and items that will get rough handling.

- Fluorescent Inks. These semi-transparent inks must be printed on a white surface to provide maximum brilliance. They are suitable for jobs such as labeling, packaging, and direct mail.

INVOICES, HANDLING When an invoice arrives, depending on your school's system, you may forward it to the business office or accounting department, or you may have to process it yourself. If you are responsible for paying bills:

- Keep a copy of the invoice and mark it: ''Paid by check #_____ (date),'' then keep the copy on file.
- Before writing the check, make sure that the invoice has not already been paid.
- Make sure that the merchandise has been received in good order or that services have been rendered satisfactorily. If you have doubts, check before paying the bill.
- It is usually easier to pay bills once a month but some companies give discounts if a bill is paid within ten days of the billing date. In such cases, follow your school's established procedure or check with the administration.
- When you write a check, note the invoice number on the face of the check and on the check register. This can speed up the search for any misplaced or questionable items.

J

JUSTIFYING LINES   There may be times when you will need the right hand margin to be even or "justified" with all the type characters in perfect alignment. If you have an executive model typewriter with variable spacing, you can easily achieve a professional look. If, however, you have a typewriter with fixed spacing, here is a method for justifying lines:

1. Set up the required margin stops. Type your copy. Do not go beyond the margin. (This will be a draft copy.)
2. Fill in spaces between the end of the typed line and the margin with asterisks.
3. Glance over the copy and see where you can skip spaces the least noticeably. Indicate these areas by check marks.
4. Spread out the skips so that they are irregularly placed within the copy.
5. Retype the copy, skipping the spaces indicated by the check marks.

LAYOUT

For Printing

A printer's layout is the plan of the way the finished product will look. You will be able to get help from the printer or graphic designer working with you on the project, but it is helpful if you can visualize the completed piece and therefore explain your requirements carefully as to the effect you are trying to achieve. Remember to consider blank space; too much text or copy will seem crammed and hard to read. Unless you have had some experience with layouts, it is best to rely on the professional whose eye is trained to read such elements of design as composition, spacing, color, and scale.

For Typing

Before cutting a stencil or typing any project that must have a professional, crisp appearance when completed, it is wise to make a draft layout:

1. Set up a dummy page of tissue thin paper and draw in the margins leaving at least one-half inch at the top and bottom and five-eighths inch at each side.

2. Use tissue or thin paper and type up the copy.

3. If you are using an illustration, place it under the dummy and trace its outline in the area in which you wish it to be located.

4. Place your copy, signatures, or handwriting on the dummy, spacing them appropriately.

5. If you are cutting a stencil, place the dummy between the stencil and the

backing to see the exact location of various components. Mark the stencil accordingly with correction fluid before typing the copy.

6. If you are typing on paper, you can see exactly how the finished piece will look and save time and energy by making alterations or corrections in advance.

Here are some additional tips for producing a good-looking typing layout:

- Avoid a crowded appearance.
- Break up solid pages of typing by using caps or underlining for headings. Variety keeps the eye interested and an interested eye means an interested reader.
- Indent important paragraphs or passages or draw boxes around them— anything that will set them off from the main body of text.
- If you are using paper that is narrower than 8½ inches, and you are doing a layout for a stencil, use the upper left hand section of the stencil to type your copy.

LETTERPRESS   A method of printing that employs *relief*. It is the oldest and most flexible form of printing in use today. It is used in books, magazines, newspapers, and packages. Revision of the copy can be made at any stage of the process. In the letterpress process, the printing is done directly from type, which makes it very economical. *Flexography* is a letterpress process that uses flexible rubber plates and quick-drying ink that enables it to be used for printing on hard-surfaced materials such as plastic films and foil. *Thermography* or raised printing is another form of letterpress and is often used in formal invitations, business cards, announcements, and letterheads. It gives the effect of embossing or engraving at a fraction of the cost.

LOANS TO STUDENTS   Students may forget bus fare, lunch money, or other necessary funds. Most schools have a petty cash reserve for this purpose. Do not permit students to abuse this privilege by (1) borrowing funds needlessly, or (2) by forgetting to return borrowed monies. You can prevent these abuses by setting up a sign-out card system when funds are loaned. If a form is used, students are more likely to borrow only when necessary and to repay promptly. The form will also allow you to reconcile petty cash receipts more efficiently. You might also consider setting the policy that if a loan is still outstanding, no further monies can be borrowed until the loan has been repaid. This method teaches responsibility to younger students and prevents older students from taking advantage. When the loan form is filled out, be sure that the student signs for the money; then there can be no doubt as to the date and amount borrowed. Always check to be sure the amount has been filled in correctly before you give out any cash. Each week follow up on any outstanding loans. If the borrower is a minor, it may become necessary to contact the parent to arrange repayment.

LOCKERS AND LOCKS   Teachers usually assign locks and lockers, but you may have to keep the master list. A simple way to proceed is for the teacher to use a class roll sheet to record the locker and/or lock number as assigned, right next to the student's name. You will then need only to gather the lists and file them. Make extra copies of the locker lists for teachers, and always make an extra master copy for the administrator in case your list is misplaced. Students frequently change lockers at random without permission. This can cause chaos in your record keeping and you should insist that all locker changes be approved. Any unauthorized locker changes that come to your attention should be brought to the attention of the administrator in charge.

If your school uses combination locks, the lock company will provide you with a copy of the master combination list and/or a set of master keys. The master list and keys should always be kept locked up when not in use and should be accessible only to authorized persons.

LOST AND FOUND   In most schools, the lost and found room is kept locked and is open to students during specific hours. The number of lost items can be staggering, especially when there are so few claims. Clothing is usually hung on racks while other items are best kept in boxes sorted by category. If an article has a name tag, leave a message for the student to come and pick up the item. Students should be encouraged to check the lost and found room for their belongings. At specific periods throughout the year, sort through the items, return those with names, and make arrangements to distribute the rest. These are often turned over to parent groups or charitable organizations. Valuable items should be kept for longer periods of time and every effort made to locate the owner.

MAIL, SORTING Mail may be delivered by the postal service, by inter-school messenger, or by commercial package delivery services. In some cases, large schools have mail departments that will handle the routing. If it is your responsibility to distribute the mail, first sort it into three basic piles—administrative, faculty, and other.

Administrative Mail

Unless letters are marked "personal" or "confidential," the secretary usually opens the administrator's mail. Some administrators prefer to see all their mail, while others prefer the secretary to screen and direct the mail to appropriate people, leaving a much smaller pile to deal with. The administrative mail is usually sorted as follows:

1. Confidential or personal mail unopened and on top of the pile.
2. Letters needing an immediate response.
3. Letters that may be dealt with at a later date.
4. Advertising mail, brochures, or trade publications.

Place the mail in a folder marked "Mail" and place it on the administrator's desk. Using a folder for opened mail maintains confidentiality.

After opening a letter, staple the envelope to the reverse side. This provides a record of delivery dates should they become needed. Keep administrative mail that you will be answering in a separate pile. Discuss with your administrator in advance the type of letters that you will be personally responsible for answering.

Faculty Mail

Most schools have teachers' mailboxes—a series of pigeonholes with faculty names arranged in alphabetical order. After you have sorted all the mail into the three categories, take the faculty mail and distribute it in the faculty boxes. There is no need to alphabetize the mail if the boxes are in alphabetical order. Usually the secretary will have her own mailbox in which to receive notes and requests from the faculty. It is a good idea to check your mailbox several times a day to keep abreast of messages. Faculty mail should be delivered unopened. Mail addressed to "Department Chairman" may be distributed to the appropriate department and may require opening to determine correct routing.

Other Mail

Other mail may include letters that require forwarding or mail that is not addressed to a particular person. If mail is addressed to an employee who no longer works for the school, forward the mail to the new address or return it to the sender. Open the miscellaneous mail, quickly scan it, and route it to the appropriate person or department. If mail arrives that is too large for a teacher's mailbox, leave a note letting her know that a bulky package has arrived and needs to be picked up. It is a good idea to have a designated area for the storage of such packages that is not visible to visitors and may be secured with a lock if necessary.

MAILING

Bulk Mail

Large quantities of first-class mail get processed faster through the post office if you use postal trays, available on loan from the postal service, at no charge. Place your first-class mail in them with all the address sides facing the same direction; the service will be much faster than if you use mail sacks. It is a requirement that all third-class bulk mail be sorted by ZIP code and bundled or placed in a sack before being brought to the post office.

Efficiency Tips

1. Keep abreast of changes in the postal system that affect you or your school. Your local post office is as near as your telephone, and postal employees are usually well-informed, courteous, and ready to help you with any mailing questions or problems. Make use of their knowledge and expertise.

2. Even if your school is not nonprofit, you can still qualify for bulk mail rates if you are mailing 200 or more *identical* pieces at a time. Brochures, catalogs, flyers, and announcements all fall into this category. Check with your local post office if you need help with details.

3. If you use a postage meter, run a frequent check to be sure that impressions are legible and that they do not overlap. Since metered mail may only be presented for mailing on the date shown on the metered postmark, get in the habit of advancing the meter's date at a fixed time each day to avoid errors.

4. Double-check your mailing scale for accuracy periodically. If it is too high, you are paying too much postage. If it is set too low this could mean postage due for the addressee. A quick way to check your postal scale's accuracy is to place nine pennies on it; they should weigh exactly one ounce—adjust accordingly.

5. Pre-stamped envelopes or metered mail envelopes that are written in error but not mailed can receive a ninety-percent rebate from the post office. It is usually easier to collect at least a few dozen; then see your postal representative.

6. Carefully choose mailing envelopes to avoid confusion in the post office, and be sure to match the envelope size to its contents. When you are mailing in the large first-class manila envelopes, use specially marked ones with the distinctive green diamond border whenever possible, or clearly mark "First Class" in large letters on both sides of the envelope. Regular mailing envelopes should be no smaller than $3\frac{1}{2} \times$ 5 inches and no larger than $6\frac{1}{8} \times 11\frac{1}{2}$ inches.

7. Know the pickup and delivery times for your location. You can often save a whole day's delivery time by mailing before the pickup deadline.

8. Try to mail as early in the day as possible, rather than waiting until late afternoon when the post office will be overloaded.

9. The postal service will lend mail sacks and trays to large-volume users, and they also have dozens of free and helpful pamphlets and booklets to help you. Use your postal service wisely and take advantage of the free help offered to you.

10. Always use the correct ZIP code on your mailings. The post office mail sorting machines are able to read ZIP codes and this results in fast and accurate delivery. Always include your ZIP code in the return address. Refer to your *National ZIP Code Directory* when in doubt, and always keep your mailing lists up to date with current ZIP codes.

11. When using metered strips for parcels, place the metered stamp strip diagonally over the right corner of the address label.

12. You can enclose a first-class letter with a parcel without having to pay first-class rates for the entire package. Tape the letter (with its own postage on it) to the front of the package as the address label, or include the letter inside the package and mark the package "First-Class Mail Enclosed." Include the postage rate for the letter when applying postage for the package.

Metered Mail

When you use a mail meter, you are stamping and postmarking at the same time. This saves steps and time at the post office, and mail can be processed faster and dispatched earlier. If your school uses a mail meter, here are ways to obtain maximum benefits:

– Be sure the meter date is changed daily. If you set a specific time for this task (first thing in the morning or last thing in the afternoon) it can save you time and trouble.

– Select the correct postage. Overpaying wastes money and underpaying can result in embarrassing postage due charges to the addressee and cause delays in delivery. If you are unsure of the correct postage, contact your post office for help.

– Double-check to make sure the meter has made a clear and readable impression.

– Face mail in one direction and bundle according to ZIP codes or "local" and "out of town" categories before mailing. Five or more pieces of mail require bundling.

– Use fluorescent postage meter ink because it enables the postal machines to sort more quickly and accurately. The machine scans the special ink and knows that the envelope has already been cancelled.

Nonprofit Mail

The United States Postal Service allows qualified educational and other non-profit institutions to apply for special third-class mail rates. The United States Postal Service Form 3624, together with papers supporting the nonprofit status, must be filed with the Postal Service to obtain permission to use this special rate.

Packaging

To obtain the most from packaging, it is essential to use the proper container. Fiberboard boxes such as those found in the supermarket are strong enough to suit most school needs. The bottoms of most fiberboard cartons have printed indications of strength and mailing capabilities. For example,

Bursting test	175 lbs per square inch
Gross Weight Limit	40 lbs

The bursting test number tells you the carton's ability to resist rupturing or breaking. The gross weight limit lets you know the *maximum weight including materials for packaging* that the carton will hold. High-density objects such as metal equipment may require stronger boxes than average items.

Fiberboard Container Selection Guide

For Average-Density Items

Burst Test Strength	Weight Limit of Item
125 lbs	up to 20 lbs
175 lbs	up to 40 lbs
200 lbs	up to 65 lbs
275 lbs	up to 70 lbs

For High-Density Items

175 lbs	up to 20 lbs
200 lbs	up to 45 lbs
275 lbs	up to 70 lbs

If in doubt about an object, treat it as high-density when mailing it.

The selection of the container depends on the WEIGHT of the object being mailed; the SIZE of the object; the DURABILITY or fragility of the object; whether it is LIQUID OR SOLID; the SHAPE of the object.

Other packaging options besides fiberboard boxes include: metal cans, wooden crates, and fiber mailing tubes with metal ends. When choosing the container, consider the following:

- The container should be large enough to hold the contents and have room for cushioning, but should not be large enough to allow shifting of the contents.
- Liquids should be in leakproof containers.
- Items with a strong odor should be securely sealed. (Science supplies often fall into this category.)

Proper packaging and cushioning materials absorb shocks and prevent the contents from shifting. When packaging more than one item, be sure to keep them separated. Such fillers as shredded or crumpled paper, fiberboard inserts, styrofoam pellets, and packing plastic (with air bubbles) are suitable cushioning materials.

It is best to avoid using wrapping paper on a package whenever possible, since it could be torn off during shipping. If you do use paper, be sure to mark the address on the container itself as well as on the wrapping paper. The best package closure material is pressure-sensitive filament tape; twine is acceptable but can catch in mail processing equipment and is best avoided.

Clearly mark all packages with waterproof ink showing the name of the sender and receiver. If no waterproof ink is available, cover the address with scotch tape. It is a good idea to place a card with the receiver's and sender's name and address *inside the package* in case the outer address becomes damaged or unreadable.

Alert postal employees to the special nature of package contents by placing the appropriate markings on parcels such as "Fragile," "Perishable," "Do Not Bend," etc. It is illegal to send through the U.S. mail any hazardous items. Contact your local post office for information regarding safety or legality of mailing specific items that may be hazardous (perhaps science supplies) if you have any doubts.

Types of Mail Service Available

The United States Postal Service has a variety of rates and services available including:

- <u>First-Class Mail</u>. This is suitable for posting letters and general correspondence.
- <u>Presort First-Class Mail</u>. This rate allows a small saving (currently two cents on first-class letters and one cent each on postcards) if mail is presorted by ZIP code. This is usually done in large organizations by mail room computers. Nonprofit schools can benefit more from the special third-class rate for bulk mailings.
- <u>Parcel Post</u>. This is the most economical means of mailing packages.
- <u>Express Mail Next Day Service</u>. This serves most major cities and the package is delivered by the next day. Packages of up to seventy pounds can qualify for this service. Express Mail Service is guaranteed. If mail does not arrive on time, you can claim a refund (unless the delay was caused by a strike). If you send letters as part of a package shipment there is no extra charge for regular postage. Any post office that handles Ex-

press Mail will provide you with appropriate shipping labels and a receipt of the shipment. If you require a fixed regular Express Mail pickup service, this can be arranged with your post office for a nominal fee. Shipping charges are figured by weight and distance and $500 insurance is included at no extra charge. Express Mail Service is also available to major cities in the United Kingdom, the Netherlands, Brazil, Australia, Japan, Belgium, France, and the city of Hong Kong.

— Priority Mail. Packages are separated from regular parcel post packages and are handled like First-Class letters. If going to a nearby location, preferential overland transport is used; for distant locations air delivery is used. Within a 150-mile radius the package will usually be delivered the next day. To use this method, mark "PRIORITY" on all sides of the package. For a foreign delivery be sure to specify "AIR."

— Mailgram Service. This is a joint service by Western Union and the United States Postal Service. Messages are routed by ZIP codes via computers to a post office near the destination and are delivered the next business day by postal carriers.

— Insurance. This provides protection against loss or damage to domestic mail.

— Return Receipts. These provide proof of delivery and show to whom and when mail was delivered.

— C.O.D. "Cash on delivery" means that merchandise can be ordered and the price of the merchandise plus postage will be collected from the addressee.

— Certificate of Mailing. This provides proof of mailing only. It does not provide insurance, nor is a signed receipt obtained from the addressee.

— Special Delivery. This service provides delivery during hours that extend beyond normal delivery hours.

— Second-Class Mail. Only newspapers and other periodical publications that meet post office criteria as to size and weight may be mailed at second-class rates. However, catalogs and course listings are allowed under the term "periodical publications," so if your school regularly sends out course catalogs, this could well be the least expensive mailing method for you. Check with your administrator or local post office.

— Third-Class Mail. Nonprofit educational institutions and some other nonprofit institutions may qualify for third-class rate mailing privileges. An application and fee must be filed with the post office prior to using this class. Check with your administrator or the postal service if in doubt. Reduced rates can also apply to educational materials, books, and films that are mailed.

COMPANY	PRIMARY SHIPPING METHOD	AREA SERVED	PACKAGING PROVIDED	DOOR TO DOOR SERVICE	GUARANTEE	NOTICE OF DELIVERY	LETTER RATE	DELIVERY TIME
Air Couriers International 2150 E. Thomas Phoenix, AZ 85016	Air	World	Yes	Yes	Refund	No	No	Next Commercial Flight
DHL Corporation 1818 Gilbreth Burlingame, CA 94010	Air	World	Envelopes	Yes	No	No	No	Overnight
Emery Air Freight Old Danbury Road Wilton, CT 06897	Air	World	Yes	Yes	No	No	No	Overnight
Federal Express Memphis Intl. Airport Memphis TN 38130	Air	Nation	Yes	Yes	No	Yes	Yes	Overnight
Flying Tiger Line 7401 Worldway West Los Angeles, CA 90009	Air	World	No	Yes	Refund	Yes	No	Overnight
Greyhound Lines Greyhound Tower Phoenix, AZ 85077	Land	U.S. Canada	Yes	Yes	Partial Refund	No	Florida only	3-4 days
Purolator Courier Corp. 333 New Hyde Park Rd. New Hyde Park, NY 11042	Air Land	Nation	Yes	Yes	No	Yes	No	Overnight
Trailways 1500 Jackson Street Dallas, TX 75201	Land	Nation	Yes	Yes	Partial Refund	No	No	3-4 days
United Parcel Service 51 Weaver Street Greenwich, CT 06830	Air Land	Nation	No	Yes	No	No	No letters	2 days

FIGURE 19

Comparative Chart of Package Delivery Services

Alternative Mail Services

There are several alternatives to the United States Postal Service. If you have an urgent local delivery, there are numerous messenger services that can be located through your local telephone directory. These have radio-dispatched messengers to give you almost immediate service. For a comparative chart of alternative package-express services refer to Figure 19.

MEETINGS

Board Meetings

The Board of Supervisors or Board of Directors meets to discuss the processes of administration, financing, and maintenance of the school. The board is usually broken down into committees such as Finance Committee, Buildings and Grounds Committee, Academic or Curriculum Committee and so on. In the case of private institutions, a Nominating Committee may be assigned to recruit board members. The committees report directly to the board and usually give a report at each board meeting. In the past, board minutes were usually held in the strictest confidence, although there is a current trend toward making copies of the minutes available to faculty and/or parent bodies. Always check with the administrator before repeating anything gleaned from a board meeting. In certain instances, a board may choose to meet in executive session where only specific members may be present and recorded minutes may not be kept. If this occurs, the chairman may give you a prepared text to insert into the minutes.

Committee Meetings

These are usually less formal than board meetings and deal with a specific area. A committee may be formed for various reasons such as overseeing plans for new construction; studying the curriculum; preparing accreditation guidelines. Committees usually have no power to act, but study a proposal and then make recommendations to the board.

Faculty Meetings

A school secretary is often asked to record the minutes of faculty meetings. Faculty meetings may be departmental, interdepartmental, or general full faculty meetings. Although these are usually informal, an agenda is helpful for maintaining order and is usually used. Faculty meetings may include such topics as: curriculum planning; scheduling conflicts; discussions of awards programs; announcements and important dates; interdepartmental conflicts; student behavior problems; discussions about learning disabilities or new teaching methods; seminar information; guest speakers. Faculty meetings are forums in which to discuss the technicalities of teaching, to resolve problems that may arise, and to gain faculty input on ideas and methods as well as a time for implementing programs and making announcements.

Parent/Teacher Meetings

Parent/teacher meetings are usually held on a regular basis and involve interaction between the two groups in such areas as outings and field trips, curriculum questions and answers, fund-raising activities, and an exchange of ideas and suggestions. Many parents like to feel a sense of involvement with their child's school or at least have a passing knowledge of it. Teachers often find it helpful to meet parents on a regular informal basis rather than only during times of crisis. The school secretary is not usually expected to take minutes of parent/teacher meetings, but may be invited to attend.

METRIC CONVERSION TABLES   This chart will give only approximate equivalents.

To Find	When You Have	Multiply By
centimeters	inches	2.5
centimeters	feet	30
meters	yards	.9
kilometers	miles	1.6
square centimeters	square inches	6.5
square meters	square feet	.09
square meters	square yards	.8
square kilometers	square miles	2.6
hectares	acres	.4
grams	ounces	28
kilograms	pounds	.45
metric tons	tons	.9
milliliters	fluid ounces	30
liters	pints	.47
liters	quarts	.95
liters	gallons	3.8
cubic meters	cubic feet	.03
cubic meters	cubic yards	.76

	Exact Temperature	
Fahrenheit	Celsius	9/5 (+32)
Celsius	Fahrenheit	−32 5/9 X remainder

To Find	When You Have	Multiply By
inches	millimeters	.04
inches	centimeters	.4
feet	meters	3.3
yards	meters	1.1
miles	kilometers	.6
square inches	square centimeters	.16
square yards	square meters	1.2
square miles	square kilometers	.4
acres	hectares	2.5
ounces	grams	.035
pounds	kilograms	2.2
tons	metric tons	1.1
fluid ounces	milliliters	.03
pints	liters	2.1
quarts	liters	1.06
gallons	liters	.26
cubic feet	cubic meters	35
cubic yards	cubic meters	1.3

MICROFILM   In 1958, the United States Congress passed the Uniform Photographic Copies of Business Records in Evidence Act which allowed microfilm copies of business records to be used in legal procedures. Since that time, the microfilm industry has made rapid progress in all phases of business and education storage and retrieval methods. As a result of the incredible speed with which our technology is progressing in such areas as microfiche and micropublishing, microfilm can now be a far less expensive medium than paper. Improvements in quality and a better understanding of methods have helped to assuage doubts about the permanence of microfilm records. More and more major educational institutions are switching to microfilm as a medium for maintaining permanent records for the following reasons: (1) It can reduce costs and save money. Storage space can be reduced by up to 98 percent. A desk drawer can house the microfilm records of over 10,000 letter-size records that would require at least a four-drawer filing cabinet. Also, microfilm can be faster and less expensive to duplicate than paper. (2) It is easy to duplicate and store records so extra copies can be filed in several locations, thereby facilitating file security. (3) Microfilm and the school computer work well together in the sense that records or data that would be too costly to reduce to computer programmable information can easily be stored on microfilm; the computer has the ability to interact with microfilm systems and can quickly pinpoint the precise microfilm image in the microfilm file.

The microfilm process is a photographic process whereby data is reduced in size and stored. While too small to be read by the naked eye, the film is easily read by scanner. There are two basic processes involved in microfilming: SOURCE DOCUMENT MICROFILMING where the images are photographs of the actual paper documents made with the use of special photographic equipment, and COMPUTER OUTPUT MICROFILM (COM) where the microfilm images are prepared from data stored on magnetic disks or tape or are transmitted directly from the computer's data center.

After the microfilm is developed, it may be processed in several forms that can be applied to the special storage or retrieval needs of each institution. These are:

- Roll or Cartridge. Available in 16mm or 35mm rolls or cartridges, this method is best suited for storage of sequential records such as attendance or grades.
- Microfiche. Often called ''fiche,'' this is a sheet of film that contains multiple images in a grid pattern. Fiche can be easily duplicated for mailing, or reference purposes.
- Aperture Card. This is a standard punch card that has a hole cut in it for mounting a frame of microfilm. It is useful in areas where easy filing, retrieval, duplicating, and updating are essential.
- Microfilm Jacket. These are acetate filing jackets that contain either 16mm or 35mm size channels for the storage of microfilm strips. The jacket can be easily updated by removing obsolete film and inserting new film into the channels.

Microfilm has many applications in the field of education including the storage and retrieval of medical records, attendance records, grade records, inventories of equipment and supplies, and in the school library where micropublishing of reference materials and catalogs on microfiche is gaining rapidly in popular usage. The savings on paper and ink supplies, not to mention postage, can be immense.

MIMEOGRAPH COPIES, IMPROVING QUALITY OF If your machine is in good working order, your copies will usually be crisp and clean, but poor copies may still occur because of the typewriter or the typist. Here are some typical problems and their solutions:

PROBLEM	SOLUTION
generally poor quality	Typewriter touch may be set too light. Readjust.
o's and e's cut out	Typewriter type could be out of alignment. Call a repair person.
corrections obvious and dark	Too much pressure when retyping a correction. Lighten up.
spotty corrections	Be sure that the entire error is covered with correction fluid before retyping.
sides or bottom of copy did not print	The typing has exceeded the limits of the stencil. Retype within the boundaries.
poor handwriting or signature copy	Adjust pressure and use a writing plate and ballpoint stylus.

MINUTES OF A MEETING   Basically, the minutes are a formal record of what goes on at a meeting. They are kept on file indefinitely as a permanent record. If you are responsible for taking minutes, here are some suggestions:

Preparing for the Meeting

Anything you can do in advance to prepare for the meeting will save you time later and will make things run more smoothly. Make copies of any reports or written information being presented at the meeting so that each person present will have access to a copy. Check the date and time of the meeting and, if necessary, reserve the location. Make arrangements for necessary equipment; for example, audio-visual equipment may be needed during a presentation; adequate seating; blackboards and chalk if necessary; podium and gravel; adequate ventilation and/or heating; ash trays or "NO SMOKING" signs; conference tables or presentation stands. Notify those who will be invited to attend of the date, time, and location of the meeting. If necessary, provide a simple map or directions for reaching the meeting place. Confirm the attendance of any guest speakers. Process any necessary payment forms. Arrange for refreshments if appropriate, plus adequate eating utensils, and be sure to make any cleanup arrangements.

What to Take to a Meeting

The Minute Book. This is a record of all the approved minutes of the year. At each meeting, the minutes of the previous meeting are voted on and approved or amended. A typical minute book is a loose-leaf binder with dividers for AGENDAS, RESOLUTIONS, REPORTS, and DOCUMENTS with the minutes typed on white bond paper. Once the minutes of the previous meeting have been approved, the administrator or chairman signs and dates the minutes. The current trend is to provide each member with a copy of the minutes. The original minute book should be kept in a secure place, since it is a legal record of the actions of the board.

Roster. This is a list of all the members. Most minutes indicate those members who were present and absent from a meeting. The roster or "roll sheet" makes it easy for you to check in those in attendance. In very large groups you do not check attendance. Instead of checking in the members yourself, you could circulate a sign-up sheet with the name and date of the meeting neatly typed at the top of the page. It may be necessary to keep an accurate account of the time a member arrives and leaves. Some boards are sticklers for knowing who was present or absent when a certain action was voted on. This would be indicated: "Mr. Jones arrived at 10:45 A.M." or "Mr. Jones departed the meeting at 12:15 P.M." Also indicate the names of visitors or guests attending the meeting.

The Agenda. Bring enough copies of the agenda for everyone. Even though the members may have received copies prior to the meeting, they will often forget to bring them or lose them.

Reference Information. This would include reference books, documents, copies of proposals, slides for presentation, reports, résumés and for formal meetings a copy of *Robert's Rules of Order* may be required. Check with your administrator prior to the meeting and make a list of necessary reference materials.

Financial Information. This might include such items as lists of bills to be paid, salary information, purchase requisitions, supply orders, or maintenance or construction bids.

Writing Implements. Bring a supply of sharpened pencils with erasers, and pens in good working order.

Steno Book. Keep a separate stenographer's book for each type of meeting you record and mark it appropriately: "Board Meetings," "Faculty Meetings," "Academic Committee Meetings," and so on. When the book is filled, indicate the period of time that is covered, then file it away. For example, "Finance Committee Meetings, September 28 to March 31, 19XX."

List of Resolutions. Resolutions require an action response from the group, and must be duly moved, seconded, and voted on. A list of resolutions is usually sent to members prior to the meeting so they will have time for their consideration. Resolutions that have been acted upon can easily be located if they are numbered and dated. For example, "Resolution 21-86" would indicate the twenty-first resolution to be acted upon in 1986. You would then keep a separate file list of resolutions in the minute book for easy accessibility.

Recording and Writing Minutes

Recording Motions

Formal minutes such as for Board of Directors' meetings usually omit pro and con discussions and contain only the formal motions. For example: "Mr. Smith moved that the board accept the proposed curriculum revisions. Mrs. Jones seconded the motion which was unanimously carried." When recording motions it is extremely important to be sure you have recorded the wording correctly. Often there is discussion and rewording before a final version is put to a vote. It is good practice to read the final version as recorded before a vote is taken. Any amendments voted on must also be recorded. Meetings are often run informally and no motions are made. In such instances it is sufficient to simply state what occurred and who said it: "Miss Smith, the history teacher, presented suggestions for curriculum changes within the department."

Recording Different Points of View

Whether or not discussions regarding the pros and cons of a given issue are discussed is strictly up to your school. Usually, board meetings are more formal and do not require the recording of discussions; only the actions taken. The more informal faculty and committee meetings often require a detailed accounting of what was specifically said so that easy reference can be made at future meetings. For example: "The curriculum revision was discussed at length. Each department briefly reported. The following points were made: (1) the French Department will remain unchanged; (2) the English and Humanities Departments will instigate an experimental program of team-teaching; (3) the Mathematics Department will study the possibilities of teaching basic computer skills; (4) the History Department will increase emphasis on United States History."

Recording Resolutions

It is essential to verify the working of resolutions before final recording takes place. Resolutions are usually indicated as follows:

Resolution 21-86   John Smith moved that the board adopt Resolution 21–86 financing the faculty-chaperoned student trip to the Science Exposition in New Haven. Mary Brown seconded the motion, which was unanimously adopted.

The resolution would then be formally written as follows:

> RESOLUTION 21–86
> The Board of the John Doe School hereby approves the funding of the faculty-chaperoned student trip to the Science Exposition in New Haven to be held March 14–18, 19XX. All student and faculty expenses will be paid by the school.

Outlining the Minutes

The following information should be included in your outline:

- date and place of the meeting
- list of those persons present and absent
- who called the meeting to order? at what time?
- state the action taken on the minutes of the previous meeting meeting: for example "unanimously approved," "approved as corrected," "approved as submitted," "the reading of the minutes was omitted"
- proceed to clearly and simply state the business transacted in order as indicated on the agenda
- list any items of unfinished or carried over business
- list any important dates or announcements
- use a complimentary close such as "Respectfully submitted"; then sign your name
- indicate the date the minutes were typed
- leave a space for the chairman's or administrator's signature and date when the minutes are approved

When writing the minutes, be factual, be concise, and write clearly. (See Figure 20 for an example of minutes.)

Seeking Approval of the Minutes

After you have done a rough draft of the minutes, submit them to the chairman or the administrator for editing and verification. If controversial or inflammatory topics are covered or questionable statements made, it is wise to submit a rough draft of that section for approval by the person in question and by the chairman or administrator. This is far better than having to correct or alter the final version. Once all preliminary approvals have been received, the minutes are ready for final typing. They will then be presented for formal approval at the next meeting and will subsequently be signed by the chairman or administrator.

Typing and Distributing the Minutes

The original should be typed on white bond paper. Most groups prefer that cop-

```
        MINUTES OF THE BOARD OF DIRECTORS MEETING OF

                THE HOWARD ABBOTT SCHOOL


The meeting was held in Conference Room "A" at The Howard Abbott
School on March 14, 19XX.

Those present: Alan, Brown, Cross, Douglas, Evans, Ferris, Gough,
               Lock, Ryder, Smith, Trask

Those absent:  Carter, Langfeld


The meeting was called to order by Mark Trask, Chairman of the Board,
at 11:45 a.m.

1.  The minutes of the February 14 meeting were unanimously approved.

2.  DIRECTORS' REPORTS

    A.  CAIS
        Mary Brown reported on recent trends in private education.
    B.  NAIS
        Nancy Evans had no report.

3.  COMMITTEE REPORTS

    A.  Academic Committee

        Michael Cross reported that curriculum revisions were
        currently being studied.  A complete report will be
        available for the April meeting.

    B.  Finance Committee

        John Smith moved that the board approve Resolution 21-86
        financing the faculty chaperoned trip to the Science Exposition
        in New Haven.  Mary Brown seconded the motion which was
        unanimously approved.

RESOLUTION 21-86
The Board of The Howard Abbott School hereby approves the funding of
the faculty chaperoned student trip to the Science Exposition in
New Haven to be held March 14-18, 19XX.  All student and faculty
expenses will be paid by the school.

    C.  Buildings and Grounds Committee
        Nancy Gough reported that the proposals adopted at the January
        meeting had resulted in improved building maintenance.

    D.  Nominating Committee
        There was no report.

    E.  Development Committee
        Morris Langfeld was absent.  There was no report.
```

FIGURE 20

Sample minutes showing committee reports, and the correct way to record a resolution.

4. ALUMNI ASSOCIATION REPORT

   Elizabeth Ferris reported that plans are underway for a spring reunion.

5. PARENTS ASSOCIATION REPORT

   Marla Lock reported that the Spring Fling is in the planning stages. A full report will be available for the April meeting.

6. FACULTY REPORT

   Robert Ryder reported that the faculty salary scale had been approved.

7. PRINCIPAL'S REPORT

   Principal Douglas reported briefly on fall enrollments and volunteer teacher aides.

8. CHAIRMAN'S REPORT

   Chairman Mark Trask reported on the recent inter-school conference. He requested that the Finance Committee study tuition increases and prepare a report by the May meeting.

9. NEW BUSINESS

   There was no new business.

There being no further business to discuss, on motion duly made and seconded, the meeting was adjourned at 1:30 p.m.

                              Respectfully submitted,

                              Marcia Straub, Secretary
                              March 16, 19XX

APPROVED: DATE:

FIGURE 20, *continued*

ies of approved minutes be sent to all members for their files. The approved original will be filed in the minute book. The approved final draft of the minutes should be free from visible corrections, and should bear the signature of the chairman or administrator and the date signed. If you carefully prepare the agenda and type it in outline form you can practically write the minutes as the meeting progresses.

NEWSLETTERS

Distribution

If you are responsible for distributing the school newsletter, here are some hints to make it a relatively painless job:

- Build or maintain a master list of names for mailings.
- Try to get help from students, parents, or volunteers to help with distribution.
- Avoid mass mailings during your busiest times. For example, if you will be heavily involved with report card distribution, do not schedule newsletter mailings at the same time.
- Keep your mailing lists updated at all times. Do not wait until a stack of changes builds up or chaos can result.
- Give your helpers clear instructions in writing. The few minutes it takes to type a ditto of instructions is well worth it. Do not rely on memory; it fails too often.
- Keep a record of what was sent and to whom. This can be as simple as making a notation on your desk calendar, or keeping a sample of the mailing piece with a notation—"sent on (date) to all parents and alumni," or whoever received it.
- Keep at least one extra set of addressed envelopes ready for emergency mailings.

Typing Newsletters   See also LAYOUT.

The first thing to do when faced with typing a school newsletter is to consider the usual layout format. Is it formal and professional looking or is it casual, including student art work and contributions from the community at large? The layout format should be consistent from issue to issue. When putting the newsletter together, be simple and direct. Avoid unusual and hard-to-read typefaces and complicated arrangements. Strive for a balance between printed and plain areas. Titles are easier to read when you use upper and lower case letters. If you have your newsletter printed, choose simple easy-to-read typefaces, but be flexible enough to allow variety. Avoid vertical typesetting; it is hard to read. Remember to include the issue and volume numbers or the date of each issue. Type the body copy so that it is easy to read and logical to follow. Begin and end columns at the same point on the page. Position artwork and illustrations flush with the margins. When preparing the school newsletter it is helpful to consider the following: (1) Purpose—Why is this newsletter being published? Are you passing along information? Are you requesting volunteer help? Is it a chance for students to practice journalism? The reason or reasons could have an effect on the overall image you wish to project; (2) Audience—Is the newsletter mainly for students? faculty? staff? parents? the entire school community? Again, the answer to this question could have a bearing on the finished product; (3) Evaluate—Perhaps most important of all is your evaluation of each completed issue. What do you like about it? What could be improved? Keep a copy and make notes as you review it; then incorporate the changes in your next issue.

NURSE, SUBSTITUTING FOR THE   Some schools have regular visits from health department nurses or have a part-time or full-time nurse available to handle student illness or injury. Many times, however, the school secretary is expected to fill the role of school nurse. In this case, it is most helpful to have at least a passing knowledge of basic first aid techniques. (See FIRST AID.)

Whether people are five years old or fifty years old, when they are ill or injured they need to be treated with extra patience and consideration. Your desk may be piled with paperwork, but an injured person takes precedence. A bandage or first-aid spray solves most problems that the school secretary who is filling in for the nurse will come in contact with, but anything more than a minor injury requires immediate action. Suspected breaks, sprains, contagious illness or severe burns require immediate medical attention and/or parent notification. This helps to limit the school's liability. Emergency medical records should be available for each student indicating: (1) drug or other allergies; (2) the physician's name and address; (3) the parent or guardian's name and emergency numbers (in the case of minors); (4) a blanket permission for medical treatment of minors in case the parents cannot be reached (this is essential if you have to accompany a minor student to the hospital).

How to Determine the Extent of an Injury

- If an injury appears serious, you should immediately notify and get help from an administrator. This minimizes your liability risk and reduces your burden.
- Observe the injured person. If he is writhing in pain, gasping, or protectively clutching an injured part, the injury is probably serious and deserves immediate medical attention. If any symptoms of shock are evident, immediate medical attention is required.
- Ask the injured person how he feels, where it hurts, if there is dizziness.
- Always consider head injuries as potentially serious and follow the directions given in the FIRST AID section.
- If a wound or injury seems minor, chances are that it is, and requires only first aid treatment on your part. However, when in doubt get professional help.

What to Do When Faced with a Medical Emergency

- <u>Remain calm</u>. Even if you are very upset about an injury, try not to show your fear to the injured person.
- <u>Be encouraging</u>. Your attitude in an emergency can greatly affect the injured person. Reassure the person that she will be fine, that help is on the way, and that everything is under control.
- <u>Be confident</u>. It is especially important for an injured person to feel that you are competent and efficient. Even if you have no idea what to do, do not let the injured person know this. A positive attitude is very important to prevent further trauma to the injured person.
- <u>Respond quickly</u>. In a real emergency, speed is essential. If necessary, call the ambulance, police, physician, fire department, poison control center, or whoever can be of the most and quickest help. Speedy medical aid saves lives; your job is to keep the injured person calm until trained medical help arrives.
- <u>Note</u>: Remember never to give first aid unless you are absolutely sure of the technique. Misinformation does more harm than good. Get fast medical help if you need it. Once the emergency is under control, you will probably need to file a liability or accident report with the insurance company or make out a report for the central office. (See ACCIDENT REPORTS.)

If the Injury Is Serious:

- Contact your administrator immediately. Do not leave the injured person alone; send someone for help.

- Have emergency numbers by your telephone for police, fire, ambulance, poison control center.
- Refer to the student's medical file for emergency numbers such as physician, or parent.
- Attempt to notify the parent or spouse right away.
- If the student is a minor and needs medical attention but the parents cannot be located:
  1. Notify the administrator of the situation.
  2. Make a photocopy of the parental medical permission form to take to the hospital. You may not get treatment without it.
  3. Make arrangements for someone (or you) to accompany the student to the hospital.
  4. Make arrangements for someone (or you) to continue trying to reach the parents.

When Notifying Parents of an Injury:

- First, before placing the call, get control of yourself. Make sure that you are fairly calm.
- Have all the necessary information close at hand such as:
  - the name of the injured person
  - the type of injury (break, burn, sprain)
  - the extent of the injury if known
  - the present location of the injured person (returned to class after medical treatment; is en route to the hospital emergency room)
  - the name of the hospital or medical center where the person has been taken
- When placing the call:
  - Identify yourself.
  - Be encouraging. Do not overemphasize the unpleasant details of the injury. Merely state the facts and try to let the person know that things are under control and that the injured person has received (or will soon be receiving) appropriate medical care.
  - If you have to relate bad news over the telephone, try to empathize with the person receiving the news. Do not sound alarmed or afraid or you will transfer that to the parent or spouse who will already be upset enough by your call. You should calmly say something like, "Mrs. Brown, this is Mrs. Fitch of Howard School. Bobby fell at school and injured his head. Everything is under control. Since we weren't able to

reach you by phone, we took him to the hospital for treatment. He's doing just fine.'' Then you can follow up with details if asked. Or you might say, ''Mrs. Brown, this is Mrs. Fitch of Howard School. Bobby fell at school. We think his arm might be broken and he needs a doctor. He's resting comfortably but could you come right away?'' You can then follow the parent's instructions and arrange to meet her at the school or at the hospital if necessary. Usually, however, it is the parent's responsibility to take over once she has been notified.

Medication in School

Usually, public schools will not allow the distribution of any medication by anyone except a physician. Private institutions do, on occasion, permit the distribution of aspirin or prescription medicines. If a young child is taking prescribed medication at school, it is often left with the school nurse or secretary so that it is not lost or abused by other students. It is best to check with the administration before giving medication to anyone for any reason.

Communicable Disease Control

The health departments of each state differ in their requirements for reporting contagious diseases. Also, these requirements are constantly changing. Bulletins are usually issued to each school stating requirements and changes. If you do not know the requirements, check with city, state, or county authorities, or your administrator. At the discretion of the school administration, bulletins may be issued to parents identifying any reported cases of extremely contagious illness. Any student who is suspected of being infected with a contagious disease should be removed from the school until checked and cleared by competent medical personnel.

O

OFFICE PARTIES   In general, office parties should be discouraged. It is best to keep your business and personal life as separate as possible. Bridal showers, baby showers, and birthday gifts can quickly become a huge drain on everyone's budget and the planning of parties can consume your work day leaving you with a mound of unfinished work at closing time. If celebrations at school are a necessity, keep them to the cards-and-light-refreshment level and hold them at a time when everyone can be invited. If some people must remain on duty and miss the party, be sure to save them a piece of cake or some of the refreshments. Collections for gift giving should be discouraged also, since that can become a monetary drain. Gift giving should be handled on a personal basis.

ORIENTATION OF NEW EMPLOYEES   Try to be friendly and put the new employee at ease. If you have had an opportunity to glance at the new person's file, there may be information that can help you relate quickly on a personal level. You might have similar backgrounds, job experience, or interests. If there are co-workers close by, introduce the new person to a few people. Try to make him feel at ease. If you keep first-day introductions to a few key people, the new person is less likely to feel overwhelmed by the first day on the job. If there is a job description, go over it point by point with the new employee. Answer any questions clearly. If no description is available, try to outline the overall purpose of the job, then proceed to show the new person each duty slowly and clearly. Let the new person know the location of restrooms, telephones, necessary keys, the cafeteria, supplies, and other necessary data right away. This will help him to feel more at ease. Be encouraging as you instruct the new employee and give ample opportunity to grasp one concept before moving to the next. If you are required to evaluate the new employee after a time, such a report usually includes information as work habits, dependability, attitude toward work, efficiency rating, attitude toward co-workers, punctuality, and attendance.

OUTLINES An outline is a very helpful way in which to record the salient facts of a particular topic. When well done, an outline is easy and fast to scan,

```
                    SAMPLE OUTLINE FORMAT


  I.  Topic

      A.  Subtopic

      B.  Subtopic

      C.  Continue with as many subtopics as needed.

          1.  Information related to subtopic C.

          2.  Additional related information.

              a.  Information related to item 2.

              b.  Additional information related to item 2.

              c.  Still more related information.

                  (1) Further breakdown on information related

                      to 2c.

                      (a)  Further breakdown of information

                           related to c. (1)


 II.  New Topic

      A.  Subtopic

      B.  Subtopic

      C.  Subtopic

      D.  Subtopic

          1.  Additional data

          2.  Additional data

      E.  Subtopic
```

FIGURE 21

Sample outline format showing the correct positioning of topics and subtopics.

and a good method for speedy retrieval of information. Outlines are used frequently in education, not only by students in preparation for term papers and reports, but by faculty and administration in preparation for speeches, programs, academic reports, and many other projects. There is a proper form to follow when typing an outline: (1) all topics of equal importance should be indented equally and phrased in a similar manner; (2) topic headings should be clear and concise; (3) topics should be organized in the following manner—Roman numerals (I, II, III,), followed by capital letters (A, B, C), then Arabic numerals (1, 2, 3), and finally lower case letters (a, b, c). If more subdivisions are needed, repeat this order but enclose them in parentheses—(I), (A), (1), (a), and so on; (4) use periods after all letters; (5) do not use periods after parentheses; (6) use at least two subheadings per topic; (7) capitalize the first letter of the first word of each topic and subtopic; (8) use periods after complete sentences. (See Figure 21.)

P

PAPER CHARACTERISTICS Following is a listing of terms used to describe paper:

- Grain. Refers to the position of the fibers in the paper Paper folds smoothly with the grain, but can crack when folded against the grain. Paper is stiffer in the direction of the grain. In books or catalogs, the grain should be parallel to the binding.
- Basis Weight. Papers are identified by their basis weight. It is the weight in pounds of a ream (500 sheets) when cut to the basic size for that particular grade of paper. Paper is commonly referred to in terms of its ream weight; for example, 20-pound bond.
- Strength. The nature of the fiber determines the strength of the paper. A paper with high rag content will have good strength and long life.
- Color. Color is an important factor as it affects the reproduction of the final version. Type is easiest to read against a soft white, but colors reproduce at their most accurate against a neutral white.
- Brightness. This affects the overall brilliance or sparkle of the printed copy. Fluorescent additives can attract attention but can also be repellent.

Finish

Finish refers to the smoothness of the paper. The following terms are listed in order of increasing smoothness:

1. Antique
2. Eggshell
3. Vellum
4. Machine Finish (MF)
5. English Finish (EF)

Stock

The variety of paper stock used in printing is great. Following is a guide to the most common papers to help you choose the best product for each job:

- Bond (Watermarked). Bond usually has at least twenty-five percent rag content. It takes erasures well and is used for letters and report typing. It is available in white and colors, and makes a good choice for letterheads since it takes engraving and raised printing well. There is also a fifty percent rag content bond that has a long life and is suitable for permanent documents.

- Bond (No watermark). Unwatermarked bond is suitable for volume work and reproduction purposes.

- Duplicator. Duplicator paper is available in white and colors and is used with the spirit and gelatin duplicating machines.

- Ledger. Ledger paper comes in white, green, and buff. It is used for bookkeeping and posting forms and can also be used for letterpress. It is glare-free, erases well, and stands up under rough handling.

- Mimeograph. Mimeograph paper has excellent opacity. It is curl-resistant and has a uniform surface that provides sharp clean copies without feathering. It is used for stencil copies of bulletins, forms, and similar material. It is available in white and colors and is used with the letterpress or offset processes.

- Xerographic. Xerographic paper is specifically designed for reproduction using the xerography process. It is available both watermarked and unwatermarked. Its special smooth surface makes a positive contact with the selenium drum to produce sharp copies with easy handling for collating purposes.

Types of Board

- Bristol Board. This is suitable for file cards, tickets, report covers, brochures, and direct mail pieces. It comes in white and colors. Vellum bristol has a textured finish; matte bristol has a level surface recommended for letterpress, offset, and gravure; gloss bristol has a high-gloss surface good for halftone (photograph) reproduction—it makes transparent inks appear radiant.

- Chipboard. Chipboard is gray and used for backing tablets and as a protector.

- Paperboard. This is suitable for mailing cards (postcards) and various other purposes requiring a lightweight board.

- <u>Tagboard</u>. Tagboard is suitable for tags, envelopes, tickets, brochures, and file folders. It is available in white and colors.

PARENTS

Substituting for Parents

If the area in which you work permits you to develop a rapport with the students, you will at some point find yourself in the position of surrogate parent. Students will seek your advice and help for a variety of reasons including divorce, death, absentee parents, or lack of communication between parent and child, as well as a host of less urgent problems. Surrogate parenting is difficult and demanding, but it can be rewarding too. There is no better feeling than knowing you have helped someone to overcome a problem, or in sharing a success. Volumes could be written on this subject alone, but it is sufficient to say that surrogate parenting must be approached with patience, understanding, and courage on your part. But you must be aware of a drain on your own emotions and know when to say, "Enough!" There aren't enough hours in the day to permit you to give attention to all the people who demand it. Sometimes the best you can do for the student is to refer him or her to a counselor, parent, clergyman, physician, administrator, or teacher. Use good judgment and common sense in this area. Strive to be pleasant and concerned without allowing the students to take advantage of you or prevent you from completing your other tasks. Remember, you are not the parent, and certain things such as values and morality are best left up to the parent.

In the course of a day, you may be bombarded with demands, requests, and claims on your attention. With experience you will be able to intuitively respond to real emergency pleas for help and to handle other student requests so naturally that it will require little effort on your part. How do you reach this point? The obvious answer is that by dealing with students for months or years, you know how to separate those who really need your help from those who are just killing time or trying to avoid class. However, there are ways to help the newcomer judge student needs:

- Listen to what the student says—then listen to what the student SAYS. This double-talk simply means that you need to go beyond the content of the student's words and listen to the meaning behind them. Knowing the student can help immeasurably in this area. An elementary student may say that he has a stomachache when he really is afraid of taking a test or has just had a fight with a friend.
- If a student has a problem or complaint, listen carefully, then ask ques-

tions that will help you to determine the extent of the problem. For example, if a young student lingers around your desk excessively, careful concerned questioning could reveal a problem at school or at home. You may then be able to help directly or to refer the student to someone who can help.

— Body language and behavior can give you clues to how a person is feeling, especially if you know the person well enough to notice a sudden change. Droopy posture, listlessness, a protective stance (arms folded as though hugging oneself), sudden hostility with no apparent cause, are all signs that something may be really wrong.

— Tears can fool you. Outbursts of crying are everyday occurrences in schools with adolescent girls. At this age tears flow easily, and while it is wise to make sure that nothing serious has occurred, usually the tears are over as suddenly and inexplicably as they began.

— Follow your intuitive feelings and common sense to determine when to listen. Temper concern with practicality; after all, you do still have to get your paperwork done.

— Common sense will dictate that if you do not feel comfortable or competent in dealing with a student problem, it is time to seek guidance and aid from an administrator or counselor.

— It is natural for people to show concern to their friends or loved ones, but what about students who are practically strangers to you? It is best to follow your natural inclinations. If you force a show of concern, the student will soon know it and may resent your being dishonest, thereby ruining your chance to help.

Working with Parents

The role of parents within the schools has changed considerably during the past few years. In the past, parents respected the teacher and were a source of aid when discipline problems came to light. In this age of consumer awareness, education seems to be thought of more as a commodity than a learning experience. If a student goes to a school for a specific number of years, it is not guaranteed that he will receive an education. Knowledge cannot be force-fed.

Learning requires motivation and old-fashioned hard work on the part of the student. This is the part of education that is frequently overlooked today. Some parents place the blame on the teacher or the system of education, when they should consider other factors that contribute to the state of education today such as the large number of working parents, and changes in the communications media leaving the student with less parental supervision and more electronic babysitting. It is tough to be a working parent, no doubt about it, but many of the values that used to be taught in the home are now lacking; this puts an undue burden on the school and on school personnel who are frequently expected to cross the line between teacher and parent. Since the role of the parent in society is undergoing changes, the effects are felt within the school community. Parents now make greater demands on the school, and in some cases even bring lawsuits because of real or imagined inequities. This affects the school secretary in various ways. You may be required to deal with growing numbers of irate parents, to deal with parent requests, to fill out increasing numbers of surveys, forms, and reports, to help with parent/teacher organizations, and to respond to a daily barrage of questions and demands. Here are some guidelines to help you successfully cope with parents:

1. When responding to questions, give factual information only. Do not speculate. Do not repeat rumor or gossip. Do not give out confidential information. Do not overstep your boundaries of responsibility. If you have doubts, refer the question to the administration.

2. Listen politely and carefully. Write down any requests accurately. If you need help in filling the request, consult your administrator.

3. Do not permit the parent to threaten or harass you into an awkward position. In cases such as this, refer the matter to the administration.

PARENT/TEACHER ASSOCIATION, WORKING WITH You may choose to do volunteer work for parent/teacher organizations. This may include such tasks as typing and cutting stencils, or helping out with social or special events. You may also act as a clerical consultant in giving ideas or directions to volunteers whom you may then oversee. Just be sure that your volunteer duties do not conflict with your work schedule. Be prepared to say "no" if you start being taken for granted. The list of unreasonable requests that a school secretary receives could circle the world. Any or all of the following items might be found in this category:

– Expecting you to do personal work for parents or faculty.
– Expecting you to loan school equipment to unauthorized persons.
– Expecting you to alter records or transcripts at the request of parents.
– Expecting you to babysit for children left at school.
– Expecting you to chauffeur students to medical or other appointments. "Couldn't you just drop Susie off on your way home?"

– Expecting you to grant a student early dismissal from school without proper authorization.

It is necessary to use good judgment and be ready to say ''no'' nicely but firmly if unreasonable requests are made of you.

PASSES   The secretary is usually responsible for issuing passes to tardy students or to students returning to school after an absence. A pass should include: (1) the date; (2) the student's name; (3) the time of departure or arrival; (4) the

Admission Pass

STUDENT _____

TIME _____ a.m. p.m.   DATE _____ 19 _____

SIGNATURE _____

Corridor Pass

STUDENT _____ DATE _____ 19 ..

TO _____ TIME _____ a m p m

TEACHER _____ ROOM _____

COUNTERSIGNED _____ TIME _____ a m p.m

VISITATION PASS

Visitor _____ Date _____ 19 ___

Purpose _____

Area(s)/Person(s) to Visit _____

_____

Permission by _____ Time _____ A.M. P.M.

Countersigned _____ Time _____ A.M. P.M.

PASS MUST BE RETURNED TO OFFICE

FIGURE 22

Sample passes and building visitation log in which all visitors to the school are recorded.

○   ○   ○

INSTRUCTIONS 1 All visitors report to Office upon arrival and exit   2 Information is completed for all visitations (e g ,   3 Pass is completed for all visitors
                                                                            parental, sales, service, repair, etc)

BUILDING VISITATION LOG

DATE	VISITOR'S NAME	TITLE FIRM RELATIONSHIP TO PUPIL OR EMPLOYEE	PURPOSE OF VISIT	AREA/PERSON TO BE VISITED	TIME ARRIVAL / EXIT	AUTHORIZING OFFICIAL NAME	COMMENTS

Figure 22, *continued*

reason for absence or tardiness. Passes are also used by teachers if they have kept a student after class or if they wish to have a student excused from class. In the case of a minor student it is essential that all absentee excuses be verified. If you do not have an excuse letter from the parent or a note from a doctor or dentist, make every attempt to verify the absence before readmitting the student to school. If no verifiable excuse is available, follow your school's set policy or contact your administrator.

Passes may also be issued to visitors on a temporary basis. Such passes usually include the visitor's name, the date, the reason for the visit, the areas in which they are cleared to visit, and a signature of authorization. Visitor's passes are to be returned to the office when the visitor leaves. See Figure 24 for sample passes.

PAYCHECKS, HOW TO PREPARE This is a very simple procedure if your data is accurate. You should have a record for each employee showing the base rate of pay, allowable deductions, and an indication of whether married or single, plus the number of dependents. All you need to do is:

1. Multiply the base rate of pay times the amount of time worked and add in any overtime or additional salary to arrive at the gross total.

2. Follow your tax withholding charts (available through your local Internal Revenue Service and state agencies) to arrive at the proper deductions. Subtract from the gross total.

3. Subtract any additional deductions such as medical, retirement, or other insurance plans, to arrive at the net total. Issue a check for the net amount.

4. Keep accurate records of all totals and individual employee breakdowns in the permanent file.

Tips for Writing Checks

1. Avoid abbreviations on the payee line. Some initials can easily be altered or misconstrued and cashed by check forgers.

2. Either type or write a line or a series of asterisks before and after the written amount on the check:

   ************Two hundred and forty-five************

   This method leaves no room for alterations.

3. Do not mail altered checks. If you make a mistake, void the check and rewrite it.

4. Indicate the invoice number or the service covered by the payment right on the face of the check. This will help to insure that the correct account will be credited.

5. If you use lightweight envelopes through which the check is visible, either fold the check in half before inserting it, or slip the check inside a copy of the invoice or a blank sheet of paper. This can prevent theft of checks from the mails.

6. Before having the checks signed, always double-check the date and verify that the numerical and written amounts agree.

PAYROLL Most schools have a specialist who handles payroll functions. This may be a person, or a group that works within the school facility, or it may be a payroll service that operates from an external data-processing facility. It has been estimated that one full-time person is necessary to process the payroll for every two hundred employees. There are two basic methods of meeting payroll requirements: (1) employees are paid a flat salary for an *expected* number of hours worked; (2) time records are kept and the employees are paid for *actual* time worked. Faculty members and some other school personnel are usually hired on a contractual basis and the annual salary is divided and dispensed on a ten-or twelve-month basis. Maintenance or clerical personnel may be required to "clock in" on time cards and be paid for actual time worked. While this may not appear fair on the surface, faculty members and administrative personnel often work many hours beyond the school day in attending meetings, course preparation time, and in correcting papers and tests. The whole industry is notoriously underpaid.

Symbols Used in Payrolls

Following are typical headings from a statement of earnings and deductions which accompanies most payroll checks:

DATE	date of check issuance
REGULAR HOURS	the number of expected hours or actual hours worked (35, 40, etc.)
OVERTIME HOURS	a listing of overtime worked which may be paid at a higher rate
RATE OF PAY	how much is paid per hour, week, etc.
OTHER PAY	this category is reserved for sums earned that are not covered by regular or overtime pay (perhaps a bonus)
GROSS PAY	the total amount before deductions
FED. W/H TAX	federal withholding tax (income tax)
FICA	Social Security deductions
SDI	state disability insurance (if applicable)
STATE TAX	state income tax (if applicable)
OTHER DEDUCTIONS	perhaps for a pension plan or health insurance payments
NET PAY	the total amount of gross pay less deductions

Payroll Record Keeping

A general ledger is kept showing gross payroll amounts, payroll deductions, and net payroll figures. This may be done by a bookkeeping machine, by computer, or by hand, depending on the size and structure of the school. Unless the school is very small, it is unlikely that the school secretary will be involved with posting the general ledger, since this is really a job for a bookkeeper or accountant. Whenever a paycheck is issued, it is necessary to keep a duplicate record for the files showing such information as

- the name of the payee
- the date of issuance
- federal or state withholding tax
- other withholding (retirement, medical insurance)
- inclusive dates covered by the payroll check
- gross total
- net total
- wage base rate (hourly, weekly, monthly)

These records should be kept accurately and are usually audited annually by an independent accounting firm. If the records are kept efficiently and accurately, auditing procedures should run smoothly.

PERMISSIONS   Parental permission is usually required for the minor student to take part in any field trips or potentially hazardous school activities such as contact team sports. Some private schools that use contract agreements signed by the parents often include a blanket permission in the agreement. Such a blanket permission could read: "The undersigned gives permission for the above named student to attend any and all field trips and excursions in connection with the school program and agrees not to hold the school responsible for accidents and injuries arising from school activities held under reasonable supervision." In some cases, it will be necessary to write separate permission forms for each event, or use a standard form in which the necessary information relating to the event can be filled in and given to the parent for her signature.

PETTY CASH   Many people do not bother to keep petty cash records. This is not a good idea since it is too easy for money to become "lost" or unaccounted for. It takes just a minute each time you use the cash box to keep an accurate accounting. Keep a file card or check register in the cash box. Mark the amount on the top right corner of the card showing the beginning cash contents of the box. Each time you use money from petty cash, indicate the date and amount used and what the money is being used for, then subtract this amount from the total to give the new running balance. If funds are added to petty cash, indicate the date and the amount added, and add this to the running total. If you follow this procedure, you should be able to balance the actual cash to your record at any given time. Balance your petty cash account on a regular basis, perhaps once a month.

PHOTOCOPYING MACHINES   There are four basic types of photocopying machines: (1) diffusion transfer method; (2) dye-line method; (3) thermography; and (4) xerography.

Diffusion Transfer Method

In this method, the master copy is made by typing or drawing on a sheet of transparent paper and is then placed upon sensitized paper and exposed to light. The negative is then placed in contact with a sheet of positive transfer paper and fed over a developer. When these two sheets are peeled apart, the image is transferred to the positive paper. The machine operates automatically, requiring the operator only to push a button and feed in the master.

Dye-Line Method

The principle here is similar to the diffusion transfer method, except that dye-line requires a translucent original and uses only one sheet of sensitized paper. It is one of the cheapest of all photocopying methods. There is a dry dye-line process which uses ammonia fumes rather than light to develop the image and reduces paper shrinkage. This machine also operates automatically. Again, the operator is required only to place the master into the machine and push a button.

Thermography

In this method, the paper and the original copy are placed in contact with each other and run through a machine where they are exposed to infrared heat rays. The original copy absorbs the rays in areas darkened by print, line drawings, or writing, and the impression is made on the heat-sensitive surface of the copy paper. This method is often time-consuming since the original must be repeatedly placed through the machine to make the desired number of copies. However, this type of equipment is often found in schools since it can be used to make transparencies that can then be used on overhead projectors and for other audio-visual presentations. 3M Corporation's Thermo-Fax series uses this process.

Xerography

In this method, the document is placed face down on a glass plate. A photograph is taken and the picture is reflected via a series of mirrors onto a selenium drum in which both a positive and negative electrical charge are present. Toner powder is then cascaded over the impression and an electrical charge causes it to stick to the drum. The toner then reaches the paper and leaves an imprint.

The "fuser box" then fuses the powder to the copy paper via fuser oil. (Bad copies can smear because of failure to fuse properly, but this usually happens only when the fuser oil is running low. You have only to add the proper amount of fuser oil to solve this problem in most cases.) Wiper blades then clean the drum to free it for the next impression. This method has several advantages over others: it is fast and clean; it can produce unlimited quantities of copies in seconds; it can be used to copy books and other large or unusually sized documents; it can copy directly onto letterhead paper as well as paper of a variety of colors and weights; certain types of xerography equipment can reproduce in color; transparencies can be made. While several companies produce equipment that uses this method, the Xerox Corporation is probably the best known. A recent survey has shown that thirty percent of all service calls could have been handled by the secretary, so Xerox offers a series of free "Key Operator Classes" in which the secretary can become thoroughly acquainted with the operation of her particular Xerox equipment. It is always wise to protect copy machines from use by untrained persons in areas such as paper loading and re-inking. If done incorrectly, these procedures can severely damage equipment.

PLURALS GUIDE

- Most nouns can be made plural by adding "s" to the singular. trees, chairs, keys

  however:

- If a common or proper noun ends in "ch," "sh," "s," "ss," "x," or "zz," add "es" (usually).
  birches, wishes, foxes, buzzes, masses, Joneses

- If a common noun ending in "y" is preceded by a consonant, change the "y" to "i" and add "es."
  faculties, babies

- Some nouns ending in "f," "ff," or "fe" change their endings to "v" then add "es."

half	becomes	halves
loaf	becomes	loaves
calf	becomes	calves

- If a noun ends in an "o" preceded by a consonant, add "es" (usually).

echo	becomes	echoes
potato	becomes	potatoes

– Some nouns change their stems to form a plural.

foot	becomes	feet
goose	becomes	geese
mouse	becomes	mice
tooth	becomes	teeth
woman	becomes	women
louse	becomes	lice
man	becomes	men

– Three nouns have plurals ending in "en."

brother	becomes	brethren or brothers
child	becomes	children
ox	becomes	oxen

– Some nouns of foreign derivation retain their original plural endings:

adieu	adieux or adieus
alumna	alumnae (female)
alumnus	alumni (male or mixed male and female group)
analysis	analyses
bacillus	bacilli
basis	bases
beau	beaux or beaus
cherub	cherubim
crisis	crises
criterion	criteria or criterions
genus	genera
madame	mesdames
phenomenon	phenomena or phenomenons

Sometimes a foreign plural denotes a different meaning such as:
antennas (radio or TV)
antennae (insect)

– Compound words that are written as a single word form their plurals like any other word with the same ending.

werewolf	werewolves
garbageman	garbagemen
hatrack	hatracks

- If a compound word is formed by a word group such as
  NOUN + ADJECTIVE OR EXPRESSIVE PHRASE
  form the plural by changing the noun as if it were alone.

mother-in-law	becomes	mothers-in-law
attorney-general	becomes	attorneys-general
maid of honor	becomes	maids of honor

- Nouns ending in "ics" usually retain the same ending whether singular or plural is intended.

  mathematics, acoustics, electronics
- Some nouns are always written in the plural form.

  scissors, cattle, clothes
- Plurals of symbols, letters, or numbers are usually formed by adding an apostrophe and an "s."

  l's, 3R's, A's

PREFIX GUIDE   Prefixes are usually formed into compound words without the use of a hyphen except when using "self" which requires a hyphen and "anti" which requires a hyphen when it is followed by a capital letter. For example,

nonentity

overdone

self-indulgent

anti-Nazi, but antidote

PRINTER'S MEASUREMENTS   For your information, here is a brief glossary of printer's measurements to help you communicate more efficiently with a printer.

- <u>Point</u>. A unit of measure for type. A point is 1/72 of an inch. There are 72 points to the inch.
- <u>Pica</u>. This is used for <u>linear</u> measure of type. There are 12 points to one

pica, or 6 picas to the inch. For example, a text might be referred to as 15 picas wide by 30 picas long—never inches.

- Em. This is the square of any given type size and measures the quantity of type. It is used to estimate composition. For example, a 10 pt. em is 10 points wide and 10 points high.

- Agate Line. This is the standard for measuring depth of space. There are 14 agate lines to the inch. This term is used frequently in the newspaper field and refers to column inches.

PRINTING COPY The printing copy is the text that you submit to be printed. It should be as free from corrections as possible. An accurate text is the best guarantee of an accurate printing job. The typesetter will set the text *exactly* as you submit it—including any errors. If you have errors in the text, you will have errors in the finished product. Check and recheck for spelling, punctuation, capitalization, grammar, clarity of message, and accuracy of information. Type the copy on 8½ × 11-inch standard white bond. Type on one side of the paper only, making sure that the type is clear and double-spaced. Make corrections above the line neatly by typewriter or in ink, not pencil. Do not make corrections in the margins, on the back of the sheet, or on attached slips which can easily be misunderstood or lost. Identify each sheet by using the school name, title, and any other pertinent information. Number consecutive sheets. If there is more than one sheet, indicate "more" or "2 of 5" at the bottom of the page. If sheets are added or removed after numbering, be sure to adjust the page numbers accordingly. If you simplify the typographer's job you will save time and money. Manuscript corrections are much less expensive than author's alterations made after the item has been typeset.

Copyfitting

Copyfitting refers to the space occupied by the text—the composition of the product. This job is best left to the typographer although you can certainly give suggestions. It is best to heed the professional as this is a difficult job and requires accurate measurements and a thorough knowledge of typeface sizes. (See also PRINTER'S MEASUREMENTS.)

Placing the Order

You are buying a service when you get something printed. Be as careful when selecting a printer as you would be when buying any product. Comparison shop. Get recommendations from other schools and ask the printer for samples of completed work. Get two or three price quotes. Once you have found a printer who is reputable, reasonable, and reliable, stick with him. He will learn the particular needs of your school and you will develop a rapport that will make working on school printing jobs easier for both of you. In public schools it is often required that large printing jobs be contracted for and at least three printing bids must be made ıf ʃou have questions about your school policy, ask the administrator.

When you have chosen the printer, make sure you give him adequate instructions. Give the printer a list of specifications prior to asking for the estimate so that he can give you an accurate quote. Here are some guidelines to follow when placing a printing order:

- Number of Copies. A major factor in printing costs is typesetting. A thousand copies cost little more than five hundred since the expense of typesetting is the same. Get advice from the printer, but consider this: if the item being printed is one that will have continuous use, such as a report card or school advertising brochure, it could be to the school's advantage to have a larger number printed rather than a series of smaller batches.
- Proofreading Responsibility. Insist that the printer submit accurate proofs. You are responsible for submitting error-free copy to him; he should be responsible for setting error-free proofs. Make sure the original text is free from errors.

- Packaging Instructions. Let the printer know how the goods are to be delivered; whether loose, boxed, in rolls, in pads, or whatever.
- Deadlines. Plan on a reasonable delivery date with the printer. If you have a rush job, see how much extra this will cost.
- Note: Make sure that all specifications and ordering instructions are typed in duplicate: one for the printer, the other for the school's file.

Preparation of Printing Specifications

It is important to be precise when dealing with the printer. The more information you can give about specifications, the more likely you are to be pleased with the finished product. You will need to decide on:

- the type of paper
- the typeface
- the finished size
- the color of the stock and ink

- the best printing process for the project
- the cover
- divider pages
- binding
- the total number of finished pages

and you will need to consider the cost variables involved.

Usually you can rely on the printer for suggestions in all of these areas, but it will be to your advantage to familiarize yourself with printing terms and other information relating to printing contained in this book. (See also INKS, and PAPER CHARACTERISTICS, Finish, and Stock.)

PROFESSIONAL ORGANIZATIONS   Many administrators belong to service clubs, community groups, or professional or trade organizations. You may be required to help the administrator in relation to such groups. Here are some suggestions:

- Keep a separate file folder for each organization that your administrator belongs to.
- If the administrator holds an office in one or more of these groups, be prepared to do typing, telephoning, or to help on special projects.
- Maintain a list of the names, addresses, and telephone numbers of these groups so that you can reach your administrator in an emergency.
- Remind your administrator of any dues or professional fees necessary and be sure to bring to his attention any important information that comes through the mail or via the news media pertaining to the group. He may already know the information, but it shows that you are interested in his activities.
- Be prepared to help if your administrator is asked to give a speech, or a lecture, or is asked to participate in a community-sponsored event. If the amount of work you do involving these external organizations begins to conflict with your other duties, or causes you to feel undue pressure, tactfully mention the problem to your administrator.

PROGRESS REPORTS   Progress reports are interim reports used between regular report card periods, or they may be issued at unspecified times for problem students or students who are being tracked for special academic studies.

STUDENT'S NAME

CLASS GRADE

SUBJECT

PROGRESS REPORT

YOUR SCHOOL NAME
ADDRESS AND PHONE NUMBER
PRINTED HERE

DATE

TEACHER

ADVISER COUNSELOR

PARENT OR GUARDIAN NOTIFICATION

This report is designed to help you understand your child's progress to date A check mark in the box indicates that your child is experiencing difficulty in performing at the level expected of other children in his/her grade

Please feel free to request additional information, or an appointment with the teacher who issued this evaluation report

Parents should be familiar with the homework expected in the subject and with the school's grading system

PERSONAL & SOCIAL DEVELOPMENT	WORK HABITS	PERFORMANCE
☐ Accepts responsibility	☐ Is Attentive	☐ Exemplifies knowledge of basic skills
☐ Exerts self control	☐ Follows Directions	☐ Works to potential
☐ Works well with others	☐ Works Independently	☐ Achieves on tests
☐ Positive Self Image	☐ Work is neat/complete	☐ Completes Assignments
☐ ________	☐ ________	☐ ________

RECOMMENDATIONS

☐ Regularity of attendance ________

☐ Assist pupil to generate more effort ________

☐ Schedule teacher conference ________

☐ Schedule extra help for after school ________

☐ Tutoring or help from outside the school ________

PRINTED IN U S A
SHIREFORMS
TRADEMARK

AUTHORIZED SIGNATURE TITLE

STUDENT'S NAME

CLASS GRADE

SUBJECT

REPORT OF STUDENT PROGRESS

YOUR SCHOOL NAME
ADDRESS AND PHONE NUMBER
PRINTED HERE

DATE

TEACHER

ADVISER COUNSELOR

DEAR PARENT,

This report is designed to help you understand your child's progress to this date The number circled indicates the statement which best applies to your child's work

1 ABOVE AVERAGE 2 AVERAGE 3 BELOW AVERAGE 4 SUBSTANTIALLY BELOW AVERAGE

GENERAL PERFORMANCE 1 2 3 4

SCHOOL BEHAVIOR		WORK HABITS		PERFORMANCE IN SUBJECT	
Attendance	1 2 3 4	Preparation of Assignments	1 2 3 4	Working to Potential	1 2 3 4
Cooperation	1 2 3 4	Class Preparation	1 2 3 4	Tests	1 2 3 4
Influence on Others	1 2 3 4	Attention	1 2 3 4	Homework	1 2 3 4
Health Habits	1 2 3 4	Self Motivation	1 2 3 4	Basic Skills	1 2 3 4

RECOMMENDATIONS

☐ Conference with Teacher

☐ Greater Concentration at Home

☐ After School Help

☐ Tutoring

TEACHER'S COMMENTS:

____

PARENT'S SIGNATURE

SIGNATURE OF TEACHER

FIGURE 23

Courtesy, Newshire Forms Inc.

Sample progress report forms using both the structured and unstructured format.

Figure 23, *continued*

Progress reports may be done on pre-printed forms or may be in the form of individually typed letters. They usually include such information as behavior, work habits, and evaluation of performance as well as optional teacher comments. See Figure 23 for a sample progress report.

PROOFREADING   Proofreading used to be done by two people: one reading the original out loud, the other following the galley proof. In an effort to save time and money, proofreading is now usually done by one person reading the original and the proof alternately.

Proofreading Checklist

– Check the number of pages received. Are they all there? Is anything out of sequence?

– Check to see that you have an original page for every galley proof. Whenever possible, make a photocopy of the original before sending it to the printer since originals can get lost.

Proofreader's Marks

MARK	EXPLANATION	EXAMPLE
ℛ	TAKE OUT CHARACTER INDICATED	ℛ Your proof.
∧	LEFT OUT, INSERT	u Yor proof.
#	INSERT SPACE	# Yourproof.
9	TURN INVERTED LETTER	Your proof.
×	BROKEN LETTER	× Your proof.
eq#	EVEN SPACE	eq# A good proof.
⌒	CLOSE UP: NO SPACE	Your proof.
tr	TRANSPOSE	tr A proof good.
wf	WRONG FONT	wf Your proof.
lc	LOWER CASE	lc Your proof.
≡ / caps	CAPITALS	Your proof. / caps Your proof.
⎺ / ital	ITALIC	Your proof. / ital Your proof.
rom	ROMAN, NON ITALIC	rom Your proof.
∼∼ / bf	BOLD FACE	Your proof. / bf Your proof.
⋯⋯ / stet	LET IT STAND	Your proof. / stet Your proof.
out sc.	DELETE, SEE COPY	out sc. She Our proof.
spell out	SPELL OUT	spell out Queen Eliz.
¶	START PARAGRAPH	¶ read. Your
no ¶	NO PARAGRAPH: RUN IN	no ¶ marked. Your proof.
⎵	LOWER	⎵ Your proof.

MARK	EXPLANATION	EXAMPLE
⎴	RAISE	⎴ Your proof.
⊏	MOVE LEFT	⊏ Your proof.
⊐	MOVE RIGHT	⊐ Your proof.
‖	ALIGN TYPE	Three dogs. Two horses.
＝	STRAIGHTEN LINE	＝ Your proof.
⊙	INSERT PERIOD	⊙ Your proof∧
⅋/	INSERT COMMA	⅋/ Your proof∧
:/	INSERT COLON	:/ Your proof∧
;/	INSERT SEMICOLON	;/ Your proof∧
∨	INSERT APOSTROPHE	∨ Your mans proof.
∨∨	INSERT QUOTATION MARKS	∨∨ Marked it proof∧
=/	INSERT HYPHEN	=/ A proofmark.∧
/	INSERT EXCLAMATION MARK	/ Prove it∧
?	INSERT QUESTION MARK	? Is it right∧
?	QUERY FOR AUTHOR	was Your proof read by∧
⊏/⊐	INSERT BRACKETS	⊏/⊐ The Smith girl∧ ∧
(/)	INSERT PARENTHESES	(/) Your proof∧ ∧
⅟m	INSERT 1-EM DASH	⅟m Your proof.∧
□	INDENT 1 EM	□Your proof
□□	INDENT 2 EMS	□□Your proof.
□□□	INDENT 3 EMS	□□□Your proof.

Courtesy, Hartco Products Co., Inc.

FIGURE 24

This chart shows the correct marks to be used when correcting copy. It is especially useful when dealing with printers.

- Check the number of paragraphs on each page for omissions.
- Check the last word of each proof page with the first word of the next page for continuity and context.
- Concentrate as you read; does it make sense?
- Draw lines through errors, and type or print the correction in ink above the line.
- Double-check hyphenations in the dictionary. Make sure words are divided correctly.
- Check titles, headings, and subheadings with the original.
- There is less likelihood of error if two people proofread. If you must do it alone, swing your eyes from the original to the proof line for line.
- At the end of each page, indicate "OK" or "OK as corrected"; then initial it.
- Unless there is an error, do not rewrite materials on the galley proof. The additional charges for typesetting can be horrendous.
- Check the table of contents to be sure that page numbers and titles are the same on the original and on the proof.

Also:

- Check punctuation.
- Check capitalization.
- Check spelling. Use the dictionary if you have doubts.
- Check abbreviations if they are used, but try to avoid them.
- Check the overall text for content. Is the message clear?
- Check titles and headings.
- Make sure all intended deletions are omitted.
- Check for skipped lines in the text.
- Check for transpositions of letters and numbers.
- Check for continuity of page numbers.
- Check the typeface and paper stock. Are they what you ordered?
- Check printing specifications, delivery instructions, and deadlines.

PUBLIC, WORKING WITH THE   If you work at the school's front desk, you will come into contact with the public on a daily basis. Visitors, tradespeople, delivery people, security personnel, and salesmen will all pass your desk. It will probably be a part of your job to perform the duties of receptionist in greeting and assisting these people. It is common practice in schools to require visitors to obtain clearance from the office before being allowed free access to the school grounds. Reasons for this are obvious, since the students and property must be protected from unsavory characters and unauthorized persons. Greet all visitors in a friendly manner. If you are busy and cannot help them immediately, *acknowledge their presence* and let them know that you will help them soon. If the visitor is unknown to you, it will be necessary to identify him before issuing a visitor's pass or giving him clearance.

1. Give the visitor a friendly greeting.
2. Ask the nature of the caller's visit.
3. Ask for a business card. If the visitor hesitates when asked to identify himself, or if you have the slightest doubt about the person, ask to see some identification.
4. If you have serious doubts about a caller, verify the identification before clearing the person. Call the office listed on the business card and ask for a description of the person, or use whatever means seem reasonable at the time. It is better to make this type of telephone call privately, but legitimate visitors should not object to having their credentials verified if you handle the situation in a tactful manner.
5. If the visitor's identity cannot be verified, or if any serious problems arise, contact the administrator, or if necessary, security personnel.
6. While you are scrutinizing references, always be courteous. A person's credentials may be valid, even though difficult to authenticate. Do not alienate the visitor by appearing to mistrust him. Keep in mind that your job requires you to scrutinize visitors. However, it is important to maintain a businesslike attitude while performing this task.

PUNCTUATION

Apostrophe

The apostrophe is used to show plurals of figures, alphabet letters, and words written about as words.

3 e's

No if's, and's, or but's.

The apostrophe combines variously with ''s'' to show possession.

Marcy's hat   mother-in-law's car

boys' gym

The apostrophe is used to show omission of one or more letters or numbers.

isn't (is not)
aren't (are not)
o'clock (of the clock)
the gold rush of '49

Colon

The colon is used before a clause that illustrates or clarifies preceding matter.

Get plenty of exercise; don't smoke; eat regularly: these are necessary for good health.

The colon is used after salutations, in expressing time, and in biblical and other citations.

Dear Ms. Thompson:
2:40 P.M.
Proverbs 25:11

The colon is used for separation in bibliographic entries and book titles and subtitles.

New York: Pentathlon Press
Nathaniel Hawthorne: *The Inward Eye*

The colon is used in stating proportions, ratios, and relationships.

Concrete mixed 5:3:1
1:2::3:6
Nose:Nasal::Ear:Aural

The colon is used after introductory lines or expressions in tables or listings.

Leading scorers: Anderson (24), Penquite (18), Aswegan (4)

The colon is used to introduce formally any matter that forms a complete sentence, question, or quotation.

The following question became the central issue: Who will choose the textbooks for the school?

Comma

Use commas to separate items in a series.

Tom's equipment included a camera, flash bulbs, a gadget bag, and plenty of fresh film.

Use commas to set off interrupters.

- <u>Appositives</u>: Smithson, a journalist by trade, wrote the message swiftly.
- <u>Words in Direct Address</u>: Jean, I want you to know we like your work.
- <u>Parenthetical Expression</u>: Your credentials, of course, are the finest.
- <u>Special Introductory Words</u>: Yes, I accept your backing.
- <u>Items in dates and addresses:</u> By Monday, June 1, 1789, the petitions had been signed and returned.
- <u>Nonrestrictive Clauses</u>: Bob Johnson, who played centerfield for the Bruins, will be traded to the Astros.
- <u>Nonrestrictive Participial Phrases</u>: The quarterback, glancing quickly at the coach, turned and threw to the tight end.

Use a comma before *and, but, or, nor, for, yet* when they join main clauses, except when the clauses are very brief.

Bert paid expensive fees and high tuition, but he received a good education in return.

He came but he did not conquer.

Use a comma after an introductory participial phrase, an introductory adverbial clause, or a series of introductory prepositional phrases.

Crashing into the wall, Kelly's car turned over twice and burst into flames.

While the dog howled, Cardenza continued to sing.

At sea, on the land, in the air, the Dragoon patrol is ever vigilant.

Use a comma after the salutation of a friendly letter and after the closing of any letter.

Dear Gail,

Yours truly,

Dash

The dash is used to mark a sudden break or abrupt change in thought.

He said—and no one contradicted him—"the battle is lost."

It was Johnson—no, maybe it was Nesbit—who forgot the license.

The dash is used to indicate an unfinished word or sentence.

"Such an idea can scarcely be—

The dash is used to show omission of letters or words.

We can offer you one h—— of a deal.

He left the book with Monsieur S—— at the rue de Main.

The dash is used to precede a credit line.

Every man's work shall be made manifest.

—*Corinthians* 3:13

The dash may be used instead of commas or parentheses if the meaning may be clarified.

There are shore deposits—gravel, sand, and clay—but great oil deposits are under them.

The dash may be used before summarizing statement or word.

Freedom of speech, freedom of worship, freedom from fear—these are fundamentals of moral world order.

Exclamation Point

The exclamation point is used to mark surprise, disbelief, or other strong emotion.

I couldn't believe it!

"Great!" he shouted.

Ouch!

What!

The exclamation point is used to help assert an order or strengthen a command.

Do it now!

Get going!

Block that kick!

The exclamation point is used to suggest cynicism, doubt, or irony.

"Sure you can!" he said derisively.

Our school has such good athletes (!) that it makes the coach's job easy.

Big deal! So he won the Grand Prix!

Parentheses

Parentheses are used to indicate that material has been added. This material may include illustrations or other helpful information that does not seem to belong in the text.

> The concession stand sells a variety of refreshments (sandwiches, beverages, cakes, etc.).

> You can find it neither in the dictionary (at least not in my dictionary) nor the thesaurus.

> Portland (Oregon) Chamber of Commerce.

Parentheses are used to enclose numbers or letters in paragraphs or listings.

> You will note that this sword is (1) old-fashioned, (2) still sharp, and (3) unusually light.

> The order of delivery will be (a) food, (b) clothing, (c) tents and household goods.

Period

The period is used after a declarative sentence that is not exclamatory, or after an imperative sentence.

> He was assigned an auditorium seat.

> Do not be late.

The period is used in place of parentheses after a letter or number denoting a series.

> a. Bread well baked   1. Report Cards
> b. Meat cooked rare   2. Progress reports
> c. Cubed apples stewed   3. Attendance sheets

Periods have several other conventional uses: after abbreviations and initials, unless otherwise specified:

> Sept.   bldg.   Minn.   Dr. J. C. Porter, Jr.

Between dollars and cents when the dollar sign is used:

> $4.75 $ .98   (but 98¢ or 98 cents)

Question Mark

The question mark is the end stop of a direct question.

> Did he do it?

> He did that?

The question mark may indicate a direct query even if not in the form of a question.

> Can the money be raised? is the question.

The question mark may be used to express doubt.

> He said the opposing center was eight (?) feet tall.
>
> The statute (?) was on the statute books.

Quotation Marks

Quotation marks are used to enclose a direct quotation (a speaker's exact words).

> "We are on our way," the President declared.

Quotation marks are used for other purposes: To mark titles of articles, book chapters, short poems and stories.

> He reads "The Raven" at least once a year.

Quotation marks are used to mark nicknames, ironical use of words and phrases, or words discussed as words.

> Theodore "Cappy" Thompson was no stranger to the Lighthouse Tavern.
>
> Thoreau's "palace" was a tiny hut at Walden.
>
> Please avoid using "irregardless" even though it is commonplace in comic strips.

A single quotation mark is used to enclose a quotation within a quotation.

> The principal said, "When you say, 'I'm going to work harder,' I expect you to do just that."

Quotation marks are used at the beginning and end of a paragraph in lengthy quotations, except when the quotation runs more than one paragraph, in which case quotation marks are placed at the beginning of each paragraph, but only at the end of the last paragraph.

Semicolon

The semicolon is a hybrid, part comma, part period. It is used to separate clauses containing commas.

> Reptiles, amphibians, and predatory mammals swallow their prey whole or in large pieces, bones included; waterfowl habitually take entire shellfish; and some birds have gizzards that grind up the hardest seeds.

To separate statements too closely related in meaning to be written as separate sentences, and also statements of contrast.

It is true in peace; it is true in war.

War is destructive; peace constructive.

To separate main clauses joined by connectives such as *hence, thus, for example, in fact, consequently,* and so on.

Jerry is never dull; in fact, he is always the life of the party.

PURCHASE ORDER A purchase order (PO) is your authority to tell an outside vendor that you can buy a certain item and that the school or board of education will pay for it. Public schools use numbered purchase orders, while some private institutions simply use the authorized person's name instead of a number. Purchase orders are issued based on requisitions made by a teacher, a staff member, or a department of the school. Requisition forms must be signed by the teacher or person requesting the purchase. Individuals should not expect

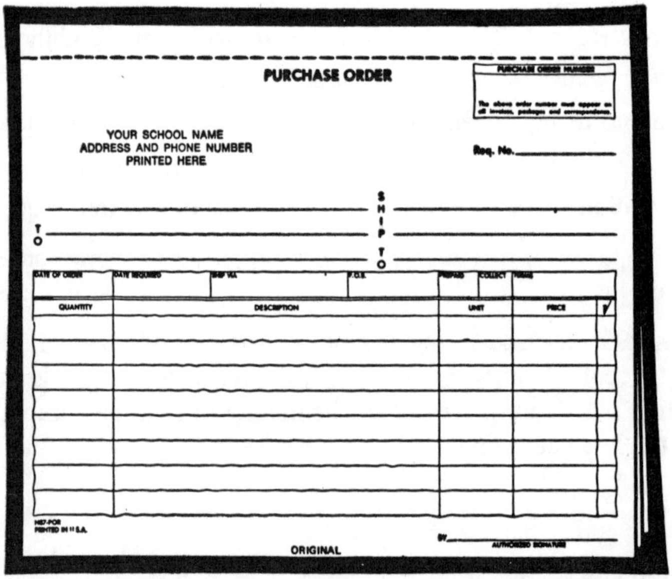
PURCHASE ORDER

PURCHASE ORDER NUMBER

The above order number must appear on all invoices, packages and correspondence.

YOUR SCHOOL NAME
ADDRESS AND PHONE NUMBER
PRINTED HERE

Req. No.

TO

SHIP TO

DATE OF ORDER	DATE REQUIRED	SHIP VIA	F.O.B.	PREPAID	COLLECT	TERMS

QUANTITY	DESCRIPTION	UNIT	PRICE	✓

ORIGINAL

BY AUTHORIZED SIGNATURE

Courtesy, Newshire Forms Inc.

FIGURE 25

Sample purchase order forms

FIGURE 25, *continued*

to be reimbursed for purchases unless they have been given authorization via a purchase order number. Funds must be cleared in conjunction with available budgets before authority to purchase is given. The vendor will request the purchase order number (or name) when the order is placed and that number will appear on the invoice. Any additional correspondence or telephone conversations about the order should always include the purchase order number. See Figure 25 for sample purchase orders.

QUITTING YOUR JOB When it is time to move on to other things, there is a right and a wrong way to quit your job. Even though you are leaving, remember that you still may need a recommendation or letter of reference from your present employer. Do not get sloppy after you have given your notice, but strive to maintain your usual high standards. It is often unfair but true that the last few tasks you do may remain in your administrator's memory more than all the previous years of work put together. It is always better to leave on a pleasant note and be remembered for your efficiency and professionalism.

QUOTATIONS, TYPING A quotation is a word for word copy of information from a published work or from a speech. Here is the format for typing quotations:

- <u>Quotation of Three Lines or Less.</u> Type it into the body of the text and enclose it in quotation marks.
- <u>Long Quotation.</u> Set it off from the body of the text. Indent the first line seven spaces and all other lines four spaces from the left hand margin. Do not use quotation marks if you use this type of indentation. If the quotation is being used for publication or for a speech, double space it. Copy all quotations exactly, including punctuation and paragraphing. If a portion of the quotation is being deleted, indicate this by using an ellipsis (. . .). You may also use quotation marks instead of indenting long quotations. In this case, place quotes at the beginning of each paragraph but only at the end of the last paragraph.

RAISED IMAGE PROCESS   A method of printing in which the master copy is made by typesetting machine. Work requiring this type of process is usually sent out to a printer for typesetting.

REQUISITIONS.   See PURCHASE ORDERS.

RESOLUTIONS.   See MINUTES.

RIBBONS, TYPEWRITER   Basically there are two types of typewriter ribbons—fabric (usually nylon) and film (also called carbon ribbon). Fabric ribbons are less expensive, but film ribbons provide a high-quality "printed" appearance and are the best choice for use with photo-reproduction equipment. There are a few typewriters that have interchangeable fabric/film ribbon systems, but in most cases, the typewriter will use only one or the other. Fabric ribbons can be used many times over as they automatically reverse when they come to the end of a spool, but film ribbons can be used only once.

RIGHTS, JOB   There is a large pay differential between men and women, although schools are often the exception because both men and women are notoriously underpaid. This is because, in the past, women have not been taken seriously in the job market. They often held lower-paying jobs and worked only temporarily, until they began raising their families. Yet the federal law states that men and women are entitled to equal pay when work is equal or substantially equal. This equality also applies to advancement and retirement benefits.

The states may have laws governing minimum wage, equal pay, and fair employment practices, that grant more than those of the federal government. To learn more about your state law, contact your state's labor department or human rights agency. If you believe that you are the victim of discrimination, you are entitled to file a complaint with the appropriate administrative agency. Procedures for making complaints vary, but a telephone request is enough to set in motion an investigation into substandard wages or unequal pay, whereas a formal verified complaint is necessary under some antidiscrimination laws. There are time limits on filing, so it is important to act promptly. Be sure to include a clear and concise statement of the facts, including dates, that might be relevant to your complaint.

Title VII of the Civil Rights Act of 1964 prohibits discrimination in employment based on sex as well as on race, color, religion, or national origin. This act makes it unlawful to discriminate in hiring or firing; wages; fringe benefits; classifying, referring, assigning or promoting employees; extending or assigning facilities; training, retraining, or apprenticeships; or any other terms, conditions, or privileges of employment. As amended in 1972, it covers most employers of fifteen or more employees, public and private employment agencies, labor unions with fifteen or more members, and joint labor-management committees for apprenticeship and training. Indian tribes are exempt as employers. Religious institutions are exempt with respect to employing persons of a particular religion, but are covered with respect to discrimination based on sex, race, color, or national origin. You have a right to complain if:

- an employer refuses to let you file an application but accepts others;
- a union or an employment agency refuses to refer you to job openings;
- a union refuses to accept you into membership;
- you are fired or laid off;
- you are passed over for promotion for which you are qualified;
- you are paid less than others for comparable work;
- you are placed in a segregated seniority line;
- you are left out of training or apprenticeship programs;

AND the reason for any of these acts is your sex, race, color, religion, or national origin.

The Age Discrimination in Employment Act prohibits discrimination on the basis of age against any person between the ages of forty and seventy in hiring, firing, compensation, or other conditions of employment. The law applies to all public employers, private employers of twenty or more employees, employment agencies serving covered employers, and labor unions of more than twenty-five members. It does not cover situations in which age is a bona fide occupational qualification (such as modeling "junior miss" fashions) nor does it affect bona fide seniority systems. It does prohibit using employee benefit plans as a basis for refusing to hire older applicants or retiring older employees. The law does not permit involuntary retirement of workers under seventy.

The Equal Pay Act of 1963 amended the Fair Labor Standards Act (FLSA) to prohibit unequal pay for men and women who work in the same establishment and whose jobs require equal skill, effort, and responsibility. Differentials based on a seniority or a merit system or on a system that measures earnings by quantity or quality or production are permitted. Employers may not reduce the wage rate of any employee in order to eliminate illegal wage differentials. In addition to covering employees subject to the minimum wage requirements of the FLSA, the law applies to state and local government employees; executive, administrative, and professional employees; and outside salespeople. A number of court cases have established that jobs need be only substantially equal, not identical, in order to be compared for purposes of the Act. It is illegal to fire or discriminate against employees exercising their rights under the law.

The Federal Wage Garnishment Law, enforced by the Wage and Hour Division of the U.S. Department of Labor, limits the amount of your disposable earnings which may be subject to garnishment. (Garnishment is the procedure whereby the earnings of a debtor are withheld in order to pay creditors.) The law also protects you from discharge because of garnishment for any indebtedness.

Maternity Leave

Under guidelines issued by the federal government, a reasonable leave must be granted for childbearing. You must be reinstated in your original job or in a position of like status and pay without loss of service credits when you decide to return within a reasonable time following childbirth. The law requires that women affected by pregnancy, childbirth, or related medical conditions be treated the same for all employment related purposes, including receipt of benefits under fringe benefit programs, as other persons not so affected but similar in their ability or inability to work. If your employer is subject to Title VII, you cannot be refused employment because of pregnancy; you cannot be fired because of pregnancy; you cannot be forced to go on leave at an arbitrary point during pregnancy if you are still able to work; and you cannot be penalized because of pregnancy in reinstatement rights, including credit for previous service and accrued retirement benefits and accumulated seniority.

ROLL SHEETS   A roll sheet is an alphabetical listing of students on which each class teacher records attendance. After the teacher records the absences, the sheets are sent to the attendance office. The secretary may then process the roll sheets or forward them to the computer center for processing.

How to Make a Roll Sheet

- Determine the number of students in each class.
- Head each column with the appropriate class title.
- Do a rough draft and list the students alphabetically with last name first, leaving enough space beside each name for recording attendance information.
- Make a master for each class roll list.
- Run off enough copies to last for the term, plus a few extras. (Some teachers like to use the roll sheets for other things such as reminder lists, field trip check lists, and book check out, so it is a good idea to make extras.)
- Roll sheets can also be used for keeping a record of bus fares or money owed by the student, and for locks and lockers issued to them.

ROMAN NUMERALS

I	1	XLV	45
II	2	XLIX	49
III	3	L	50
IV	4	LV	55
V	5	LIX	59
VI	6	LX	60
VII	7	LXV	65
VIII	8	LXIX	69
IX	9	LXX	70
X	10	LXXV	75
XV	15	LXXIX	79
XIX	19	LXXX	80
XX	20	LXXXV	85
XXV	25	LXXXIX	89
XXIX	29	XC	90
XXX	30	XCV	95
XXXV	35	XCIX	99
XXXIX	39	C	100
XL	40	CL	150

CC	200	M	1000
CCC	300	MD	1500
CD	400	MM	2000
D	500	MMM	3000
DC	600	MMMM or M$\overline{V}$	4000
DCC	700	$\overline{V}$	5000
DCCC	800	$\overline{M}$	1,000,000
CM	900		

Sample Dates:

MD	1500	MCMXL	1940
MDC	1600	MCML	1950
MDCC	1700	MCMLX	1960
MDCCC	1800	MCMLXX	1970
MCM	1900	MCMLXXX	1980
MCMX	1910	MCMXC	1990
MCMXX	1920	MM	2000
MCMXXX	1930		

S

SCHEDULES In large institutions and colleges, computers take care of scheduling. The student receives a computer printout showing which classes have been assigned, and the student in conjunction with the teacher is responsible for submitting class changes, additions, or for dropping or withdrawing from the school. In small schools or in elementary level programs, it is necessary to keep a close watch over the scheduling procedure as it is usually executed by hand. First, a master schedule is made into which all classes, room numbers, and teachers are blocked. Verification of each section is made to be sure that there are no conflicts. Next, each student is scheduled into appropriate classes, whether "solids" (academic requirements) or "electives" (classes that may be chosen by the student). Schedule cards are then issued to each student, showing the class and room number for each period of the day. Additional copies of the schedule cards are usually filed with the principal, counselor, and student's file. In the smaller school, it is helpful if the secretary keeps a copy of the schedules within easy reach, so that students can be located quickly and easily in times of emergency.

SEATING CHART, HOW TO READ A Some instructors use the alphabetical seating method; some prefer random choice, ability grouping, or some other method.

If there is a seating chart that you need to read (as in the case of substitute teaching) remember that each square on the chart corresponds to a chair in the room. When the chart is facing you and you are facing the class, the bottom left square corresponds to the first seat in the far left row. The rest follow in sequence. Seating charts can be particularly helpful to new or substitute teachers. Children are less likely to misbehave if you can call on them by name.

SECURITY The occasional playground fight or a few broken windows or scribblings on the bathroom wall used to be the extent of violence in the school; times have changed. In California alone, $80–$100 million is spent annually on school vandalism in comparison to $142 million spent on books. It has been estimated that $1 billion is spent annually on school vandalism nationally. Many school districts are unable to buy fire insurance because of prohibitive rates caused by the high-risk factors. The Safe School Study conducted by the National Institute of Education in 1977 found:

- The risks of assault and robbery to urban youngsters aged twelve to nineteen are greater in school than out.
- In a typical month, a minimum of 157,000 cases of crime and disruption occur in American public schools.
- Schools report 50,000 offenses a month to police.
- Schools do not report to police two-thirds of the assaults requiring medical attention.
- Almost half a million secondary school students are afraid at school most of the time.
- In a typical month, approximately 125,000 secondary school teachers are threatened with physical harm; about the same number hesitate to confront misbehaving students for fear of harm to themselves.
- Annual replacement and repair costs because of school property offenses are estimated at about $200 million.
- According to a recent four-year study, violence and vandalism have increased 273 percent for teenagers.

In the light of these statistics, a preventive rather than a reactive approach to school security is imperative. Actions that prevent teachers, students, administrators, parents, school personnel, security personnel, and often innocent bystanders from becoming victims of school crime must be given the highest priority.

Factors Associated with School Violence and Vandalism

- The principal's firmness in enforcing rules, and the amount of control in the classroom; the more firmly a school is run, the lower the incidence of violence.
- Fairness in the enforcement of rules; the absence of fairness, as perceived by students, seems to provoke violence.
- The school's proximity to students' homes may make it a convenient target for vandalism.

- The presence of nonstudent youth around the school; they often cause problems and increase the school's risk of property loss.
- School size; in larger schools, property losses are higher.
- Coordination between faculty and administration; good coordination helps reduce the incidence of crime.
- Class size; the implication is not that teachers have better control over small classes, but that more continuous contact with the same students helps reduce violence.
- Students valuing their teachers' opinions of them; schools in which students identify with their teachers and have a good sense of self-worth have less vandalism.

Prevention Techniques

- Keeping the school occupied.
- Keeping the school watched.
- Controlling access to the school.
- Designing or modifying the school with crime prevention in mind.
- Repairing damage immediately.
- Working with the courts and local law enforcement.
- Prosecuting offenders and demanding restitution for damage.
- Having adequate key control.
- Having adequate alarm systems.

Target Areas of Vandals and Thieves

- Principal's office and administrative offices
- Industrial arts shop
- Cafeteria and food storage areas
- Library and audio-visual storage area
- Band room and instrument storage area
- Business equipment storage area
- Laboratories
- Gym and locker rooms
- Hallways
- Service areas
- Custodial supply storage area

- Mechanical and electrical rooms
- Educational supplies
- Grounds equipment storage areas

Working with Security Personnel

Contract security guards (also known as "rent-a-cop") can present an effective deterrent to prevent vandalism in schools, especially when present during large gatherings; but their purpose is often stopgap. Their accountability is lower, their preparation and training to react to critical situations are less comprehensive, and often the commitment and turnaround rate are less than desirable. It may be more beneficial in the long run for schools to hire permanent professional security personnel. In any event, the school secretary is often asked to work directly with security personnel in helping to familiarize them with the school plant via maps and diagrams, or in filling out damage reports and performing other clerical duties.

SPELLING, BASIC RULES OF

- Adding a suffix to a one-syllable word

  If the word ends in a single consonant preceded by a single vowel, double the final consonant before a suffix that begins with a vowel: redder (red + er).

  If the word ends with two or more consonants or one consonant preceded by two or more vowels, do not double the final consonant before adding the suffix: wilder (wild + er).

- Adding a suffix to a word that has two or more syllables

  If a word has two or more syllables, the accent is on the last syllable, and if it ends in a single consonant preceded by a single vowel, double the final consonant before adding the suffix: permitted (permit + ed).

  If the word ends with two consonants or if the final consonant is preceded by more than one vowel, do not double the final consonant before adding the suffix: comfortable (comfort + able).

  If the accent is placed on any syllable except the last, do not double the final consonant before adding the suffix: consideration (consider + ation).

- Adding a suffix that begins with a vowel to a word that ends in a silent "e"

  Drop the silent "e" (usually) before adding a suffix beginning with a vowel: meditation (meditate + ion).

Exceptions: If words end in "ce" or "ge," retain the final "e" before adding the suffixes "able" or "ous":

changeable (change + able)

outrageous (outrageous (outrage + ous)

traceable (trace + able)

If a word ends in silent "e" but could be mistaken for another word by adding a suffix, retain the final "e":

dyeing (dye + ing). If the final "e" were dropped it could be   con fused with "dying."

If the word ends in "ie," drop the "e" and change the "i" to "y" before adding the suffix "ing." (Never use two "i" 's together.)

— <u>Adding a suffix beginning with a consonant to a word ending in a silent "e"</u>

Retain the final "e" (usually): politeness (polite + ness).

Exceptions: abridgment, acknowledgment, argument, awful, duly, judgment, truly, wholly

— <u>Adding a suffix to a word ending in "c"</u>

Usually, add the letter "k" after the "c" before adding the suffix: panicky (panic + "k" and y)
Do not add "k" to clinic (clinical).

— <u>Is it "ie" or "ei"?</u>

You can still usually rely on the old adage "I" before "E" except after "C." When in doubt consult the dictionary.

STATISTICAL REPORTS   School statistical reports can seem endless and may include any or all of the following topics:

— School population breakdown by age, sex, grade level, race, religion

— Attendance statistics reports

— Ability level statistics

— Medical statistics:

immunizations by type and date

incomplete medical records

contagious disease reports

— Graduate admissions to other schools and colleges

— Graduate employment statistics

– Financial records:

fund-raising, grants (applied for, awarded, refused), tuitions (paid and outstanding), departmental budgets and on and on.

When compiling data or typing up such reports, common sense points the way to efficiency. A statistical report is the structure that rests on the foundation of accurately maintained records. You cannot prepare the best possible report unless all the records leading up to it are precise and complete. The small amount of extra time it takes to keep your records exact and current can pay off big dividends in efficiency.

STENCILS A stencil is made of thin, tough porous material that is specially coated so that ink will not pass through. When you type or write on the stencil sheet, the coating is pushed aside so that only the shape of the letter or drawn character remains. Stencils are "run off" on mimeograph machines. There are different kinds of stencils for different needs. Your supplier can give you specific information but the basic stencil categories are:

– All-Purpose Stencils

Long-run ability; high quality; able to withstand heavy typing pressure, underscoring, wear and tear; some are available with a form on the stub for filing and running information.

– Artist Quality Stencils

A special coating makes them suitable for art techniques such as detailed lettering, tracing, and free-hand drawing. They can also be used for typing.

– Stubless Stencils

These are available in sizes from 8½″ × 4″ to 8½″ × 14⅝″. Because they have no stubs, even the large size may be filed in standard file cabinets.

– Photographic Offset Stencils

Designed especially for use as negatives for making photographic offset plates; they may also be used for typing.

– Continuous Stencil Sheets

These are for use with tabulators and sprocket-fed printing equipment; various sizes are available.

– Electronic Stencils

These enable you to mimeograph material instead of paying to have it printed. These ready-to-run plastic stencils can be prepared from your printed original or from fine line work such as forms, letterheads, catalog pages, and so on.

There are also special stencils to fill specific needs:

– Addressing Stencil Sheets

These are used for typing labels. You just type the name and address in the spaces provided, then run off the stencil on special gummed perforated label paper.

– Newspaper Stencil Sheets

These are specially designed for mimeographing newspapers, newsletters, and any work requiring columns. They eliminate the need for time-consuming measuring and layout.

– Folder Stencil Sheets

The special guidelines on these sheets eliminate the need for measuring and copy positioning while enabling you to prepare professional looking programs and bulletins.

– Handwriting Stencil Sheets

These provide guidelines for handwriting and are especially good for teacher/classroom use.

– Music Stencils

Music staffs are already in place and music notes can be written in with a stylus.

– Outline Map Stencils

A large selection of outline map stencils is available. These can be filled in with any information desired.

How to Use Stencil Guide Marks

Proper use of the stencil guide marks will help you to quickly and accurately position your copy. Most stencils indicate a top and bottom edge paper guide and a side margin guide as well as numbered typewriter line spaces (usually six per inch). Warning numerals are indicated to let you know how many lines you can type before reaching the bottom of the page.

How to Correct Stencils

You will need special stencil correction fluid for this job. Essentially, the fluid replaces the coating which has been pushed aside, and fills in the indentation in the stencil. It is best to burnish the error before applying the correction fluid as this will prevent the fluid from seeping through and sticking to the cushion. To burnish, simply rub the error gently with the rounded end of a paper clip. Then, insert a pencil between the stencil and the cushion to hold them apart and apply the correction fluid. If you are using a film over the stencil, it must be peeled back before the correction fluid is applied. Allow the fluid to dry for a few seconds, then retype. After you have finished typing the copy, hold the stencil up to the light and make sure that the corrections are visible, and that no errors are "bleeding through."

How to Prepare Stencils for Handwriting

It is easy to write or draw on stencils; all you need is a stylus and a steady hand. Choose a stylus with a ball tip and you can use it just like a ballpoint pen. Hold the stylus almost vertical so that the ball is even. Use firm pressure and keep it as even as possible. Any little quiver or falter of your hand will show up on the mimeographed copy. Use a signature plate or writing plate between the stencil and the backing, then place it on a smooth surface and write.

How to Type Stencils

Place the typewriter in a stencil position by disengaging the ribbon control system and placing it in neutral. Clean the typewriter keys by brushing them with a circular motion. (Some stencils come with a mylar film cover that reduces the possibility of letters "punching out" and makes it unnecessary to clean the type before typing a stencil.) Push your paper bail rollers aside. Insert the cushion sheet if specified with the particular type of stencil you are using. Insert the stencil into the typewriter as if you were inserting paper. Line up the stencil with the guides. Check to be sure the stencil is straight and free of wrinkles. Corrections are easier if you proofread before removing the stencil from the typewriter.

Typing Postcard Stencils

Cards are fed into a mimeograph machine lengthwise from the center of the machine feed table. Therefore, the copy for a card is typed on the top center of the stencil. Most stencils show special guides for postcards. If the copy is to run the narrow way on the card:

- Lay the card on the stencil, aligning it with the top edge of the paper guide.
- Mark the perimeters of the card on the stencil with dots of correction fluid.

- Leave at least one-half inch from each edge for margins.
- Remove the card and cut through the stencil, cushion, and backing about two inches below the area to be typed.
- Fold a piece of paper over the stencil back and insert it into the typewriter. The paper protects the stencil as it is being inserted into the typewriter. After insertion, discard the paper.
- Type your stencil and remove it from the typewriter.
- Cement the cut piece of stencil back to the original by using mimeograph cement.
- Run as usual.

STRESS, HOW TO RELIEVE   Stress is any physical or emotional strain. During periods of stress the body's metabolism is altered, changing the person's physical condition and mental outlook. Short periods of stress may result in a jittery feeling, a headache, muscle cramps, "tight neck," or upset stomach. Prolonged stress can result in ulcers, hypertension, allergic reactions, heart attack, constant fatigue, depression, and a host of other ailments. In order for you to do the best possible job, you must maintain yourself in the best possible health. Here are some stress-reducing exercises that you can do at work; some right at your desk. They can really do wonders for your disposition and your efficiency.

All exercises are to be done with caution and common sense. If any exercise causes you to feel pain, discontinue it at once and check with your physician. If the back of your neck sometimes feels tight and stiff or your muscles feel sore and tense at the end of the day or your fingers cramp from too much writing or typing, try some of these exercises for relief:

The Neck Roll

This exercise relieves tension in the neck and shoulders that is often associated with extensive periods of writing or typing (often called "secretary's neck"). The exercise may be done from a sitting or standing position. Slowly and gently rotate your head downward until your chin touches your chest or as far down as you can comfortably go. Slowly rotate your head in a complete circle five times counterclockwise. Repeat five times in a clockwise direction. Repeat slowly as often as necessary to relieve tension.

The Arm Stretch

This exercise relieves tension in the arms and back. Sit or stand erectly. Raise arms straight over your head. Slowly and gently stretch. Hold the stretch for a few seconds. Release. Relax for a few seconds. Repeat five times.

The Throw-Away

This exercise relieves cramps in the hands and fingers. Shake your hands vigorously for several seconds until they tingle. Make a fist, then open your hands and stretch the fingers as if throwing something away. Alternate these movements (shaking, fist, and throwing away) until cramping is relieved.

The Giant Stretch

If you have a private office, you may wish to try this exercise there; otherwise, the restroom or lounge will suffice. If fellow employees think you are a little strange, you might encourage them to share the benefits of this exercise; it provides general tension relief. From a standing position, raise yourself on your toes with your arms overhead. Slowly and gently stretch, reaching your arms up toward the ceiling. Slowly and gently bend over and try to touch your palms to the floor or as far as you can comfortably go. Repeat five times.

The Grimace

Save this one for really terrible days. It releases pent-up hostilities and tension. Go to a really private place such as a restroom enclosure. Stand with your feet slightly apart about two feet from a wall. Place your palms against the wall, lean and push with all your strength. Imagine that the source of your tension is the wall and that you are going to destroy it. Grimace and really try to feel the hostility leaving your body and going into the wall. Don't feel foolish; no one can see you. Repeat this until you feel better.

Breathing Properly

One of the simplest and most effective forms of tension relief can be achieved by breathing properly. We all take breathing for granted but for most adults effective breathing must be relearned. Babies and small children breathe naturally, using their full lung capacities, thereby enabling maximum oxygenation of the brain and bloodstream. Somehow, through the passage of the years and the build-up of tension most of us become chest breathers, using only a small percentage of the lung in breathing, and therefore cheating ourselves of the relaxation and energy-giving benefits of oxygen. Learning to breathe deeply can have both immediate and lasting health benefits. When practicing the following exercises initially, do not overdo it. You may become dizzy if your body is unaccustomed to receiving such large amounts of oxygen. As in the previous exercises, slow and gentle is the rule. When you breathe naturally, the chest should not move during a breath. The lower part of the lungs in the back and the abdominal area should slowly expand with each inhalation and contract with each exhalation. Deep breathing causes an immediate overall relaxation and calming effect. When practiced daily, it is a great boon to an overall sense of well-being. It takes just a few minutes to become a happier and more efficient person. When performed properly, the following exercise is guaranteed to calm and relax you, refresh your mind, and ready you to continue your duties with renewed energy. Why not try it on your next coffee break instead of pumping yourself full of caffeine?

Deep Breathing Exercise

In this exercise, the greatest benefits are achieved from a sitting position but it may also be done from a standing position. Your head and back should be erect but not rigid. All breathing is done through the nose, not the mouth. Begin by exhaling slowly. Imagine all impurities and tensions leaving your body. Close your eyes if this helps you to concentrate. Do not force the air out; just let it flow naturally and easily.

Do not allow your chest to rise and fall. All expansion and contraction should occur in the rib cage and abdomen. Slowly breathe in. Do not force. Just let the air flow in at its own pace. Imagine that the air is rushing in through a hole in the middle of your back and that the lower parts of your lungs are filling with clean pure air. Continue inhaling until you reach a feeling of fullness without strain. Pretend that you are getting ready to fill a giant balloon. You will feel your lungs and rib cage expand; then your abdomen. When your lungs are comfortably full, hold the breath for two or three seconds. Avoid any straining. Exhale slowly. Do not force. Allow an equal amount of time to fill and empty the lungs. Slowly and rhythmically continue to inhale and exhale deeply a few times. Do not hurry. Repeat this until you feel relaxed. At first you may really have to concentrate, but as you become more accustomed to deep breathing, one or two breaths properly executed will bring immediate relief.

STUDENTS, WORKING WITH   If you have not had any contact with students for a few years, get ready for a surprise. Students have changed in the past decade or so, both in their attitudes toward teachers and staff, and toward their place in the educational system. There was a time when the typical student behaved like a captive who was forced to memorize pages of dates and data and who, at the first opportunity, would escape from the confines of his imprisonment. While there are still a few students with this attitude, the majority want an education, enjoy the new inductive learning methods, and are (as are their parents) very consumer-oriented. They want their education to relate to their lives and goals, and often demand that curricula be revised to that end. They have an awareness of the world far beyond that of the previous generation—partly because of their early exposure to television. They can spot a phony in a second and relate best to an honest and straightforward approach. In spite of their sophisticated attitudes, they are still young people and are still plagued by the insecurities and anxieties that come with the territory. Young people often send out the conflicting message: "I'm grown up. I don't need you. Help me!" The students you deal with may range from elementary school through adult, but your role in working with them will probably not differ much. When working with people of any age group, there are more similarities than differences.

From the school secretary's viewpoint there is surprisingly little difference in dealing with a kindergarten student or an adult student. Of course, you will alter your speech for a very young child who will need clear and patient explanations, but the following guidelines can be applied when working with students of all ages:

1. Be patient. Smile and seem interested. Take time to understand what is being said and to be sure that what you say is understood.

2. Listen. Take time to give full attention when a student is making a request. Do not keep on typing or working when a student is speaking to you.

3. Respond. Try to fill requests to the best of your ability. Do not let the student think you are too busy to help or that he is a pest.

4. Care. If there were no students you would be out of a job. Strive to achieve a balance between your paperwork and human needs. Do not allow the paperwork to overshadow the fact that a student may really need your help.

5. Be honest. Your attitude toward the student should always be based in honesty—a student can spot a phony very quickly.

6. Never belittle students. If a problem arises, do not belittle a student in front of his peers. If you need to reprimand a student, do it in private.

SUBSTITUTE TEACHER, ACTING AS A   Depending on the size of your school and its particular function, you may be asked to act as a substitute teacher frequently, from time to time, or not at all. The first time you walk in to take over a class can be a terrifying experience, since students traditionally take advantage of "the sub" and feel much freer to misbehave. Ask any teacher and he will tell you that "subbing" is one of the most difficult of all teaching assignments. The student feels safe in his anonymity to play pranks, and you, in your new role, might feel insecure, especially when you have no formal training in that area. Remember, though, that as a regular member of the staff, you are known and have a better chance of maintaining order than an unknown substitute who is unfamiliar with students' names and routines. You have a better chance of commanding respect and attention than a stranger, even though you may not have developed the techniques of an educator. Just in case you run into problems, here are few tips on how to handle discipline in the classroom:

- Be pleasant but firm right from the start.
- Be sure to deal with insubordination immediately. A firm "Don't do that again" might be all that is required if said right away.

Keeping Control of the Class

Each professional teacher develops his own style of maintaining control. Some can be buddies with the students and maintain order, while others are very stern in their manner. Even though this may be your first experience as a teacher, there are some methods that can help you:

- First, mentally prepare yourself. You are the teacher. You have control. You will maintain control.
- Set down your rules at the beginning of the class. Let the students know right away what you will not tolerate if anyone misbehaves.
- Let the students know that you are keeping a list of names of anyone who misbehaves to give to the regular teacher.
- Keep students in their seats and keep them working separately. Do not allow them to work in groups unless you have had sufficient experience to handle the situation.
- Do not allow anyone to leave the classroom for any reason (except to go to the bathroom) unless they have a signed pass, or unless you have a way of verifying their destination. Those going to the bathroom should go alone.
- If the class should get out of control, call an administrator immediately (send a reliable student to notify the office) or get help from the teacher next door.
- Never allow even a slight transgression to slip by in the beginning or you soon might have a chaotic situation on your hands.
- If things progress well, you can always soften your attitude, but if you begin as a "softie" it is virtually impossible to regain control.
- Be fair in your judgments. If you have not actually witnessed an action, do not place blame because of a bad reputation. Even the "bad guys"

behave sometimes. Sometimes students will test you to see how much you will tolerate. If you make it plain right away that you will not stand for any nonsense, your experience as a substitute can be very pleasant. It is not necessary to act as an ogre, but be assertive; you are the teacher, and it is your job to maintain order.

- If a student is particularly unruly after you have made repeated efforts to alter his behavior,

- Make direct eye contact and tell him once again that you will not allow further unacceptable behavior. Be cold and firm. Do not appear ruffled; just be matter-of-fact. If he continues, it is time to remove that student from the classroom. In the case of young children, a few minutes in the hall might get the point across. With older students, the threat of detention or a trip to the principal's office might be in order. Be sure to check your local regulations regarding disciplinary action and punishment before entering the classroom as a substitute teacher.

SUPPLIES

Faculty

Teachers are usually given supplies, but you will still need to keep track of usage. A simple way to do this is to make 4×6 index cards for each teacher, or keep a sheet for each teacher, which is then kept in the supply room. When a teacher picks up supplies, write the number and type of supplies taken and have the teacher sign for them. Faculty and student supplies may overlap at some points since paper, pens, erasers, and pencils are standard equipment, but some typical supplies for faculty use only include:

class record books	staples
chalk	thumb tacks
blackboard erasers	push pins
ditto masters or stencils	first aid supplies
transparencies	specially requested items such as art or science supplies
scotch tape	
masking tape	

Paper Clips and Fasteners

See Figures 26 and 27 for samples of the most common types of paper clips and fasteners and the most efficient uses for each.

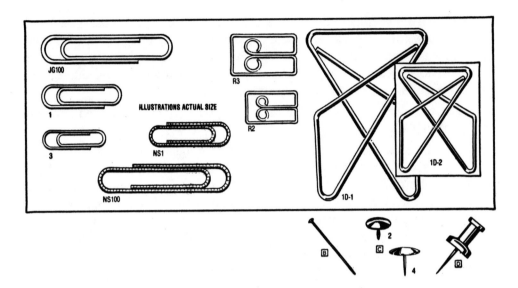

JG100
JUMBO SIZE PAPER CLIPS
Same as above except heavier gauge wire. Illustrated actual size.

1
3
GEM PAPER CLIPS
Genuine Gem clips, standard size, premium quality. .Full gauge .036 wire assures firm gripping power, resists undue bending even with frequent use. Not to be confused with lighter, shorter "economy" clips, genuine Gems have white tinned, rust-proof finish with rounded ends and smooth edges. Illustrations shown actual size.

NS1
NONSKID GEM CLIPS
Feature corrugated edges for extra gripping power. Same high quality as standard gem clips. Illustrated actual size.

NS100
JUMBO SIZE NONSKID GEM CLIPS
Same as above except heavier gauge wire.

R2
R3
REGAL PAPER CLIPS
Constructed of strong, polished nickel steel wire with turned-in ends to protect paper. Provides positive double grip.

LARGE SIZE
ID-1

MEDIUM SIZE
ID-2
IDEAL CLIPS AND CLAMPS
Here is the clip with the greatest expansion for use where a large number of papers must be held together. Constructed of tough, heavy gauge steel wire with turned ends to prevent paper damage.

Ⓑ **STEEL BANK PINS**
Constructed of the finest quality triple plated steel. Packed in ½ pound boxes. Shown actual size.

Ⓒ **THUMB TACKS**
Finest quality solid round head thumb tacks of special tempered steel.

Ⓓ **PUSH PINS**
Ideal for use where pins are often moved. Specially designed extended "handle" head for easy removing. Ground steel points are ⅜" long.

FIGURE 26

Chart of sample paper clips and pins

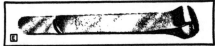

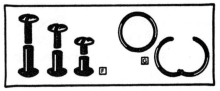

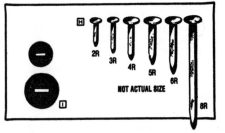

A BALL-BEARING CLIPS
Scientifically accurate in design and construction. Easy to operate. Ball-bearings set in special sockets reduce friction providing extra strong gripping power. Jaws cannot get out of alignment.

B ACCO CLAMPS
Made of rust-proof cadmium plated metal. Provide exceptional holding strength. Jaws have turned-in smooth edges. Hook in handle permits hanging for display uses.

C HUNT BULL DOG CLIPS
Made of durable blue spring steel with nickel plated handles. Designed with barrel-type hinges. holes in handles for hanging.

D BINDER CLIPS
Made of tempered blued steel with nickel plated wire arms. After clip is applied, arms may be reversed and snapped against documents for carrying. When used at side of papers a complete book is made. One arm may be reversed against the papers and the other forms a hook. Wire arms remove for permanent binding.

E BANKERS' CLASPS
Constructed of bright-finish highly tempered stainless steel. Smooth rounded ends. Raised short end permits easy slip-on for holding letters. check stubs, papers, etc.

F ALUMINUM SCREW POSTS
For use in binding all sorts of papers. swatches, etc. Made of strong aluminum alloy, light and rust-proof. 3/16" diameter with round. flat heads.

G LOOSE-LEAF BOOK RINGS
Easy to open and close nickel plated steel rings. Ideal for loose-leaf sheets and many other uses.

H BRASS PAPER FASTENERS
These paper fasteners are made of quality brass. Shanks are rigid and smooth, points are sharp, eliminating the aid of a punch for piercing through papers. Heads are round.

I BRASS WASHERS
Provides a neat binding job when brass fasteners are used. Recommended for top and bottom use.

FIGURE 27

Chart of sample paper fasteners. All are actual size unless otherwise stated.

Student Supplies

Often schools sell supplies and textbooks to students from the bookstore or supply room. The complexity of maintaining supplies and keeping track of sales depends on the size and scope of your school. In some schools, older students are hired to work in the bookstore: students may work under your supervision; or you might be solely responsible. In large schools and colleges, the bookstore is usually a separate operation, out of your jurisdiction. If you must maintain the student supply room, the key to efficient management is good organization. You will need to keep an accurate accounting of supplies and sales as well as an inventory of supplies.

- List the supplier's name and any order numbers or catalog numbers for each item.

- Accurately maintained lists will make taking inventory much easier.

- Reorder before your supply becomes low. Delays in shipping occur frequently enough to warrant reordering in plenty of time.

- Flag your supplies so that you know when to reorder. One way to do this is by first determining when you will need to reorder, based on the time it takes to use up the supply. If, for example, you will place a new order when you open the last carton of an item, mark one carton "Last Carton—Reorder" and place it on the bottom of your supply. As you replenish your working stock, you can quickly tell when it is time to reorder.

- Remember to charge sales tax on items sold if applicable in your city or state, and keep a record of items sold or charged.

- Some schools require cash-only sales, in which case a receipt is issued at the time of sale. Other schools allow a charge system in which students may carry a running tab, which is billed monthly, or as convenient. In either case, you will need to be as accurate as possible when issuing sales slips.

- Periodically, you will need to take inventory of the supplies and tally the total of goods sold with the sales slips (which should balance and cancel each other out).

A typical student supply room might contain:

textbooks (usually segregated by grade or subject)	graph paper
reference books (dictionaries, thesauruses)	specialized equipment such as drafting or graphics supplies
notebooks	erasers—pencil, ink, art gum
	folders and binders

loose-leaf paper, lined and plain

colored construction paper

pencils

pens

rulers

reinforcements, gummed or self-stick

specialty gift items—T shirts, tote bags with school name

SUPPLIERS OF EDUCATIONAL MATERIALS   Check the Yellow Pages of your telephone directory for additional suppliers in your area.

SCIENTIFIC SUPPLIES

Edmund Scientific
101 E. Gloucester Pike
Barrington, NJ 08007
(609) 574-8900

Rascher & Betzold, Inc.
5410 N. Damien Avenue
Chicago, IL 60625
(312) 275-7300

FIRST AID AND MEDICAL
SUPPLIES

H.L. Moore
P.O. Box 156
New Britain, CT 06050
(203) 225-4621

A.J. Masuen Co.
11 Central Avenue N.W.
Le Mars, IA 51031
(712) 546-4563

AUDIO-VISUAL EQUIPMENT
AND MATERIALS

R.V. Butterworth, Inc.
P.O. Box 4893
Hayward, CA 94540
(415) 785-4230

6959 California Avenue
Portland, OR 97211
(503) 288-6733

5417 NE 30 Avenue
Seattle, WA 98136
(206) 938-4677

Wholesale Educational Suppliers Co.
63 South Fourth Avenue
Mt. Vernon, NY 10550
(914) 664-8200

Photo & Sound
(locations in 7 states)
Corporate Headquarters
116 Natoma Street
San Francisco, CA 94105
(415) 421-0410

Northeast AudioVisual Inc.
548 Donald Street
Bedford, NH 03102
(603) 668-5511

<u>GRAPHIC SUPPLIES AND
EQUIPMENT</u>

Hartco Products Company, Inc.
357 W. Pearl Street
West Jefferson, OH 43162
(614) 879-8315

<u>INSTITUTIONAL SUPPLIES</u>

Belmont Jobbing & Supplv
2775 Shermer Road
Northbrook, IL 60062
(312) 564-3850

SUSPENSION REPORT   When a student has exceeded the limits of acceptable behavior, suspension from school may be the result. If so, a suspension report will need to be made out. These reports usually contain a statement about the offending incident, remarks from witnesses, parents, or faculty, and a brief statement as to the punishment; for example, ''Suspension—2 weeks'' or, in extreme cases, ''Expelled (date).'' Expulsion reports or suspension reports may have to be forwarded to other district offices and will remain in the student's permanent file; so they should be neat and accurate.

SYLLABICATION GUIDE   Syllabication is the division of a word into syllables so that it can fit into a given space. The dictionary gives the correct syllabication for words and should be consulted if you are in doubt about a specific word. If you learn the following rules of syllabication, however, you can save yourself much time and perform your writing tasks more efficiently.

1. Divide words between double consonants.
   cof-fee, mas-sage, tot-ter

   If a root ends in a double consonant, divide after the root word: fulfill-ment

   If the last consonant of a root word was doubled in order to add the suffix, then divide between the double consonant: drip-ping:

2. Divide between two vowels when they are pronounced separately:
   cre-ate

3. Divide between compound words:
   trades-man, waste-basket, water-logged

   If the compound word is hyphenated, divide at the hyphen:
   desert-dweller, crow's-feet

4. Divide after a prefix of three or more letters:
   semi-colon, micro-organism

5. Divide before a suffix of three or more letters:
   considera-tion, consider-able

6. Divide between pronounceable syllables:
   en-cour-age-ment, i-so-met-ric, i-sos-ce-les

   This is the trickiest rule and you may require dictionary help for some words.

   If two consonants are between two vowels and the consonants are pro-nounced separately, divide between the consonants: sub-mit, tid-bit

   If the two consonants are not pronounced separately, do not divide between the consonants: weath-ered

7. When one consonant is between two vowels:
   If the first vowel is long, place the consonant with the second vowel: sta-bilize

   If the first vowel is short, place the consonant with it: vig-i-lance

Syllabication Don'ts

Do not divide one-syllable words.

Do not divide a word so that only one or two letters remain at the end of a line.

Do not divide any part of a proper name. Start a new line.

Do not divide contractions or abbreviations.

Do not separate a figure from its accompanying symbol.

Do not divide the last word of a paragraph.

Do not divide the last word on a page.

T

TEACHER CERTIFICATION RECORDS   Teacher certification and teaching credential requirements vary from state to state and are often not required at all in private schools. If your school or district requires that teachers be certified in order to teach, the teacher is usually asked to supply proof of certification at the time of employment. This may be in the form of a photocopy of the actual certification or credential, or only the credential number and the state in which it was issued. The issuance must then be verified and such data placed in the teacher's individual file or forwarded to a centralized personnel location.

TESTING

Glossary of Terms

academic aptitude	The type of learning ability that is needed for school work.
achievement test	A test of acquired information, abilities, or skills.
aptitude test	A test used for estimating ability to learn or obtain skills.
battery	A group of tests used together.
converted score	A score such as an IQ, percentile, or grade equivalent that is taken from a raw score.
correction for guessing	A reduction in score for wrong answers.
grade equivalent	The public school grade level, expressed in years and tenths of years, and corresponding to an achievement test score. It represents the minimum

desired knowledge to be acquired by a specific time. For example, 9.6 indicates that the knowledge demonstrated by the test score indicates that the student has an equivalency of the sixth month of the ninth grade.

group test	A test that can be administered to a large number of pupils simultaneously by one test proctor.
individual test	A test given to one individual at a time.
intelligence quotient (IQ)	An index of learning ability, which reflects a combination of inherent and learned characteristics.
inventory	A questionnaire rather than a test, which is used principally in testing interest and personality.
mean	The average score of a group.
median	The middle score obtained by a group being tested. It corresponds to the 50th percentile.
mental age (MA)	The level of development in intelligence expressed as equivalent to the learning abilities of an average child of that age. For example, if a child is chronologically thirteen years old, he may have a mental age higher or lower depending on learned skills, etc.
multiple-choice	A type of test question where the student chooses the right answer from a group of possible answers.
norm	A single score or range of scores that represent the usual performance of a given group. A norm serves as the reference gauge for those who take the test.
norm group	The group used as the criterion of gauging test scores.
objective test	A test that can be scored by using a test key as opposed to an essay-type examination that requires subjective judgment when grading.
percentile	A rating with a possible range of 1 to 100 that indicates the percent of individuals that fall below a set score. Percentiles do not represent the percentage of questions answered correctly.
profile	An overview of a group of tests that gives a graphic picture of a student or group.

quantitative aptitude	The ability to learn symbols or numbers.
raw score	The basic test score obtained before it is converted to a scaled score. It is usually the number of correct responses.
reliability	The degree of stability of a test's scores.
standard deviation	A basic measurement of variability allowing for differences both up and down from the average score.
standardized test	An objective test that is given subject to specific stringent rules and is scored accordingly, thereby facilitating the establishment of standard norms.
stanine	A ranking system consisting of nine steps. The word is derived from a *sta*ndard *nines* ranking system.
validity	The success of a test—its ability to do its job and measure what is desired.

Testing Programs

Admissions Testing Program
of the College Entrance Examination
Board
Box 592
Princeton, NJ 08540

Advanced Placement Program
of the College Entrance Examination
Board
Box 977
Princeton, NJ 08540

American College Testing Program
P.O. Box 168
Iowa City, IA 52240

Graduate Record Examinations
Educational Testing Service
Box 955
Princeton, NJ 08540

The Independent School Testing
Program Educational Records
Bureau
160 Speen Street
Framingham, MA 01701

Independent Schools Admissions
Testing Program
Educational Records Bureau
3 East 80 Street
New York, NY 10021

Law School Admission Test
Educational Testing Service
Princeton, NJ 08540

The Medical College Admission Test
American College Testing Program
P.O. Box 168
Iowa City, IA 52240

PSAT/NMSQT   Secondary School Admission Test
Box 589   Educational Testing Service
Princeton, NJ 08540   Princeton, NJ 08540

Abbreviations of Test Titles

ACT	American College Testing Program
Binet	Stanford-Binet Intelligence Scale
California	California Test Bureau test series
CLEP	College-Level Examination Program
College Boards	College Entrance Examination Board Scholastic Aptitude Test or Achievement Test
Cooperative	Cooperative Tests and Services, Educational Testing Service
CTP	Comprehensive Testing Program of Educational Records Bureau
ERB's	Educational Records Bureau tests
GRE's	Graduate Record Examinations
GSAT	General Scholastic Aptitude Test
Iowas	Iowa Test of Basic Skills (elementary level) Iowa Tests of Educational Development (secondary level)
K-A	Kuhlmann-Anderson Intelligence Test
Otis (OLMA)	Otis-Lennon Mental Ability Test
PSAT/NMSQT	Preliminary Scholastic Aptitude Test/National Merit Scholarship Qualifying Test
QUESTA	Questionnaire for Students, Teachers, and Administrators
SAT	Scholastic Aptitude Test of the College Entrance Examination Board
SCAT	School and College Ability Test
SRA	Science Research Associates tests
SSAT	Secondary School Admission Test
Stanford(SAT)	Stanford Achievement Test
STEP	Sequential Tests of Educational Progress

Strong	Strong-Campbell Interest Inventory
Wechsler	Various Wechsler intelligence tests such as WISC (Wechsler Intelligence Scale for Children); WPPSI (Wechsler Preschool and Primary Scale of Intelligence); WAIS (Wechsler Adult Intelligence Scale)

Filing of Test Scores

Test scores may be kept in a separate file, alphabetically; filed in the student's individual file; and/or copies kept in the central file and at key locations such as the guidance office. The test scores referred to here are, of course, major test results such as the SSAT (Secondary School Achievement Test), the ERB (Educational Records Bureau) test, or the GRE (Graduate Records Examination). Sometimes, final examinations are kept on file but most other tests are returned to the student.

TEXTBOOKS

Ordering Textbooks

In the smaller school the secretary is often responsible for ordering textbooks. Following is a typical format:

- Set a deadline by which time teachers must turn in textbook requests to you.
- Double-check the teachers' forms to be sure that they are complete. You will need to know (1) the complete book title; (2) the author's name; (3) the publisher; (4) the edition number or year of publication; (5) the number of books required per teacher; (6) is a teacher's edition needed? (The teacher's edition supplies the answers to quizzes and gives other special information not included in the student edition.)
- You may then need to submit the forms to your administrator for budgetary approval, or forward them to a central location.
- Next you will need to coordinate the orders. For example, if you have three classes of forty students each who all use the same textbook, you would submit only one order for 120 books to the publisher.
- When you place your order, try to give the publisher as much accurate information as possible including:
  - Title, author, edition (or date of publication)
  - Number of books being ordered

- Your shipping address
- Your billing address if different from the shipping address
- A notation of whether you wish to be billed or that the payment is enclosed
- Your name and telephone number in case of questions
- Always keep a copy of all orders

When the books arrive:

- Check for damage. If the carton is severely damaged, ask the delivery person to wait while you check the contents. Once you sign for a delivery it often indicates that you have received it in good order. Another alternative is to sign right away but mark on the delivery receipt "Damaged Goods" so that you will not be held responsible later.
- Check that the number of books delivered corresponds to the number ordered.
- Separate the books according to the teacher's orders and arrange for their transportation to the bookstore, classroom, or follow your school's established procedures.
- Textbooks are often stamped with the school's name on the inside front cover and on a designated page. This may be done by the office staff or by the teachers.
- In schools where books are loaned rather than sold, the books are usually numbered and a list is kept of which number is assigned to which student. Books are turned in at the end of the year. If a book is lost, the student is responsible for replacing it. Faculty members usually take care of checking the books.
- If a shipment is incorrect or incomplete, notify the publisher immediately in writing or by telephone. Keep a record of the call.

Textbook Publishers

Addison-Wesley Publishing Co.
Jacob Way
Reading, MA 01867
(617) 944-3700

Ginn & Co., A Xerox Publishing Co.
191 Spring Street
Lexington, MA 02173
(617) 861-1670

Harcourt Brace Jovanovich, Inc.
757 Third Avenue
New York, NY 10017
(212) 888-4444

Harper & Row Publishers, Inc.
10 East 53 Street
New York, NY 10022
(212) 593-7000

Houghton-Mifflin Co.
2 Park Street
Boston, MA 02107
(617) 725-5000

J.B. Lippincott Co.
Educational Publishing Division
E. Washington Square
Philadelphia, PA 19105
(215) 574-4200

McGraw-Hill Publishing Co.
1221 Avenue of the Americas
New York, NY 10020
(212) 997-1221

Macmillan Educational Corporation
866 Third Avenue
New York, NY 10022
(212) 935-2000

Charles E. Merrill Publishing Co.
1300 Alum Creek Drive
Columbus, OH 43216
(614) 258-8441

Prentice-Hall, Inc.
Englewood Cliffs, NJ 07632
(201) 592-2000

Scott, Foresman & Co.
1900 E. Lake Avenue
Glenview, IL 60025
(312) 729-3000

Steck-Vaughn Co.
P.O. Box 2028
Austin, TX 78768
(512) 476-6721

TIME MANAGEMENT   No matter how busy you are, allow some time for planning your day. The more rushed and pressured you feel, the more important it is to allot your time wisely. Five to ten minutes at the beginning of each day spent in planning your activities can work wonders in reducing tension and making you a more efficient secretary. *Plan in the morning when you are alert*. The plans will be fresh in your mind; you will gain momentum as you perform your tasks; and you will be less likely to become sidetracked. Each Monday, make a short list of the main things you must accomplish or that you want to do during the week. Then quickly refine the list by marking each item "M" through "F" according to the day on which it should be done. For example, M = Monday, W = Wednesday and so on. If some of the items are designated "TH" or "F" they can then be postponed until Thursday or Friday. By then they may have become an "M" priority for the following Monday; they may be further postponed because of unforeseen changes; or they may have become obsolete altogether and be eliminated. If a project is lengthy, it is wise to allot additional time, thereby moving it up one or two days in priority. If an item is to be done daily, mark it "M–F."

Once you have made up your chart, you can tell at a glance which days will be the heaviest. Try to allot a little time for the unexpected rush assignment. Do not allow your workload to become overwhelming. If a week is so packed with assignments that you feel pressure from just looking over your time-planning chart, then discuss the workload with your administrator. Some of the items may not be as urgent as you think, and may be postponed. The time-planning chart is an invaluable tool to use in convincing your administrator of the magnitude of your workload. You might consider keeping a file of your time charts as they can be useful tools when bargaining for a salary increase.

Each morning, scan the weekly time chart and update it by adding, deleting, or altering as necessary. Try to schedule your activities to take the most advantage of your best "internal time." Do you perform best in the morning? If so, then try to schedule your heaviest workload then. If you become more efficient as the day progresses, you may prefer to schedule the bulk of your duties for the later hours. It may take a little effort and experimentation on your part to find the best path for you, but the benefits to your general sense of well-being and efficiency will be well worth it. One important thing to remember when time-planning is to be flexible. Never allow yourself to become so rigid in a schedule that you become boxed in and are therefore placed under stress by the schedule. The purpose of planning your activities is to allow yourself time to remain calm and relaxed while performing your tasks at optimum efficiency.

TIME-SAVING TIPS

- When collating or counting papers, you can speed things up by using a rubber finger tip or the tip of a pencil eraser to turn the pages.
- A speedy way to count the number of cards or papers is to pile a stack until they measure an inch in height. Count the number in that pile and you can then easily estimate the remainder. For example, if 200 papers equal an inch, then 100 papers would equal a half-inch, 50 papers would equal a quarter-inch, and so on.
- Make up a form for repeated requests. If you need to make supply requisitions, ask for assignments for absent students, and so on. Instead of writing a note each time, make up a form that can be photocopied and used again.
- Speed up your work by using postcards instead of letters whenever possible. This will also reduce mailing costs. Requests for brochures or acknowledgments and transcripts can usually be handled by postcard.
- You can speed mailings up even more if you have postcards pre-printed with a form message.
- A quick way to clean your dial telephone is to dampen several cotton balls and place them in the dial holes. Dial the telephone a few times and the dial will be cleaned.

- If you need to make several telephone calls, try to make them consecutively. This will cause fewer interruptions in your work day.

- If you staple papers before filing them, staple them at the top right corner. This way, the staple will be at the upper part of the file folder, and will be less likely to stick and tear other papers when you remove them from the file.

- If you need to send a follow-up letter for an unanswered request, save time by sending a photocopy of the original letter with a short cover note indicating that this is a second request.

- A fast way to stamp envelopes by hand is to line them up across your desk with the top right corners accessible, take a roll of stamps, moisten a few at a time, and place the first stamp against the first envelope. As the stamp adheres, hold it in place with your left thumb and tear off the rest of the strip with your right hand. Repeat this for the remainder of the envelopes.

TRANSCRIPTS   A transcript is a record of the subjects taken, grades received, attendance, awards and honors, perhaps major test scores such as I.Q. or aptitude tests, and any other information pertinent to a student's academic development. Transcripts are usually kept as a part of a school's permanent file and are required for entrance to a school and for transfers between schools. Large institutions use computer formats; all the information about a particular student is included on one sheet. Small schools may use hand-copied forms or may simply photocopy report cards and other data to make up a transcript package. Whatever method your school uses, it is essential that transcript records be maintained accurately since a student's future may literally depend on them.

TRANSPARENCIES   Transparencies are used as visual aids by many teachers. They are plastic sheets that contain written, printed, or drawn information. Transparencies are placed on the glass lens plate of an overhead projector and the image is then thrown on a screen or wall projecting the data for presentation to the class. Transparency film can produce images on clear, tinted, or opaque backgrounds, and takes only about four seconds to make on a spirit duplicating machine or xerox machine.

TUITION PLANS   The costs of private education climb annually. In order to alleviate some financial pressures, there are plans available that reimburse the student for school time missed because of illness or injury. Usually, a claim is made by the subscribing parent or student directly to the tuition plan. The school, however, is often asked to verify dates of absence, so it is important to keep accurate attendance records. (One such plan is called The Tuition Refund Plan underwritten by Commercial Union Insurance Company, Boston, for A.W.G. Dewar Inc., 141 Milk Street, Boston, MA 02109.)

TYPEFACES   Typefaces vary from six to ninety-six points with a complete *font* (assortment of any one size and type style) in each size. You may choose light, bold, and extra bold, expanded, condensed, roman and italic within most type styles. The capital letters are called *upper case* and small letters are *lower case*. Lightness or boldness, upper or lower case are variables that can dramatically alter the visual effect of the printed image even though you use a single typeface. Then again, the selection of different typefaces can radically alter the visual impact of the finished piece. There are many ways to approach the classification of typefaces. For example:

- Oldstyle. This group refers to typefaces patterned after classical Roman inscriptions. It is easy to read and has a good contrast between light and dark.
- Modern. This does not refer to modern as we know it today, but the modern of two hundred years ago. This type is similar in appearance to oldstyle but is mechanically more precise.
- Transitional. Halfway between oldstyle and modern, this type is sturdier than modern, but with characteristics of oldstyle.
- Square Serif. This contemporary style is used mainly for headlines and short texts. The geometric design and uniform strokes can be used effectively.
- Sans Serif. This fairly new and simple style is easily read and lends itself well to contemporary imagery.
- Script. This style simulates handwriting and is used for special effects. Do not use it for the body of a text. It is difficult to read and can give an unprofessional appearance.
- Text Letters. This resembles the hand-drawn letters used in old manuscripts. It is often used by religious groups, and on certificates, diplomas, and invitations.
- Decorative Types. Also called "novelty faces," these are used primarily to attract attention. A large number of decorative types is available; they tend to go in and out of fashion.

Type Size Guide

Aal 96 point

Aal 84 point

Aal 72 point

Aal 60 point

Aal 48 point

Aal 42 point

Aal 36 point

Aal 30 point

Aal 24 point

Aal 20 point

Aal 18 point

Aal 16 point

Aal 14 point

Aal 12 point

Aal 10 point

Aal 8 point

Aal 6 point

FIGURE 28

This is a guide to choosing the correct size type for your particular job. By using the point scale to the right, you can converse with the printer in a knowledgeable manner.

ABCDEFGHIJKLMNOPQRSTUVWXYZ
abcdefghijklmnopqrstuvwxyz
$1234567890 :;&?!()/—-'' fifl

ABCDEFGHIJKLMNOPQRSTUVWXYZ
abcdefghijklmnopqrstuvwxyz
$1234567890¢ ,,&?!()%*

ABCDEFGHIJKLMNOPQRSTUVWXYZ&
abcdefghijklmnopqrstuvwxyz   1234567890

ABCDEFGHIJKLMNOPQRSTUVWXYZ
abcdefghijklmnopqrstuvwxyz
$1234567890¢ :;&?!()

ABCDEFGHIJKLMNOPQRSTUVWXYZ
abcdefghijklmnopqrstuvwxyz
$1234567890¢   :;&!?()%*

𝔄𝔅𝔆𝔇𝔈𝔉𝔊𝔥𝔦𝔧𝔨𝔩𝔪𝔫𝔬𝔭𝔮𝔯𝔰𝔱𝔲𝔳𝔴𝔵𝔶𝔷&
abcdefghijklmnopqrstubwxyz   1234567890

ABCDEFGHIJKLMNOPQRSTUVWX
YZ& abcdefghijklmnopqrstuvwxyz 123456789

ABCDEFGHIJKLMNOPQRSTUVW
XYZ& abcdefghijklmnopqrstuvwxyz   1234567890

ABCDEFGHIJKLMNOPQRSTUVWXYZ
$1234567890 :;?!

ABCDEFGHIJKLMNOPQRSTUVWXYZ
1234567890   :;&?![]

FIGURE 29

**Examples of the basic kinds of typefaces. There are literally
hundreds available within each category.**

When choosing a typeface, remember to consider readability and legibility. They are not synonymous. Readability is the ease with which the text can be read; legibility is the speed with which a type character can be identified. Always choose an easy-to-read type if you want to convey a clear message. If you want a particular typeface and you know its name, specify this information on the manuscript or text page before sending it to the printer (for example, 12 pt. UNICA). Most art supply and stationery shops, and of course printers, have catalogs of type styles to choose from.

TYPING TIPS AND TECHNIQUES

Easy Horizontal Centering

1. Figure the center of your line. For example, if your margins are set at ₁0 and 70, your line would contain 60 spaces ($70 - 10 = 60$). Divide the number of spaces in half to figure your centering point (60 divided by 2 = 30).

2. Move your typewriter to the center point (in this case 30 spaces in from the left margin).

3. Now, as you look at the copy to be centered, backspace once for every two characters (including spaces and punctuation). With a little practice, you will easily get into the rhythm of this method. It is fast, easy, and it works.

How to Make Characters Not on Your Typewriter

exclamation point	type an apostrophe, backspace, then type a period (!)
division sign	type a hyphen, backspace, then type a colon (÷)
cents sign	type a lower case "c," backspace, then type an oblique line (¢)
dollar sign	type a capital "S," backspace, then type a line ($)
percent sign	type a lower case "o," type an oblique line, then type another lower case "o" (o/o)
equals sign	type a hyphen, backspace, rotate the platen slightly and type another hyphen (=)
semicolon	type a comma , backspace, rotate the platen slightly, and type a period (;)
colon	type a period, backspace, rotate the platen slightly and type anotner period (:)

Typing Shortcuts

Use your tabulator and save time. Some people seem to think that the tabulator has a special function only to be used when typing charts and statistics. Not so. Make use of your tabulator whenever you need to type paragraph indentations, or the indented date and signature lines of letters.

Spacing can be easy. If you do not have a line space measure on your typewriter, make up a chart to save yourself time and energy. Take a sheet of paper a little larger than your typing paper, and make a scale on the right-hand margin showing your typewriter's line spacing. Use the chart as a backing sheet and you can quickly tell at which number you stop typing on the first page. It is then easy to end consecutive pages at the same number and have a beautifully balanced typing project.

To keep reports uniform, make a chart indicating the locations of headings, margins, and so on. You will use the chart as a backing sheet, so be sure to use dark ink that can be seen through your typewriter paper. This method can save you a great deal of time and produces perfect-looking results.

Setting margins by eye is quicker than counting. When you have the time, experiment with your letterhead and see which margin stops produce the best-looking results for long, medium, and short letters. Then jot down the margin numbers and keep them close to your typewriter for future use.

Save time when typing form letters by proofreading typed copy as you type the next letter. Type each new letter using the one you have just typed as your guide copy. As a quick check against omitting a line, place each finished form letter against the original. The lines should match up.

Keep your work clean. If you are getting black smudges on your work, the rubber wheels on the paper bail may be worn out and need replacing. As a temporary measure, you can cover them with cellophane tape (although this will cut down on their traction).

To prevent creased carbon, back the papers with a sheet of heavy-weight paper; then place them in the typewriter.

Save filing space by using the reverse side of an original letter to make the carbon copy of the response. This can be most convenient since both question and answer can be cn one sheet of paper, eliminating the need for staples and extra bulk

<u>To type a section in a different color</u> without changing the ribbon, just set your typewriter to stencil position, place a piece of colored carbon paper over the area to be typed, and type in the characters. Then return your machine to its normal position and continue typing the rest of the copy.

<u>If using an electric typewriter,</u> forget about typing rhythm. If your fingers want to type some letters faster than others, follow your natural inclination and your speed will increase.

TYPEWRITER MAINTENANCE

- Keep your typewriter clean and dust-free. When not in use, keep the machine covered. Dust with a soft cloth every day. If particles of lint or dust become lodged in the openings of the machine, gently remove them by blowing or using a soft brush.
- Rely on a qualified repair person when your typewriter is not operating properly.
- If you must erase, move the carriage to one side so that eraser particles will not fall into the machine.
- Periodically clean the platen with a little platen cleaning fluid on a soft cloth.
- Be sure that your electric typewriter is turned off when not in use.
- Clean the type bars or typing element regularly with a stiff-bristled brush.

UNEMPLOYMENT INSURANCE Unemployment insurance is a weekly benefit paid for a limited time to eligible workers to tide them over between jobs when they are involuntarily unemployed. Federal law establishes certain minimum requirements: however, each state administers its own program, paying benefits out of a fund collected from a special tax on employer payrolls throughout the state. The federal government provides funds for benefits for its laid-off civilians and persons discharged from the Armed Forces.

To be eligible for benefits, you must have worked long enough in covered employment to meet your state's requirements, be involuntarily unemployed, be available for and seeking work, and not refuse a suitable job offer. Each state specifies its eligibility requirements and amount of weekly and total benefit payments. The general rule is that the jobless worker receives fifty percent of the average weekly wage formerly received. Most states limit payments to a maximum of twenty-six weeks. A federal program provides that during times of high unemployment, individuals who have exhausted their benefits under state law may continue to receive payments for half again as long as their regular entitlement. Since January 1978, states cannot deny benefits solely on the basis of pregnancy or recency of pregnancy (pregnant women do, however, have to meet generally applicable requirements of seeking work and being available for and able to work).

W

WEIGHTS AND MEASURES

Linear Measure:

1 inch		=	2.54	centimeters
12 inches	= 1 foot	=	.3045	meter
3 feet	= 1 yard	=	.9114	meter
16½ feet	= 1 rod	=	5.029	meters
40 rods	= 1 furlong	=	201.17	meters
5,280 feet	= 1 mile	=	1609.3	meters
3 miles	= 1 land league	=	4.83	kilometers

Square Measure:

1 square inch		=	6.452	square centimeters
144 square inches	= 1 square foot	=	929	square centimeters
9 square feet	= 1 square yard	=	0.8361	square meter
30¼ square yards	= 1 square rod	=	25.29	square meters
160 square rods	= 1 acre	=	.4047	hectare
640 acres	= 1 square mile	=	259	hectares

Cubic Measure:

1 cubic inch		=	16.387	cubic centimeters
1728 cubic inches	= 1 cubic foot	=	.0283	cubic meter
27 cubic feet	= 1 cubic yard	=	.7646	cubic meter
16 cubic feet	= 1 cord foot			
8 cord feet	= 1 cord	=	3.625	cubic meters

Dry Measure:

1 pint		=	5505 liter
2 pints	= 1 quart	=	1.1012 liters
8 quarts	= 1 peck	=	8.8096 liters
4 pecks	= 1 bushel	=	35.2383 liters
1 British quart	= 1.032 U.S. quarts		

Liquid Measure:

1 gill	= 4 fl ounces	=	.1183 liter
4 gills	= 1 pint	=	.4732 liter
2 pints	= 1 quart	=	.9463 liter
4 quarts	= 1 gallon	=	3.7853 liters

WITHDRAWALS, STUDENT Withdrawing a student from school is basically a reverse of the enrollment procedure. Make sure that all applicable fees have been paid. Make sure that all textbooks, locks, and equipment are accounted for. Make sure that all lockers have been emptied. Remove the student's name from the official roll register, indicating the date of withdrawal. Assemble all student data into his or her file and place the file in the "previous student" category of your filing system. Make out any necessary transfer papers as required by your district or local agencies.

WORK PERMITS Minor students are required to file for a permit to work during after-school hours. The requirements can vary from state to state. Permits can be issued for vacations, weekends, or after-school hours. Minors may also be approved to work in special industries such as film or TV or modeling. The school office keeps a record of each permit showing the name, address, birthdate, and grade of the minor. The board of education may also require a report on the number of work permits issued. The minor takes the request for a permit to the school for authorization, then it is taken to the place of employment. In some special cases, a temporary tutorial situation may arise (as in the case of minors making films on location), in which case the tutor usually attempts to coordinate instruction with the school.

XEROX See PHOTOCOPYING MACHINES.

Z

ZIP CODE PREFIXES

STATE/TERRITORY	ABBREVIATION	ZIP CODE PREFIX
Alabama	AL	350 369
Alaska	AK	995-999
Arizona	AZ	850-865
Arkansas	AR	716-729
California	CA	900-966
Colorado	CO	800-816
Connecticut	CT	060-069
Delaware	DE	197-199
District of Columbia	DC	200-205
Florida	FL	320-339
Georgia	GA	300-319
Guam		969
Hawaii	HI	967-968
Idaho	ID	832-838
Illinois	IL	600-629
Indiana	IN	460-479
Iowa	IA	500-528
Kansas	KS	660-679
Kentucky	KY	400-427
Louisiana	LA	700-714
Maine	ME	039-049
Maryland	MD	206-219
Massachusetts	MA	010-027
Michigan	MI	480-499

STATE/TERRITORY	ABBREVIATION	ZIP CODE PREFIX
Minnesota	MN	550-567
Mississippi	MS	386-397
Missouri	MO	630-658
Montana	MT	590-599
Nebraska	NE	680-693
Nevada	NV	890-898
New Hampshire	NH	030-038
New Jersey	NJ	070-089
New Mexico	NM	870-884
New York	NY	100-149
North Carolina	NC	270-289
North Dakota	ND	580-588
Ohio	OH	430-458
Oklahoma	OK	730-749
Oregon	OR	970-979
Pennsylvania	PA	150-196
Puerto Rico	PR	006-009
Rhode Island	RI	028-029
South Carolina	SC	290-299
South Dakota	SD	570-577
Tennessee	TN	370-385
Texas	TX	750-799
Utah	UT	840-847
Vermont	VT	050-059
Virginia	VA	220-246
Virgin Islands	VI	006-009
Washington	WA	980-994
West Virginia	WV	247-268
Wisconsin	WI	530-549
Wyoming	WY	820-831